OXFORD THEOLOGICAL MONOGRAPHS

OXFORD THEOLOGICAL MONOGRAPHS

Early Israelite Wisdom

STUART WEEKS

CLARENDON PRESS · OXFORD
1994

Oxford University Press, Walton Street, Oxford OX2 6DP

Oxford New York Toronto
Delhi Bombay Calcutta Madras Karachi
Kuala Lumpur Singapore Hong Kong Tokyo
Nairobi Dar es Salaam Cape Town
Melbourne Auckland Madrid
and associated companies in
Berlin Ibadan

Oxford is a trade mark of Oxford University Press

Published in the United States
by Oxford University Press Inc., New York

British Library Cataloguing in Publication Data
Data available

Library of Congress Cataloging-in-Publication Data
Early Israelite wisdom/Stuart Weeks.
(Oxford theological monographs)
Includes bibliographical references and index.
1. Bible. O.T. Proverbs—Criticism, interpretation, etc.
2. Bible. O.T. Proverbs—Sources. 3. Middle Eastern literature—Relation to the
Old Testament. I. Title. II. Series.
BS1465.2.W38 1994 223'.706—dc20 93–17226
ISBN 0–19–826750–9
Typeset by J&L Composition Ltd, Filey, North Yorkshire
Printed in Great Britain
on acid-free paper by
Bookcraft (Bath) Ltd.,
Midsomer Norton, Avon

To my father, David Weeks

Acknowledgements

I am greatly indebted to Dr John Day, who supervised the doctoral research upon which this book is based. Throughout, he has given freely of his time, advice, and learning. I am grateful also to Dr Richard Parkinson and Dr Stephanie Dalley, who kindly commented and advised on the lists of Egyptian and Mesopotamian material in the Appendix. None of these scholars, of course, bears any responsibility for the opinions which I have expressed, or for any errors which I have made. Many egyptologists at Oxford, students and staff, made me welcome in their classes and discussed particular issues with me. I should like to thank all of them. Finally, I owe a special debt to my wife, Frances Thirlway, who has put up with me throughout the various stages of research, writing, and revision. I am grateful for her patience, and also for her assistance when French, German or Dutch sources have descended to an obscurity far beyond my own knowledge of those languages.

Contents

Abbreviations

AA	Alttestamentliche Abhandlungen
AASOR	*Annual of the American Schools of Oriental Research*
ÄAT	Ägypten und Altes Testament
ABRL	Anchor Bible Reference Library
AK	*Archiv für Kulturgeschichte*
ANET ³	J. B. Pritchard (ed.), *Ancient Near Eastern Texts Relating to the Old Testament*, third edition with Supplement (Princeton, 1969)
ASOR	American Schools of Oriental Research
BA	*Biblical Archaeologist*
BAR	British Archaeological Reports
BASOR	*Bulletin of the American Schools of Oriental Research*
BDB	F. Brown, S. R. Driver, and C. A. Briggs, *A Hebrew and English Lexicon of the Old Testament* (Oxford, 1907)
BETL	Bibliotheca Ephemeridum Theologicarum Lovaniensium
BHS	K. Elliger and W. Rudolph (eds.), *Biblia Hebraica Stuttgartensia*² (Stuttgart, 1984)
Bi. Or.	*Bibliotheca Orientalis*
BJEPS	*Bulletin of the Jewish Palestine Exploration Society*
BWANT	Beiträge zur Wissenschaft vom Alten und Neuen Testament
BWL	W. G. Lambert, *Babylonian Wisdom Literature* (Oxford, 1960)
BZAW	Beihefte zur Zeitschrift für die alttestamentliche Wissenschaft
CB	Coniectanea Biblica
CBQ	*Catholic Biblical Quarterly*
CBQMS	Catholic Biblical Quarterly Monograph Series

CTA	A. Herdner, *Corpus des tablettes en cunéiformes alphabétiques découvertes à Ras Shamra-Ugarit de 1929 à 1939* (Paris, 1963)
ET	English translation
ET	*Expository Times*
GK	E. Kautzsch, *Gesenius' Hebrew Grammar*, second English edition revised by A. E. Cowley (Oxford, 1910)
HAT	Handbuch zum Alten Testament
HSS	Harvard Semitic Studies
HTR	*Harvard Theological Review*
HUCA	*Hebrew Union College Annual*
ICC	International Critical Commentary
IEJ	*Israel Exploration Journal*
JA	*Journal asiatique*
JAOS	*Journal of the American Oriental Society*
JBL	*Journal of Biblical Literature*
JCS	*Journal of Cuneiform Studies*
JEA	*Journal of Egyptian Archaeology*
JNES	*Journal of Near Eastern Studies*
JSOT	*Journal for the Study of the Old Testament*
JSOTS	Journal for the Study of the Old Testament. Supplement Series
JSS	*Journal of Semitic Studies*
JTS	*Journal of Theological Studies*
KAI	H. Donner and W. Röllig, *Kanaanäische und aramäische Inschriften* (Wiesbaden, 1962–4)
LSJ	H. G. Liddell, R. Scott, and H. S. Jones, *A Greek–English Lexicon*, ninth edition with supplement edited by E. A. Barber et al. (Oxford, 1968)
LUÅ	Lunds Universitets Årsskrift
LXX	Septuagint
MT	Masoretic text
NK	New Kingdom
NESE	*Neue Ephemeris für semitische Epigraphik*
OA	*Oriens Antiquus*
OBO	Orbis Biblicus et Orientalis
OT	Old Testament
OMRO	*Oudheidkundige Mededelingen uit het Rijksmuseum van Oudheden te Leiden*

PEQ	*Palestine Exploration Quarterly*
RA	*Revue d'Assyriologie*
RB	*Revue biblique*
RdE	*Revue d'Égyptologie*
RSV	Revised Standard Version
SAK	*Studien zur altägyptischen Kultur*
SAT	Die Schriften des Alten Testaments
SBL	Society of Biblical Literature
SBT	Studies in Biblical Theology
SPAW	*Sitzungsberichte der Preussischen Akademie der Wissenschaften*
SSEA	Society for the Study of Egyptian Antiquities
St. ANT	Studien zum Alten und Neuen Testament
St. Th.	*Studia Theologica*
SVT	Supplements to Vetus Testamentum
TA	*Tel Aviv*
Th. LZ	*Theologische Literaturzeitung*
TRSC	*Transactions of the Royal Society of Canada*
UF	*Ugarit-Forschungen*
VT	*Vetus Testamentum*
WMANT	Wissenschaftliche Monographien zum Alten und Neuen Testament
WZKM	*Wiener Zeitschrift für die Kunde des Morgenlandes*
ZA	*Zeitschrift für Assyriologie*
ZÄS	*Zeitschrift für ägyptische Sprache und Altertumskunde*
ZAW	*Zeitschrift für die alttestamentliche Wissenschaft*
ZDPV	*Zeitschrift des deutschen Palästina-Vereins*

Introduction

For some seventy years, biblical scholars have supposed that wisdom literature arose in Israel as a response to the educational needs of the state administration. Composed by 'wise men' within administrative circles, it imitated and drew upon works used for the education of officials in other nations, inheriting ideas and assumptions from these, and perhaps constituting part of an international 'wisdom movement'. Those parts of the earliest wisdom literature which are preserved in the book of Proverbs reflect, therefore, the pragmatism and internationalism of a particular group within Israel, and originated within an educational context.

This idea, that early wisdom literature was largely orientated toward the training of bureaucrats, might come as a surprise to anyone more familiar with Proverbs than with historical criticism. The book itself shows a wide interest in many activities and aspects of daily life, and if an administrative background is to be presumed for the earliest material, then it must also be assumed that later redaction has obscured this background, or that the administrators had a very wide range of interests. Such assumptions are, indeed, generally made,[1] and justified by an appeal to evidence outside Proverbs. Comparison and analogy with similar non-Israelite literature are of particular importance here, as are references to 'wise men' in other parts of the Old Testament.

In the nineteenth and early twentieth centuries, scholarship already associated the wisdom literature with such references, and posited the existence of a distinct class of 'wise men'. Some scholars suggested that, like the wise men of Egypt and Assyria mentioned in the Old Testament, the Israelite wise men may have played some role in the formation of state policy; but the principal

---

[1] e.g., G. von Rad *Weisheit in Israel* (Neukirchen-Vluyn, 1970), ET *Wisdom in Israel* (London, 1972), assumes varied interests; W. McKane, *Proverbs: A New Approach* (London, 1970), later redaction and reinterpretation.

role of the wise was thought to be one of moral teaching. Gathering disciples around them, and perhaps seeking out individuals, they taught in the city gate, or later in schools.[2] The non-Israelite literature was brought to centre-stage only after Budge's publication of the Egyptian *Instruction of Amenemope* in 1923 and the recognition by Erman, in the following year, of a direct literary link between this work and Proverbs.[3] A number of more broadly comparable 'instructions' were already available, as was the Aramaic *Ahikar*,[4] and Hugo Gressmann suggested that, since the authors of the instructions and the hero of *Ahikar* were all scribes, the same was probably true for the writers of the Israelite material. Since the scribe's profession was international, and since foreign scribes were often to be found at royal courts, a scribal origin would also, he suggested, explain the international character and dissemination of wisdom literature.[5] Five years later, Paul Humbert went further, and argued that the literature was written not only by scribes but *for* scribes. The appearance of wisdom literature and of a new state administration in the reign of Solomon were not coincidental: as in Egypt, and probably in imitation of Egypt, the wisdom literature was developed to serve in the training of future officials.[6]

Much subsequent discussion has been little more than refinement of Humbert's hypothesis. On the historical side, several scholars have attempted to show that Solomon imitated Egyptian administrative practices in other ways, and the nature of scribal schooling has been further discussed. Gerhard von Rad proposed that Solomon's reign had been an age of 'enlightenment' in Israel,

---

[2] See, e.g., H. Ewald, *Jahrbücher der biblischen Wissenschaft*, i (Göttingen, 1848), 95–113, and *Die Dichter des alten Bundes*², ii. *Die salomonische Schriften* (Göttingen, 1867), 12; Franz Delitzsch, *Biblischer Commentar über die poetischen Bücher des Alten Testaments*, iii. *Das salamonische Spruchbuch* (Leipzig, 1873), esp. 32 f., ET *Biblical Commentary on the Proverbs of Solomon*, i (Edinburgh, 1874), 39 f; T. K. Cheyne, *Job and Solomon* (London, 1887); C. F. Kent, *The Wise Men of Ancient Israel and their Proverbs*² (New York, 1899).

[3] E. A. W. Budge, *Facsimiles of Egyptian Hieratic Papyri in the British Museum: Second Series* (London, 1923). A. Erman, 'Eine ägyptische Quelle der "Sprüche Salomos"', *SPAW* 15 (1924), 86–95.

[4] Published in 1911. See section (li) in the Appendix.

[5] H. Gressmann, 'Die neugefundene Lehre des Amen-em-ope und die vorexilische Spruchdichtung Israels', *ZAW* 42 (1924), 272–96.

[6] P. Humbert, *Recherches sur les sources égyptiennes de la littérature sapientale d'Israël* (Neuchâtel, 1929), 181. In part, Humbert was following the ideas of P. Volz, *Hiob und Weisheit* (Göttingen, 1921), 101.

during which literature was cultivated and the royal court became a 'nursery' for international wisdom, an opinion which has enjoyed wide currency.[7] William McKane and others have discussed the relationship between wise men and prophets.[8] The interpretation of Proverbs has stressed the presence of sayings related to king and court, and key concepts have been understood in terms of an administrative or educational background. Some approaches to the redaction and composition of the book, most notably McKane's, have posited an original 'secular' stage, principally concerned with career-development and *realpolitik*.

Perhaps the most significant impact of such hypotheses has been upon the interpretation of other parts of the Old Testament. Many books or sections show affinities with the wisdom literature in form, vocabulary, or thought, and these are frequently understood to be evidence of 'wisdom influence'. The association of wisdom with the administrative profession has set such influence on a historical, rather than simply a literary level. Moshe Weinfeld, for instance, argues that the Deuteronomists, whose work shows some affinities with the wisdom literature, must have belonged to the scribal class;[9] von Rad long ago argued that the Joseph Narrative must be scribal;[10] and a scribal background has been suggested for the prophet Isaiah.[11] With these and other studies suggesting 'wisdom influence' across much of the Old Testament, there is some perception that the fashion has gone too far, and caution has now begun to prevail.[12] However, the quest for such influence has already had very considerable consequences for the interpretation of many passages.

Such a thumbnail sketch does little justice to the liveliness of discussion within the subject, and it is true that some dissent has

---

[7] See esp. G. von Rad, 'Der Anfang der Geschichtsschreibung im alten Israel', *AK* 32 (1944), 1–42, and 'Josephsgeschichte und ältere Chokma', SVT 1 (1953), 120–7. ETs in *The Problem of the Hexateuch and other Essays* (Edinburgh and London, 1965), 166–204, 292–300.

[8] W. McKane, *Prophets and Wise Men* (London, 1965); cf. J. Fichtner, 'Jesaja unter den Weisen', *Th. LZ* 74 (1949), cols. 75–80; ET in J. L. Crenshaw (ed.), *Studies in Ancient Israelite Wisdom* (New York, 1976), 429–38.

[9] M. Weinfeld, *Deuteronomy and the Deuteronomic School* (Oxford, 1972).

[10] von Rad, 'Josephsgeschichte und ältere Chokma'. See Ch. 6, below.

[11] Fichtner, 'Jesaja unter den Weisen'.

[12] See J. L. Crenshaw, 'Method in Determining Wisdom Influence upon "Historical" Literature', *JBL* 88 (1969), 129–42; D. F. Morgan, *Wisdom in the Old Testament Traditions* (Atlanta and Oxford, 1981).

been voiced, most notably by R. N. Whybray.[13] It cannot
be denied, though, that the broad hypothesis of wisdom's
origins in the education of administrators has taken on the
status of an 'assured result', and that it has had profound
effects.

It is always healthy to re-examine 'assured results' once in a
while, and in this case such a re-examination is long overdue. The
non-Israelite literature, which played such an important role in
shaping the hypothesis, is now much better known and understood;
at the same time, assumptions and methods in the study of biblical
texts have changed considerably over the years. This book is an
attempt to reconsider the evidence in the light of such changes,
and challenges many of the conclusions which have been reached.
It is my hope that this will clear the ground for the future study
of Proverbs, but I have not set out an alternative hypothesis
myself: that is a very different undertaking, which would require
much more discussion than is possible here. On particular
issues, however, I do try to offer alternative interpretations or
explanations.

The first two chapters deal briefly and selectively with the use
of non-Israelite literature and with the structure of sentence
literature. In part they are prefatory, presenting information
which will be used in subsequent chapters, but they are also
intended to highlight particular problems in current approaches to
the material. Non-Israelite sources are listed in an Appendix;
when such texts are referred to elsewhere, a Roman numeral in
brackets indicates their place in the list. The rest of the book
examines specific issues and theories relevant to the origins and
setting of wisdom literature.

Except where otherwise indicated, I have assumed throughout
the conventional divisions of the material in Proverbs. I have not,
however, attempted to rank the various sections chronologically.
The usual, late dating of chs. 1–9 rests principally upon form-
critical and stylistic assumptions which are now generally acknowledged to be false. Other grounds for such a dating are very slight,
and it seems to have been maintained through a mixture of
conservatism and intuition. While sharing that intuition, I can see

---

[13] R. N. Whybray, *The Intellectual Tradition in the Old Testament* (Berlin,
1974).

no compelling evidence for placing those chapters, or any part of the book, substantially later than the rest. For comparative and other purposes, I have tried to take account of the fact that the material may be as early as the tenth or as late as about the fourth century BC. We can probably be more precise than this, but not certainly so.

I

Using the Non-Israelite Sources

In 1924 Adolf Erman pointed out that a series of parallels between sayings in Prov. 22. 17–23. 10 and the Egyptian *Instruction of Amenemope* (**xiii**) were so close and so concentrated that it was necessary to acknowledge some relationship between the texts.[1] In the Saite or Persian period, he supposed, a Jew living in Egypt must have become familiar with *Amenemope*, which was then in use as a school-book, and adapted it to produce a work in Hebrew which was compatible with Jewish ideas. This book was in turn taken up by the collectors of Proverbs, who cannibalized it, ignoring the original structure and features. They did, however, unwittingly preserve clues to its origin, most notably an obscured reference to 'thirty sayings' in 22. 20, reflecting the thirty chapters of *Amenemope*.[2] Although the nature of the relationship and the number of parallels have been the subject of much debate, subsequent scholarship has generally accepted the existence of a link. No comparable relationship with any other text has been discovered, but many structural similarities and close parallels between specific sayings are now widely recognized, and are taken to show that the writers of Proverbs were familiar with other foreign wisdom material.

It is not easy, however, to determine the exact nature of the relationship between the Israelite and non-Israelite material, either in general or in specific cases. Indeed, there are still many different explanations current even for the link with *Amenemope*, with scholars arguing variously for direct or indirect dependence

[1] Erman, 'Eine ägyptische Quelle'.
[2] The emendation of MT *šilšôm* (Q. *šālîšîm*) to *šelōšîm* in 22. 20 is a good explanation for a difficult text, but whether we should go on to seek thirty actual sayings in the section is another matter: the reference may be to an earlier stage of transmission or adaptation. See W. Richter, *Recht und Ethos: Versuch einer Ortung des weisheitlichen Mahnspruches* (Munich, 1966), 17–21, 36 f.; also O. Plöger, *Sprüche Salomos (Proverbia)* (Neukirchen, 1981–4), 266.

of the Hebrew on the Egyptian, or for a common source.[3] That the Egyptian was secondary is, at least, now ruled out by consensus of an early date for *Amenemope*, recognition of its place in New Kingdom thought, and thorough refutation of arguments for the presence of non-Egyptian expressions and ideas.[4] Anyway, if it is difficult to clarify the relationship even in this case, it is all but impossible when resemblances are broader or more isolated. In other words, we cannot claim that any extant text, except *Amenemope*, was itself probably known to the Israelite writers, and are restricted to saying that those writers seem to have been broadly familiar with certain sayings and styles of literature current in the Near East.

Such familiarity is often explained in terms of an 'international' wisdom movement, which transcended national boundaries and in which the Israelite writers participated. This is in turn associated with ideas of a cosmopolitan scribal class, representing 'wisdom' in each nation. However, lumping the texts together like this serves only to blur the issues and confuse the terminology. Although there may have been literary influence across national boundaries from an early stage, the Egyptian and Mesopotamian texts are firmly tied to the particular literate cultures from which they emerged, and are not merely ambassadors from some international movement. Although it is convenient to use 'wisdom literature' as a designation of genre in non-Israelite literature, it is not possible to isolate a specific 'wisdom school', physical or philosophical, in either Egypt or Mesopotamia. As regards the 'scribal' character of the texts, Michael Fox has rightly pointed out that its origins in the scribal élite of Egypt do not distinguish wisdom literature from most other forms of Egyptian literature, since they too, in all their variety, were produced by that class.[5] There is no reason to describe the scribal class in Egypt as the 'wisdom' class, nor any evidence to suggest that wisdom literature was produced by a specific group within that class. The situation is somewhat different for Mesopotamia, but the principle is the

---

[3] Opinions were surveyed in G. E. Bryce, *A Legacy of Wisdom* (Lewisburg, Pa., and London, 1979), 15–56. Now see also D. Römheld, *Wege der Weisheit* (Berlin, 1989).

[4] See R. J. Williams, 'The Alleged Semitic Original of the Wisdom of Amenemope', *JEA* 47 (1961), 100–6.

[5] M. V. Fox, 'Two Decades of Research in Egyptian Wisdom Literature', *ZÄS* 107 (1980), 120–35; see 128 f.

same: 'scribal' and 'wisdom' are not synonymous descriptions, and there is no distinct 'wisdom' group. In short, it is impossible to identify an international wisdom movement operating within national scribal classes, while these classes as a whole cannot meaningfully be identified as such a movement.

Accordingly, the Israelite wisdom literature cannot be placed within an international wisdom movement. Rather, it almost certainly lies within an undirected network of specific influences across a large area and a long period. The extent and direction of these influences cannot be determined, and this makes the assessment of parallels between Proverbs and other texts extremely difficult. At the heart of the problem lies a lack of evidence: it is unlikely that the material preserved in Proverbs represents the whole corpus of such material in Israel, just as it is unlikely that we possess anything like all the relevant works from Egypt and Mesopotamia; with the probable exception of *Ahikar*, we know nothing of the wisdom literature which may have been produced in the nations closer to Israel, and which may have served as a conduit for Egyptian and Mesopotamian material. Furthermore, material could have been transmitted orally, and this route, naturally, would have left no trace. The problem is compounded, finally, by the possibility of coincidence: similar thoughts and sayings may have originated quite independently in different times and places.

If we cannot adequately evaluate the relationship, how, then, can we use the non-Israelite literature to further our understanding of Proverbs? There is no straightforward answer to this, but a brief examination of some previous attempts does help to clarify the issues and set some ground-rules. My examples are drawn principally from the study of Prov. 1–9, and are arranged according to the aspect of the literature which is supposed to be elucidated through comparison with the foreign texts.

1. *Formal Features of the Literature*

(a) *Instruction and Sentence Literature*

McKane and Kayatz have drawn a useful distinction between 'instruction' and 'sentence literature', which is based upon study

of the non-Israelite texts.[6] Broadly speaking, 'instruction' is preceptive and gives direct advice, usually explained in subsequent
subordinate clauses. 'Sentence literature', on the other hand,
consists of observations in the form of statements. Thus, in Prov.
I, v. 7 is a sentence-literature form, while v. 8 is instruction.
Despite such juxtapositions, one form or the other tends to
predominate within particular sections of the book, and so Prov.
10. 1–22. 16 may be described as sentence literature, while 22.
17–24. 34 is instruction. This predominance of one or other form
characterizes the non-Israelite literature from an early time, a fact
which strongly contradicts the old view that the longer units of
instruction developed within Israel from the shorter statements of
the sentence literature.[7]

It would be unwise to push the distinction too far. McKane
regards instruction as a 'genre' which can be defined syntactically,
but it is difficult to apply such a definition to all the Egyptian
instructions, which vary considerably in style and mode of address.
More practically, statements and direct address are frequently
found together in Israelite and foreign works, while certain
instruction forms, such as the bipartite prohibition, are often
treated as though they were 'sentences' by the redactors of
sentence literature. It would certainly be wrong to presume that
a strong distinction was drawn at the time of composition. In other
words, it is convenient for us to differentiate between sentence
literature, where the units are predominantly short sentences
without subordinate clauses, and instruction, where they are
predominantly longer and formed around direct advice, but this
should not become a rigid dogma.

Sentence literature is unusual in Egypt before the Late Period
but it is the normal form in earlier Mesopotamian texts. Miriam
Lichtheim has sought to explain the change in Egypt as a consequence of foreign influence, and this is not improbable, although
she does overlook the earlier Pap. Ramesseum II (x), which shows
that monostichic sentence literature was known as early as the
Middle Kingdom.[8] In any case, it is impossible to establish a

---

[6] McKane, *Proverbs: A New Approach*; C. Kayatz, *Studien zu Proverbien* 1–9
(Neukirchen, 1966).

[7] Cf. J. Schmidt, *Studien zur Stilistik der alttestamentlichen Spruchliteratur*
(Münster, 1936).

[8] M. T. Lichtheim, *Late Egyptian Wisdom Literature in the International Context*
(Freiburg and Göttingen, 1983).

relative dating of Israelite sentence literature and instruction by
the appearance of the forms elsewhere. For our study of Proverbs,
the most important consequence of isolating the sentence literature
lies in the area of composition and structure: the non-Israelite
sentence literature may be shown to rely heavily on the use of
catchwords and similar organizational techniques. This will be
explored in the next chapter, and the approach taken there may
be justified by reference to the foreign texts.

(b) *Attribution*

The attribution of literature to a named author was unusual in
Egypt, but was a characteristic of the 'instructions' from an early
time. In part this may be due to some early relationship with tomb
inscriptions,[9] but it is also likely that the reputation of the author
was used to underwrite the value of the instruction. By the
New Kingdom, when the protagonists are less prominent men,
the practice may have become more simply conventional. In
Mesopotamia, attributions are rare, but this may be due in part to
the fragmentary nature of our texts. It is noteworthy that the
earliest of the works from there, *The Instructions of Šuruppak*
*(***xxxiii** cf. **xxxix**), is attributed to a legendary figure. In fact, it is
now widely held that a number of non-Israelite works are pseudonymous, and that the earliest Egyptian instructions are also back-
dated.[10] In some cases this is indisputable: the protagonists of
Šuruppak and *The Farmer's Instruction* (**xxxv**) are legendary
or mythical, while *The Instruction of King Amenemhet* (**v**) is
supposedly given by the king after his death.[11] It is not clear
whether the protagonists of '*Onchsheshonqy* (**xxi**) or *Ahikar* (**li**)
ever actually existed.[12] More controversially, it has been argued

---

[9] See J. Assmann, 'Schrift, Tod und Identität: Das Grab als Vorschule der
Literatur im alten Ägypten', in A. Assmann *et al.* (eds.), *Schrift und Gedächtnis*
(Munich, 1983), 64–93.

[10] Ibid., esp. p. 86; also e.g. J. Baines, 'Literacy and Ancient Egyptian Society',
Man, NS 18 (1983), 572–99, esp. 578.

[11] See references in the Appendix, section (**v**).

[12] A late text from Uruk published by Van Dijk on pp. 44 ff. of H. J. Lenzen
(ed.), *XVIII, vorläufiger Bericht . . . in Uruk-Warka* (Berlin, 1962), has often been
taken to prove the existence of a historical Ahikar, *ummânu* to Esarhaddon; see
e.g. J. C. Greenfield, 'The Background and Parallel to a Proverb of Ahiqar', in
A. Caquot and M. Philolenko (eds.), *Hommages à André Dupont-Sommer* (Paris,
1971), 49–59. However, it probably proves nothing more than the influence of the
story in the Seleucid period.

on a number of grounds that *Hardjedef, Kagemni, Ptahhotep*, and, perhaps, *Merikare* (**i–iv**) were written substantially later than they claim to have been.[13] The motivation for such pseudonymity must have been a desire to associate the instructions not only with famous or important men, but also with the past. *Ptahhotep* speaks of instruction as something written for the benefit of posterity (ll. 517–19), and the classical version of *Šuruppak*, in particular, emphasizes the great age of the instruction (ll. 1–3); from New Kingdom Egypt we have evidence of a late work actually entitled *The Instruction According to Ancient Writings* (**xv**).

If pseudonymity and back-dating are not features of all the comparable works, their occurrence in some should at least lead us to look critically at the attributions in Proverbs. For Agur (30. 1) and Lemuel (31. 1), we can go little further than this. The attributions to Solomon, on the other hand, are questionable on other grounds, as we shall see later. If they are taken to be unhistorical, then they might possibly be explained in the same terms as the non-Israelite attributions, as attempts to link the material with the past and with a man renowned for his wisdom. Whether this was influenced directly by non-Israelite conventions is another matter: while there is evidence that pseudonymity in the earlier texts was recognized,[14] it cannot be shown to have been a common feature in later Egyptian or Mesopotamian works. More generally, though, it does seem probable that the attribution of material in Proverbs followed the non-Israelite convention of naming a source for the instruction, even allowing that named attribution is not so uncommon in Israelite literature.

(c) *Prologue and Title Forms*

In his early work on Prov. 1–9, R. N. Whybray argued that a basic form underlies the 'introductions' in 1. 8 ff.; 2. 1 ff.; 3. 1 ff., 21 ff.; 4.1 ff., 10 ff., 20 ff.; 5. 1 ff.; 6. 20 ff.; 7. 1 ff. This form, he claimed, resembles the introductions to Egyptian and some

---

[13] Generally, see n. 10. For *Ptahhotep*, see E. Blumenthal, 'Ptahhotep und der "Stab des Alters"', in J. Osing and G. Dreyer (eds.), *Form und Mass* (Wiesbaden, 1987), 84–97; P. Seibert, *Die Charakteristik*, i (Wiesbaden, 1967). For *Hardjedef*: W. Helck, 'Zur Frage der Enstehung der ägyptischen Literatur', *WZKM* 63/64 (1972), 6–26, esp. 16–19, with a contrary view in H. Brunner, 'Zitate aus Lebenslehren', in E. Hornung and O. Keel (eds.), *Studien zu altägyptischen Lebenslehren* (Freiburg and Göttingen, 1979), 105–71, esp. 117 f., 122.

[14] *Amenemhet* is attributed to Khety in Pap. Chester Beatty IV.

Babylonian instructions so closely that it must itself be recognized as a prologue form, marking in each case the beginning of a distinct discourse. This is a conclusion which Whybray has recently affirmed,[15] and it is, on the face of it, a reasonable one. However, even leaving aside the question of whether a precise prologue form can be isolated in the foreign texts, Whybray's approach raises a number of serious problems. Considerable emendation, not justifiable on other grounds, is needed to uncover any single basic form in these 'introductions'. Moreover, even if we acknowledge a similarity to the prologues of other works, we need not suppose that an Israelite redactor employed a borrowed form mechanistically. Given the paucity of concrete instruction in the section, it is possible that the redactor of Prov. 1–9 is attempting a more general treatment of instruction and wisdom, such as is found in the prologues or epilogues of some other works. In that case, he may be deliberately evoking the prologue form in various guises, not to make the beginning of new sections, but to emphasize the nature of his own work. Alternatively, the influence may be from a tradition which employed resumptive prologues, as in *Šuruppak*, where the 'prologues' do not seem to mark the beginning of independent, coherent units. My point here is not that Whybray must be wrong, but that in reaching conclusions based on a link with the foreign literature he makes insufficient allowance either for the variety within that literature or for the autonomy of the Israelite text. In almost all those areas where parallels can be drawn, not least its style, Prov. 1–9 shows an inclination to vary from attested norms. Whether this reflects redactional freedom or influence from unknown sources, there is certainly no slavish dependence on any known usage.

The view that Prov. 1–9 is itself a sort of prologue has, in fact, been adopted by Kenneth Kitchen in two ambitious articles which attempt to classify all the extant Near Eastern literature.[16] The exhortatory content of the section, he argues, is comparable to the short exhortatory prologues in many instructions, and reveals it to

---

[15] R. N. Whybray, *Wisdom in Proverbs* (London, 1965), esp. 33–71. Cf. his *Wealth and Poverty in the Book of Proverbs* (Sheffield, 1990), p. 99, n. 2.

[16] K. A. Kitchen, 'Proverbs and Wisdom Books of the Ancient Near East: The Factual History of a Literary Form', *Tyndale Bulletin*, 28 (1977), 69–114, and 'The Basic Literary Forms and Formulations of Ancient Instructional Writings in Egypt and Western Asia', in Hornung and Keel (eds.), *Altägyptischen Lebenslehren*, 235–82.

be the prologue to a longer work, 'Solomon I', which extends to ch. 24. That prologues have been a major influence on the section certainly seems very possible, but Kitchen goes on to draw further conclusions of more dubious value. In particular, he believes that the length of Prov. 1–9 shows it to be a transitional stage between short exhortatory prologues and the longer narrative prologues of ʿOnchsheshonqy and Ahikar.[17] Since there is no reason to believe that the later narratives somehow developed from the quite different exhortatory sections, though they may have replaced them, this argument is quite without force, and the length of the section cannot be used to date it.

Prologues are, it so happens, an important element in Kitchen's overall classification, which divides texts into two types according to whether or not they have a prologue between the title and the main text. Since other structural elements seem to be variable, there are no other major criteria for distinguishing between the two types, both of which are found in all periods with no particular geographical bias. In that case, one may well ask (as Kitchen does not), what is it about the presence or absence of a prologue which is so significant for understanding the nature of these texts? No justification is given for the criterion, and no search made for a better one. Furthermore, a 'prologue' for Kitchen is simply anything preceding the main text, regardless of form or nature, and this itself undermines his approach.

Finally, it is worth mentioning Kitchen's treatment of titles, which are important for his division of the material in Proverbs. In particular, he considers 10. 1 and 24. 23 to be 'subtitles' rather than proper titles, on the grounds that they are too short ever to have stood independently. For very different reasons, to be discussed later, I am inclined to agree with his conclusion that they never stood at the head of separate works. Their length, however, is irrelevant: while some features, such as an attribution, are certainly standard features of title sections, the length of such sections varies considerably and is probably the least appropriate criterion for determining whether or not something is a proper title.

(d) *Parallelism*

Most of the material in Proverbs employs the poetic technique of parallelism, which is unusual in the foreign literature. Kitchen

[17] Kitchen, 'The Basic Literary Forms', 248.

takes this as a criterion for dating, suggesting that as parallelism is found primarily in the early non-Israelite texts, its use in Proverbs implies an early date.[18] Since early texts continued to circulate for many centuries, stylistic and other features can at most be used to suggest a date *post quem*, and even then the position may be complicated by our ignorance of prior traditions. This, and the presence of parallelism in some late texts, invalidate Kitchen's conclusion. Of more interest, perhaps, is the way in which extensive parallelism distinguishes Proverbs from most foreign texts, but brings it into line with normal Hebrew poetic techniques. Again, it is difficult to draw conclusions without knowing the whole corpus of Near Eastern wisdom literature, but it seems likely that the extensive use of parallelism is a national or regional characteristic.

2. *Themes and Motifs*

(a) *Women in Prov.* 1–9

The general and exhortatory nature of this section has already been noted: specific, practical advice on day-to-day matters is thin on the ground here. It is surprising, therefore, that one very specific topic, the dangers of seductive women, should come so to dominate in the second half. This becomes all the more curious when we consider the foreign parallels and the rest of Proverbs: warnings about women are common but never predominate in this way. As with parallelism, it may be that the principal significance here lies not in the similarity but in the difference between this text and comparable material. If the redactor of Prov. 1–9 is not simply a full-blooded misogynist, then it is reasonable to assume from its unusual prominence that the theme of the dangerous woman has some special meaning or relevance in the section. In view of the deliberate contrast in ch. 9 and the nature of the woman's seductions,[19] it seems very possible that the woman is

---

[18] Kitchen, 'Proverbs and Wisdom Books', e.g. 98 f.

[19] See J. N. Aletti, 'Séduction et parole en Proverbes I–IX', *VT* 27 (1977), 129–44, who points out that it is, significantly, the woman's speech which accomplishes the seduction; more recently, G. A. Yee, '"I Have Perfumed my Bed with Myrrh": The Foreign Woman (*'iššâ zārâ*) in Proverbs 1–9', *JSOT* 43 (1989), 53–68, also notes the importance of speech, but emphasizes the similarities in the portrayal of Wisdom and the foreign woman, and the eroticism which surrounds each.

portrayed as a counterpart to the figure of personified Wisdom: where Wisdom represents the path of life, and her invitations are to be accepted, the woman represents falling away from that path, and her deadly invitations are to be resisted.[20] Be that as it may, we have in this case to look beyond the mere existence of foreign parallels, and to compare extent and usage.

(b) *Maternal Instruction*

In the Egyptian texts, direct address to 'my son' occurs only once, in a very late instruction, but it is common in the Mesopotamian material.[21] Equally, we find in Mesopotamia admonitions to obey both parents, and apparent reference to the mother as a source of guidance or teaching,[22] while such references are unknown in Egypt. This suggests the possibility of Mesopotamian influence, direct or indirect, upon Prov. 1–9, where addresses to 'my son' are common and the mother appears alongside the father as a source of teaching (1. 8; 6. 20), in addition to the Egyptian influence which is commonly acknowledged. In view of this, claims that references to the mother as teacher are 'unique',[23] and their use in discussions of 'family wisdom' or of the authority of women in Israel,[24] must be treated with great caution: this is not a concept restricted to Israel, and it may simply have been inherited as a motif. That said, such references do show that 'father' here is not a cipher for 'schoolmaster', and that Prov. 1–9 is genuinely intended to be seen as parental instruction, whether this is a fiction or not. Bearing in mind also the maternal instruction of Lemuel (31. 1), the Good Wife's wise teaching in 31. 26, and the female characterization of personified Wisdom, it seems clear that the idea of women as a source of instruction was acceptable in

---

[20] This is not an original suggestion. See esp. Yee, 'The Foreign Woman in Proverbs 1–9, and perhaps R. E. Murphy, *The Tree of Life* (New York, 1990), 17 f.

[21] Cf. Kitchen, 'Proverbs and Wisdom Books', 82; occurrences in *Šuruppak, Šube'awilum* and *Counsels of Wisdom*, also in *Ahikar*, which was certainly influenced by the Mesopotamian tradition. The Egyptian occurrence is in P. inv. Sorbonne 1260 (**xxiii**), frag. a, 1. 6.

[22] See especially *Šuruppak* (**xxxiii**) 259 f., in the section reconstructed by Alster on pp. 137 ff. of *Studies in Sumerian Proverbs* (Copenhagen, 1975); cf. the similar saying in rev. 5. 1 of *A Sumerian Preceptive Work* (**xxxiv**).

[23] See Whybray, *The Intellectual Tradition in the Old Testament*, 42.

[24] e.g. C. V. Camp, *Wisdom and the Feminine in the Book of Proverbs* (Sheffield, 1985), 82; J. L. Crenshaw, 'Education in Ancient Israel', *JBL* 104 (1985), 601–15, esp. 614.

Israelite wisdom literature; it is not, however, an idea specific to
Israel.

3. *General Considerations*

There are many other areas in which foreign parallels have been
discussed or used by scholars, but these few cases serve to
illustrate the key problems. First of all, overall classification of the
texts presents many difficulties: the extant tests do not fall neatly
into identifiable groups, and no classification has been achieved
beyond the broad differentiation between instruction and sentence
literature. It is questionable whether any more precise classification of all the texts is desirable. I suggested earlier that it is a
mistake to lump these texts together as an international phenomenon, and this is borne out by those features which are found
or predominate in some traditions but not others. There is
nothing to suggest that redactors simply borrowed from a central
set of models, and every reason to believe that they shaped
material in accordance with their own ideas and cultural
contexts.

Consequently, the existence of foreign parallels is not in itself
a sufficient explanation for the presence of particular themes or
features in Proverbs, and we need to compare the ways in which
these themes are used. In the case of the seductress in Prov. 1–9,
a difference in emphasis and extent may suggest that a traditional
theme has been taken up and used almost symbolically. In a
similar way, the prologue forms in the same section may serve to
show the affinities of that section, while having their structural
function transformed. Both these issues, incidentally, raise
interesting questions about the nature and redactional techniques
of Prov. 1–9. On the other hand, very similar usage may suggest
a more straightforward borrowing of conventions: this may have
happened in the case of the addresses to 'my son', and I shall argue
later that it may also have happened with sayings about the king
in other sections of Proverbs. In short, we must allow for, but not
assume, creativity in the use of borrowed elements. This can be
judged only tentatively through a comparison with use of those
elements in the other extant texts.

Associated with this is the whole issue of acceptance and
assimilation. The universality of so much in wisdom literature

is probably the single most important reason for its wide dissemination, and many of the sayings or themes in a text could readily be adapted to suit a new context. The problem for us is that such adaptation might not always require any change in wording beyond simple translation, the actual change being in the presuppositions of the new audience. Thus a declaration that, say, the wicked will perish, may have originated in a nation where it connoted inherent causation; transferred to a culture where direct divine judgement was anticipated, the same saying would merely be read against this different background of ideas, with which it remained compatible. Again, elements which originally had some much greater significance might remain as mere poetic metaphors, stripped of ideological or mythological meaning.[25] Consequently, the presence of certain themes and motifs need not say anything about the ideology or background of wisdom in Israel, and might merely signify the broad acceptability of such things when read in the context of Israelite society and belief. This is why it would be unwise to draw too many conclusions from the references to maternal instruction.

Such problems paint a gloomy picture. We cannot establish central models against which Proverbs may be compared, but must resort to comparison with a varied and incomplete set of texts. We can never be certain whether or not a redactor is using his sources creatively, and cannot usually, indeed, pinpoint those sources precisely. It is even difficult for us to say how the redactors themselves understood some of the material which they borrowed. In sum, the foreign parallels cannot be used straightforwardly to illuminate the structure or meaning of material in Proverbs, and they do not excuse us from a proper exegesis of the text. They may, however, serve as a check and guide in some areas. So, for instance, foreign parallels prevent the assumption that instruction developed from sentence literature in Israel, highlight the dominance of parallelism in Proverbs, and suggest reasons for the attribution of material to Solomon. In general, they give us some idea of the sort of sources which Proverbs probably drew upon, and allow us, therefore, to undertake a tentative redaction criticism.

[25] See e.g. Prov. 16. 12; 20. 28 LXX; 25. 4 f: the image of the throne supported by righteousness may go back to Egyptian ideas. See Ch. 3 n. 22, below.

4. *Establishing the Nature and Purpose of Proverbs*

On a much broader level, the non-Israelite sources are frequently deployed in arguments about the nature of Proverbs. Indeed, as we have seen, analogy with them originally underpinned Humbert's influential hypothesis. There are, in fact, two issues involved here: the actual nature of the foreign material, and the propriety of drawing analogies. The second is the more important, and is frequently overlooked: the Egyptian and Mesopotamian texts arose fully within their own cultures, in response to the needs and conditions of those cultures. We violate basic principles of method if we ignore the underlying context and start picking and choosing parallels from such different societies in order to elucidate phenomena within Israel.[26] Humbert himself was writing at a time when attitudes were somewhat different and the comparative approach still flourishing, but there is no reason for modern scholarship to follow his example.

Equally, Egyptology has moved on since Humbert's time, and the 'pragmatic misinterpretation' of Egyptian instructions, which we shall discuss later, has been generally discarded. Unfortunately, there is often little recognition of this in OT scholarship, where descriptions of the instructions as manuals or 'guide-books to success'[27] are still commonplace. In fact, the genre probably belongs in the category of 'high literature' or '*belles lettres*'.[28] Its origins are obscure, but probably pre-literary, and related in some way to tomb inscriptions;[29] a party-political or propagandist purpose has been suggested for many of the Middle Kingdom texts.[30] Some instructions took on the status of classics,[31] and were

---

[26] See S. Talmon, 'The "Comparative Method" in Biblical Interpretation—Principles and Problems', SVT 29 (1977), 320–56.

[27] Eric Heaton's description, in *Solomon's New Men* (London, 1974), 116.

[28] See e.g. P. Kaplony, 'Die Definition der schönen Literatur im alten Ägypten', in J. Assmann *et al.* (eds.), *Fragen an die altägyptische Literatur* (Wiesbaden, 1977), 289–314, and R. B. Parkinson, 'Tales, Teachings and Discourses from the Middle Kingdom', in S. Quirke (ed.), *Middle Kingdom Studies* (New Malden, 1991), with references. For a similar description of the Sumerian material, see S. N. Kramer, 'Sumerian Literature: A General Survey', in G. E. Wright (ed.), *The Bible and the Ancient Near East* (Garden City, NY, 1961), 249–66.   [29] See n. 9, above.

[30] See e.g. G. Posener, *Littérature et politique dans l'Egypte de la XIIᵉ Dynastie* (Paris, 1956).

[31] See especially the NK eulogy to authors on Pap. Chester Beatty IV; there is a new translation on pp. 148–50 of R. B. Parkinson, *Voices from Ancient Egypt* (London, 1991).

used, along with other, non-didactic works, as set texts in the Egyptian schools of the New Kingdom and Late Period. Amongst those most widely attested in school copies are *Amenemhet* (**v**) and *Khety* (**vi**), neither of which is primarily didactic or a 'guide-book to success': both are classic instructions, and this use is comparable to the reading of Shakespeare or Chaucer in a modern English school. At the same time, new compositions were produced, perhaps actually addressed to sons of the authors, but with a view to a wider audience.[32]

In the light of all this, and of the highly literary style of the works, it is hard to believe that the instruction genre was simply one of textbooks or manuals. Furthermore, in addition to familiarizing pupils with classic literature, the older instructions would also have been used in schools for the teaching of Middle Egyptian, already an archaic language by the end of the Middle Kingdom and doubtless all but incomprehensible to a pupil in the Late Period. It seems incredible that such works could be supposed to function as practical manuals, when the students' principal difficulty would have been in understanding them. In general, it is possible to say that many instructions were intended to show their readers how to reach a greater attunement with the social and world order, and thus improve themselves. This is hardly, though, a narrow pedagogical purpose, and in some texts it may well be a secondary purpose. Consequently, even were we to draw a straight analogy between Proverbs and the Egyptian texts, it would not lead us to conclude that early Israelite wisdom literature was written specifically for the training of officials, nor would it justify a 'pragmatic' interpretation of the text.

---

[32] Cf. Ostracon Oriental Institute 12074 (**xix**).

2

Context in the Sayings Collections

When studying the nature of the major sections in Proverbs, it is the 'sentence literature', of which the largest collections are to be found in chs. 10. 1–22. 16 and chs. 25–9, which poses the greatest difficulties of method. Some scholars have, in fact, been inclined to disregard altogether the presentation of the sayings in collections. So McKane declares that: 'While it is important to pay attention to the principles which determine the association of sentences, it is none the less true that these are secondary groupings which do not significantly alter the atomistic character of sentence literature.'[1] At the other extreme, as we shall see below, some scholars perceive in the collections intricate and subtle patterns which are vital indications of a deeper meaning. Most often, the analysis tends to be an unsystematic combination of both these approaches, where the position of sayings is taken into account when it makes some convenient point, but otherwise disregarded. In view of this confusion, it seems important to examine the whole question of what constitutes a 'collection' in Proverbs, and to consider how significant such a concept is for interpreting the sayings and understanding the tradition.

Unfortunately, we know nothing and can deduce little about the materials which preceded and underlie the present collections. Doublets, along with the evidence for the Demotic and Sumerian collections, may suggest that a number of smaller collections coexisted and interacted, and, as I shall show, we do have some grounds for identifying two large sub-collections within each of the major collections. However, those sub-collections show a broad formal consistency, and if many earlier collections were indeed employed in their creation, they seem to have been thoroughly redacted. In any case, our ignorance of the sources makes our study of the redaction that much more difficult, and by excluding

[1] McKane, *Proverbs: A New Approach*, 413.

any assessment of the redactor's selectivity, it forces us to concentrate upon his arrangement of the material. This is not quite so restrictive as it sounds, and in the first part of this chapter I shall try to show just how much information can be garnered through an analysis of the links between sayings; in the second part I shall review some of the limitations.

1. *Nearest-Neighbour Analysis*

The approach taken here is not new, and is based upon a phenomenon often noted, that sayings are frequently linked in some fashion with one or both of the sayings adjacent to them. This is true also of much non-Israelite sentence literature. The method has an appearance of objectivity which is slightly misleading, as certain judgements have to be made about the more doubtful links, and, more importantly, about what constitutes a 'theme'. Despite this and other drawbacks, I think that it is probably the closest that we can get to an objective and controlled method, and that it offers greater insights than have previously been appreciated. I shall treat the two main collections separately.

(a) *Chapters* 10. 1–22. 16

This section contains 375 sayings, all but one of which (19. 7) consist of a single line divided into two stichs. The sentences thus formed are predominantly statements, and most employ parallelism. Many are linked to an adjacent saying, or to sayings on both sides. This linkage is achieved in various ways, of which three are particularly common:

(i) Thematic linking: adjacent sayings deal with the same subject or theme; e.g. all the sayings in 14. 6–8 deal with the fool's lack of wisdom.

(ii) Verbal linking: adjacent sayings employ the same or similar items of vocabulary; e.g. in the same passage, *wĕdaʿat* in v. 6 is picked up by *yādaʿtā* and *dāʿat* in v. 7, *kĕsîl* in v. 7 by *kesîlîm* in v. 8. The chain extends, in fact, to v. 9, where *ʾĕwilîm* picks up *wĕʾiwwelet* from v. 8.

(iii) Literal thinking: adjacent sayings share the same initial letter, or a sequence of initial letters is repeated; e.g. all the sayings in 11. 9–12 begin with the letter *beth*.

Diagram 1. Thematic and verbal/literal links in Prov. 10.1–22.6. A line to the left of the references indicates verbal and/or literal links; a line to the right, thematic linking.

```
10  1    6     12    21    33    2     6     15    28      6  12
    2    7     13    22    34    3     7     16    29      7  13
    3    8     14    23    35    4     8     17  20 1      8  14
    4    9     15    24  15 1    5     9     18    2       9  15
    5    10    16    25    2     6     10    19    3      10  16
    6    11    17  14 1    3     7     11    20    4      11
    7    12    18    2     4     8     12    21    5      12
    8    13    19    3     5     9     13    22    6      13
    9    14    20    4     6     10    14    23    7      14
    10   15    21    5     7     11    15    24    8      15
    11   16    22    6     8     12    16  19 1    9      16
    12   17    23    7     9     13    17    2     10     17
    13   18    24    8     10    14    18    3     11     18
    14   19    25    9     11    15    19    4     12     19
    15   20    26    10    12    16    20    5     13     20
    16   21    27    11    13    17    21    6     14     21
    17   22    28    12    14    18    22    7     15     22
    18   23  13 1    13    15    19    23    8     16     23
    19   24    2     14    16    20    24    9     17     24
    20   25    3     15    17    21    25    10    18     25
    21   26    4     16    18    22    26    11    19     26
    22   27    5     17    19    23    27    12    20     27
    23   28    6     18    20    24    28    13    21     28
    24   29    7     19    21    25  18 1    14    22     29
    25   30    8     20    22    26    2     15    23     30
    26   31    9     21    23    27    3     16    24     31
    27 12 1   10    22    24    28    4     17    25  22 1
    28   2    11    23    25    29    5     18    26     2
    29   3    12    24    26    30    6     19    27     3
    30   4    13    25    27    31    7     20    28     4
    31   5    14    26    28    32    8     21    29     5
    32   6    15    27    29    33    9     22    30     6
11  1    7    16    28    30  17 1    10    23  21 1     7
    2    8    17    29    31    2     11    24    2       8
    3    9    18    30    32    3     12    25    3       9
    4    10   19    31    33    4     13    26    4      10
    5    11   20    32  16 1    5     14    27    5      11
```

Diagram 1 shows the links formed by these methods. Often more than one of the methods is employed, and sometimes more than one is represented by the same features, as when a catchword is also the initial word, or embodies the theme. Verbal and literal links are closely related and frequently indistinguishable: I have treated them as a single method in the diagram, and represented the presence of verbal and/or literal links by a line to the left of the references. Thematic linking is indicated by a line to the right. As my intention is to include only those links which are reasonably certain, I have excluded literal links which join only two sayings, since there is scope for coincidence in this area.[2] The list might be increased greatly by including these shorter literal links and more

TABLE 1. *Thematic and verbal/literal links in Prov. 10. 1–22. 16.*

	Chapter													
	10	11	12	13	14	15	16	17	18	19	20	21	22	TOTAL
Verb/lit. only	1	4	2	5	7	11	16	8	3	15	14	10	4	100
Thematic only	6	7	4	2	5	2	1	2	0	0	0	0	0	29
Both	21	14	11	6	10	7	7	2	6	4	0	2	0	90
Total linked	28	25	17	13	22	20	24	12	9	19	14	12	4	219
Linked as % of all sayings	88	81	61	52	63	60	73	43	38	66	47	39	25	58

TABLE 2. *Thematic and verbal/literal links in Prov. 10. 1–22. 16, each expressed as a % of all sayings linked in these ways.*

	Chapter													
	10	11	12	13	14	15	16	17	18	19	20	21	22	TOTAL
(%)														
Verb/lit. only	4	16	12	38	32	55	67	67	33	79	100	83	100	46
Thematic only	21	28	24	15	23	10	4	17	0	0	0	0	0	13
Both	75	56	65	46	45	35	29	17	67	21	0	17	0	41

[2] The full list of sayings linked literally is: (*a*) linked by the same initial letter: 10. 2 f., 25 f.; 11. 5 f., 9–12; 12. 17 f., 28–13. 1; 14. 3 f., 32 f.; 15. 12–14, 16 f.; 16. 6 f., 27–9, 30 f.; 17. 3 f., 18 f.; 18. 1 f., 5 f., 20–2; 20. 4 f., 7–9, 12 f., 24–6; 21. 16. f.; 22. 2 f.; (*b*) linked by sequence of letters: 16. 20–2 (m, l, m, l) and 17. 12–15 (p, m, p, m).

general thematic and verbal resemblances.[3] It should be emphasized that other types of linking are found within this collection:
we are considering here only the methods which seem most
common and obvious.

Altogether, some 219 sayings out of the 375, over 58 per cent,
are clearly joined to an adjacent saying by verbal, literal, or
thematic links, sometimes forming lengthy chains of sayings. The
distribution of links is shown in Table 1, while Table 2 shows the
proportion of each expressed as a percentage of the total linked
sayings in each chapter.[4] It is clear that verbal/literal links predominate overall;[5] links which are thematic only are rare from ch.
15 onwards, and there are none at all in chs. 18–22. Except in ch.
18, where there are very few linked sayings anyway, sayings linked
only verbally or literally are the most common linked sayings in
chs. 15–22, while sayings linked both verbally/literally and
thematically are the most common in 10–14. In other words, there
is a clear difference between chs. 10–14 and 15–22 in the preferred
method of linking sayings.

Also noteworthy are the significantly higher proportions of
linked sayings in chs. 10–11 and, to a lesser extent, ch. 16. Even
in these chapters, however, there is no evidence of an attempt to
link all the sayings together as a single chain. Though chs. 11 and
15–16 include some lengthy chains, most of the chains are short,
often simply pairs of sayings. Large gaps appear often between
one chain and the next (e.g. 16. 31–17. 11; 22. 7–16); indeed, half
the unlinked sayings are found in groups of five or more. The
linked sayings are, correspondingly, often concentrated together,
even when there is no chain linking them all (e.g. 10. 2–21; 12.
12–23). Distribution is, then, somewhat uneven.

Setting these links aside for the moment, we may turn our

---

[3] e.g. Hermisson sees a broad theme of 'poverty and wealth, privation and
repletion' linking 10. 2–5. See H.-J. Hermisson, *Studien zur israelitischen
Spruchweisheit* (Neukirchen, 1968), 174.

[4] All percentages are rounded, downwards if the fraction is less than 0.5,
otherwise upwards.

[5] For the verbal links in these chapters and elsewhere, I have generally followed
the lists in G. Boström, *Paronomasi i den Äldre Hebreiska Maschallitteraturen*
(Lund, 1928). In instances where the text is in doubt (e.g. at 13. 13, where Boström
reads *ḥkm* on the basis of the LXX, and sees a link with v. 14), or where the verbal
resemblance is very slight, I have taken a more cautious approach. In the cases of
textual problems, this should not be taken to express my preferred reading in every
instance, but merely my desire to exclude controversial cases.

attention to a very striking feature of the material, which has been noted by many scholars; the distribution of antithetical sayings. Sayings which employ antithetical parallelism are fairly common throughout the section, but whereas they compete with similar numbers of sayings employing synthetic or synonymous parallelism in 16. 1–22. 16, they are far and away the most common type of saying in chs. 10–15. The actual number of antithetical sayings depends on the definition adopted, and many scholars overstate the case by including 'better than' sayings (e.g. 15. 16 f.), 'how much more' sayings (e.g. 11. 31; 15. 11), and other sayings which clearly differ from the basic form.[6] Other problems arise from interpretative difficulties (e.g. in 10. 18)[7] or text-critical considerations (e.g. in 11. 16, where the LXX contains an antithesis absent from MT). In a number of sayings, moreover, the antithesis is far from precise (e.g. 10. 13). These difficulties do not, however, make any real difference to the basic point, that the proportion of antithetical sayings falls dramatically after ch. 15.

By my own reckoning,[8] the number and proportion of antithetical sayings in each chapter is:

chapter					
10:	30 (94%)	15:	22 (67%)	20:	9 (30%)
11:	26 (84%)	16:	5 (15%)	21:	12 (38%)
12:	26 (93%)	17:	4 (14%)	22:	4 (25%)
13:	23 (92%)	18:	4 (17%)		
14:	29 (83%)	19:	6 (21%)	*Total*:	200 (53%)

[6] In chs. 10–15, Skladny finds 164 sayings (including 10. 1) which show antithetical parallelism, Pfeiffer 169, and Skehan 170; I consider all of these overestimates. See U. Skladny, *Die ältesten Spruchsammlungen in Israel* (Göttingen, 1962) p. 23 n. 141; R. H. Pfeiffer, *Introduction to the Old Testament* (1st Brit. = 2nd US edn., London, 1952) 647; P. Skehan, 'A Single editor for the Whole Book of Proverbs' (revised version), in P. Skehan (ed.), *Studies in Israelite Poetry and Wisdom* (Washington, DC, 1971), 15–26, see p. 18.

[7] The synonymous interpretation generally adopted by translators poses considerable problems. It seems more likely that the verse is antithetical, and it might be paraphrased as 'One who conceals hatred may be a liar, but one who utters slander is (far worse!) a fool.'

[8] In chs. 10–15, I take all the sayings to be antithetical except: 10. 22, 26; 11. 7, 22, 25, 29, 31; 12. 9, 14; 13. 14, 23; 14. 7, 10, 13, 19, 26, 27; 15. 3, 10, 11, 12, 16, 17, 23, 24, 30, 31. In chs. 16–22. 16 I take the following to be antithetical: 16. 1, 9, 22, 25, 33; 17. 9, 16, 22, 24; 18. 12, 19, 23, 24; 19. 4, 12, 14, 16, 21, 25; 20. 3, 5, 6, 14, 15, 17, 21, 24, 29; 21. 2, 5, 8, 11, 12, 15, 20, 26, 28, 29, 31; 22. 3, 5, 12, 15. It is, of course, possible to quibble about some of these and other sayings, but the overall picture is not really affected. Caution has led me to take 13. 19 as antithetical; it is, however, tempting to see the second stich as consequent upon the first, i.e. fools hate to give up their plans because the gratification of desire is so sweet (cf. R. B. Y. Scott, *Proverbs, Ecclesiastes* (Garden City, NY, 1965), 94).

The change in proportion from ch. 16 onwards has led most scholars to divide 10. 1–22. 16 into two sections, 10–15 and 16. 1–22. 16. The break is not, however, clean: ch. 15 has a significantly lower proportion of antithetical sayings than the preceding chapters, but it is still much higher than in the chapters which follow. This cannot be explained by a sudden influx of non-antithetical sayings at the end of the chapter, since there are as many in the first half of the chapter as in the second. The actual number of sayings involved is fairly small, and might be disregarded were it not that the end of ch. 15 and the beginning of 16 are also joined in a lengthy verbal chain. If the section is to be divided into two parts on the basis of the antithetical sayings, there appears to be a third part, a grey area, in between them.

It is interesting to compare the result with our observations about the change in the type of linking used. Here too we saw consistency of usage in chs. 10–14, with a marked change taking place in ch. 15. For a division of the text according to its formal elements, the method of linking suggests 10–14, 15. 1–22. 16, while the antithetical sayings suggest 10–14, 15, 16. 1–22. 16. The sections cannot be precisely delineated: there is no reason to suppose that they follow the chapter divisions imposed much later on the text, and there is no really satisfactory way of slicing up the text so as to determine the exact limits. Among the last few verses of ch. 14 and the first part of 15, where the end of the first collection is most probably to be sought, there are relatively few linked sayings. It is impossible, therefore, to use the switch from thematic to verbal/literal links as a pointer to the precise end of the first main collection. Since this preference for verbal/literal links is shared by the second collection, it is equally useless as a guide to the end of the grey area.

At the same time, the first collection, in its present form, is not composed entirely of antithetical sayings, and one cannot take the appearance of non-antithetical sayings as a sign in itself that the grey area has begun. Furthermore, there is no reason to assume that the grey area, which still boasts a majority of antithetical sayings, must begin with one which is non-antithetical, an error implicit in Skehan's argument[9] that the area begins with 14. 26. At most it appears probable that we are in the grey area by the

---

[9] Skehan, 'A Single Editor for the Whole Book of Proverbs'.

time we reach the three non-antithetical sayings in 15. 10–12, which are followed by a high proportion of both non-antithetical sayings and verbal/literal links. It is equally difficult to pinpoint the end, since the formal characteristics are identical to those of the second main sub-collection after about 16. 2; the chain of 'king' sayings in 16. 12–15, for instance, includes not a single antithetical saying, and such sayings are infrequent in the chain of Yahweh sayings which precedes it. The latter is a part of the unusually long verbal[10] chain which runs from 15. 28 to 16. 7. This includes a series of four sayings linked by 'hearing' (15. 29–32), the first of which speaks of Yahweh, and is followed by eight sayings in 15. 33–16. 7 which all mention the divine name. The two series are linked by *mûsār* / *mûsar* in 15. 32, 33, and the first series to the preceding saying by the righteous/wicked contrast. It seems possible that the purpose of this chain was to link ch. 16 with the preceding material. A proper description of the grey area cannot, however, be attempted on the basis of formal elements alone, and we must profess ignorance of the points at which the 'antithetical collection' ends and the other main collection starts. Nor, of course, can we say whether there is any other material lying between them.

Anyway, it is clear that there are good reasons for seeing 'sub-collections' within the material. It is possible that a single redactor has been at work, sorting out antithetical from non-antithetical sayings, but the presence of many antithetical sayings in 16. 1–22. 16 and the shift in the method of linking tell against this. It is more probable that the collection has been formed from the amalgamation of independent collections, and it is possible that these were in turn formed by the amalgamation of still earlier collections, although the general formal consistency within the major sub-collections makes this unlikely.

It is, on the face of it, likely that the collection and its sub-collections would have been liable to addition, textual corruption,

---

[10] The Yahweh and king chains are probably to be taken as verbal chains: they cover a number of different issues, and in some sayings Yahweh and the king are not really the subject-matter (e.g. 15. 33, 16. 5 f., 13). The same is true of the short chain of 'king' sayings in 25. 2–7*b* and of the chains in ch. 26 linked by the 'fool' (vv. 4–12) and the 'sluggard' (vv. 13–16). Nevertheless, there is more than simple catchword-linking involved, and perhaps they should be viewed as a sort of 'catch-theme' linking, of the sort described below.

and other minor changes. Certainly there are many places where versional or textual evidence suggests that a verse has been corrupted; it may be, for example, that the obscure third stich in 19.7 is the remnant of an original distich, if it, or the whole saying, is not an addition. The repetition of single stichs may arouse similar suspicions: the slightly implausible 10. 6*b*, for instance, looks as if it may well have come from 10. 11*b*. On the whole, this is merely a text-critical rather than a redactional matter. However, textual disruption does make a very considerable difference to the interlinking of sayings. The insertion of a single saying into a linked pair may leave three unlinked sayings, and the transposition of two verses may turn a chain of four sayings into four unlinked sayings. It is, therefore, a factor to be reckoned with in an analysis of the structure. More importantly, in the case of additions to the text, even small changes are undoubtedly a part of the process of collection. The identification of such additions is not, however, an easy matter. The presence of links to an adjacent saying is not, in itself, a reliable guide, since there is no reason why an addition should not have been placed so as to form such a link. On the other hand, the apparent disruption of a link is, without other evidence, at best a slender and somewhat subjective basis for analysis. At worst, the analysis can spin rapidly out of control; we can hardly, for instance, excise 10. 6–25 simply because 10. 4 f. could then be linked with 10. 26. The nature of the material makes the identification of additions much more difficult than in any other part of the Old Testament.

Nevertheless, we are not entirely helpless: the formal features which allowed us to identify sub-collections are also strong enough to provide a formal 'context' against which individual sayings may be judged. Thus, the fact that the overwhelming majority of the sayings in chs. 10–14 are antithetical may allow us reasonably to suppose that at some level of redaction there existed a collection composed entirely of antithetical sayings, and that the seventeen non-antithetical sayings are later additions to this collection. Their removal leads to the loss of some links, and to the creation of others; most strikingly, the removal of 11. 7 does not only leave verbal and literal links between vv. 6 and 8, but reveals a literal (and verbal) chain in vv. 5, 6, 8, immediately preceding the literal chain in vv. 9–12. The removal of 11. 29 leaves a verbal link between vv. 28 and 30, which share a similar and very distinctive

TABLE 3. *Thematic and verbal/literal links in Prov. 10. 1–22. 16 after removal of the non-antithetical sayings.*

	Chapter				
	10	11	12	13	14
Verb/lit. only	1	2	2	6	3
Thematic only	6	6	3	0	4
Both	21	14	11	6	10
Total linked	28	22	16	12	17
Linked as % of all sayings	93	88	62	52	59

TABLE 4. *Thematic and verbal/literal links in Prov. 10. 1–22. 16 after removal of the non-antithetical sayings, each expressed as a % of all sayings linked in these ways.*

	Chapter				
	10	11	12	13	14
(%)					
Verb/lit. only	4	9	13	50	18
Thematic only	21	27	19	0	24
Both	75	64	69	50	59

imagery. Two of the non-antithetical sayings resemble each other closely (14. 10, 13), and their removal leaves a chain of verbal and thematic links between vv. 9 and 14. Without going into all the details, Table 3 shows the overall distribution and proportion of links after the removal of non-antithetical sayings, with types of link expressed as a percentage of linked sayings in Table 4. On comparison with the previous figures, it becomes clear that the removal of non-antithetical sayings from chs. 10–14 results in the reinforcement of formal characteristics which were visible previously, most notably the high proportion of linked sayings in chs. 10–11, and the high proportion of links formed both verbally/literally and thematically. This is what we should expect if the sayings were indeed additions, and gives strong support to the idea that they are.

(b) *Chapters 25–29*

The one-line saying still predominates, but chs. 25–9 include several sections of 'instruction' (25. 6–7*b*, 7*c*–8, 9–10, 21–2; 26.

Diagram 2. Thematic and verbal/literal links in Prov. chs. 25–29.

25	**25**		**29**		
2	25	16	10	7	26	17
3	26	17	11	8	27	18
4f.	27	18f.	12	9	28	19
6–7b	28	20	13	10 **29**	1	20
7c–8 **26**	**26** 1	21	14	11	2	21
9f.	2	22	15f.	12	3	22
11	3	23	17	13	4	23
12	4	24–6	18	14	5	24
13	5	27	19	15	6	25
14	6	28	20	16	7	26
15	7 **27**	**27** 1	21	17	8	27
16	8	2	22	18	9	
17	9	3	23–7	19	10	
18	10	4 **28**	**28** 1	20	11	
19	11	5	2	21	12	
20	12	6	3	22	13	
21f.	13	7	4	23	14	
23	14	8	5	24	15	
24	15	9	6	25	16	

TABLE 5.   *Thematic and verbal/literal links in Prov. 25–29.*

	Chapter					
	25	26	27	28	29	TOTAL
Verb/lit. only	13	14	8	6	16	57
Thematic only	0	1	0	1	2	4
Both	2	6	2	1	0	11
Total linked	15	21	10	8	18	72
Linked as % of all sayings	65	84	45	29	67	58

24–6; 27. 23–7) and some other lengthy sayings, including one (25. 4 f.) formed by the juxtaposition of distichs. There are higher proportions of admonitions and sayings which lack parallelism than in chs. 10. 1–22. 16. If the instructional sections are counted here as single sayings, the total number of sayings is 125. Verbal,

TABLE 6. *Similitudes and antithetical sayings in Prov. 25–29.*

	Chapter					
	25	26	27	28	29	TOTAL
Similitudes	13	16	7	2	0	38
Antithetical	1	0	4	18	12	35

TABLE 7. *Similitudes and antithetical sayings in Prov. 25–29, each expressed as a % of total sayings.*

	Chapter					
	25	26	27	28	29	TOTAL
(%)						
Similitudes	57	64	32	7	0	30
Antithetical	4	0	18	64	44	28

literal,[11] and thematic links are still employed, and these are indicated, as before, in Diagram 2, with the distribution shown in Table 5. Overall, the proportion of sayings linked in these ways is almost exactly the same as in chs. 10. 1–22. 16. The preponderance of verbal/literal links is very marked—more so even than in chs. 16. 1–22. 16. Other methods of linking are apparent, though most of these play a minor role (e.g. the use of similar imagery which links 25. 5 and 26. 1 to the sayings which follow them). The exception is linking by form, where sayings of the same basic form are juxtaposed (e.g. 27. 3 f.). This appears to play a major role in the arrangement of the material here, but is difficult to quantify, as we do not know how precisely the original redactors distinguished between the different forms. At a rough estimate, around 70 per cent of the sayings are placed next to a saying of similar form. This sort of juxtaposition is much rarer in chs. 16. 1–22. 16, but it is, of course, broadly the same sort of thinking which drove a redactor to collect together antithetical statements in chs. 10–14.

No single form predominates overall, but two forms, the antithetical saying and the similitude, are far more common than any

---

[11] The full list of sayings linked literally is: 25 (4.f), (6–7*b*), 25, 26; 26. 1, 2; 27. 6, 7; 28. 8–10, 18, 19, 24, 25. As before, the diagram and subsequent calculations include only literal chains of more than two sayings. The literal link between vv. 18 and 19 in ch. 29 has, however, influenced my decision to accept the otherwise rather weak verbal link.

other,[12] and the distribution of these is shown in Table 6. Table 7 indicates the proportion of each as a percentage of the total verses in each chapter. Clearly, similitudes form the largest single group of sayings in chs. 25–7, and antithetical sayings in chs. 28–9. The distinction is very marked, except in ch. 27, where it is still, however, obvious. The situation is analogous to that in chs. 10. 1–22. 16: there seems to be a clear division within the collection between chs. 25 f. and 28 f., with a somewhat blurred area in between. The problems which surround the grey area in the other collection do not, however, trouble us here. In the first place, we are not dealing in the virtual absolutes which characterize the distinction there: chs. 25 f. do not consist almost entirely of similitudes, nor 28 f. of antithetical sayings. At the same time we have other evidence to hand: the distribution of instructional material and of simple admonitions[13] is also striking. All of the former and more than 80 per cent of the latter are to be found in chs. 25–7. Of the statements which lack parallelism,[14] on the other hand, 75 per cent are in chs. 28–9. Although the matter is not entirely clearcut, the distribution of these distinctive forms seems to support those scholars who favour a division of the material into two sub-collections: 25–7 and 28–9. The appearance of a long and unusual piece of instruction at the end of ch. 27 may mark this break.

(c) *Nearest-Neighbour Analysis: Summary and Conclusions*

The distribution of links and forms supports the conventional view that Prov. 10. 1–22. 16 and 25–9 each contain two major sub-collections with their own characteristics. In the former, the bulk

---

[12] Antithetical sayings: 25. 2; 27. 6, 9, 12; 28. 1, 2, 4, 5, 7, 10–14, 16, 18–20, 25–8; 29. 2–4, 6–8, 11, 15, 16, 23, 26, 27. I am not sure about 29. 18, 25 and have excluded them, along with 28. 21, 23. The simile-sayings, or similitudes, are presented in various ways: juxtaposition of two statements for comparison in 25. 11, 12, 14, 18, 19, 26, 28; 26. 6, 17, 23; 28. 3, 15. Juxtaposition of distichs in 25. (4 f.). Linking by '*waw* copulative' in 25. 3, 20, 23, 25; 26. 3, 7, 9, 10, 14, 20, 21; 27. 17, 18, 20, 21. *kĕ* alone in 25. 13; 26. 11, 22. *kĕ + kēn* in 26. 1, 2, 8, (18 f.); 27. 8, 19. Finally, 27. (15 f.) employs a verb of comparison. I have excluded 27. 2, 3, the distinctive form of which is paralleled in *Ahikar*, since they are not really similes.

[13] Admonitions (excl. instruction): 25. 16, 17, 27; 26. 4, 5; 27. 1, 2, 10, 11, 13; 28. 17; 29. 17.

[14] Statements lacking parallelism: 26. 13, 15, 16; 27. 14, 22; 28. 8, 9, 21–4; 29. 1, 5, 9, 12–14, 19, 21, 24.

of each sub-collection lies in chs. 10–14 and 16. 1–22. 16 respectively, but the precise boundaries cannot be determined from the evidence assessed so far. In the latter, the sub-collections correspond to chs. 25–7 and 28–9. The present collections have, then, been created by the amalgamation of at least a few smaller collections. In addition, there is evidence for the existence of secondary insertions in chs. 10–14, and they may occur elsewhere. It cannot be held that the present collections each came into being as the result of a single redaction of independent sayings.

Except in the first sub-collection, the content and theme of the sayings seem to have had little influence on the juxtaposition of sayings. Even in that sub-collection, the most obvious redactional interest is in the collection of antithetical sayings. The organization of the material, so far as it can be determined from this approach, is geared much more to the use of catchwords and the juxtaposition of sayings which are formally similar: in the vast majority of cases, a saying shares with at least one of its neighbours an initial letter, a catchword, or a form. The effect of this is to give a sort of flow to the reading or recitation of the material, the motivation for which was probably aesthetic: the links are too varied and irregular to have served as a mnemonic device.

2. *Broader Approaches*

(a) *Larger Structures*

The limitations of the nearest-neighbour approach are obvious: at the very least its somewhat statistical nature makes it inappropriate for the consideration of small portions of the text. More importantly, it certainly tells only part of the story. For example, even when two almost identical sayings are separated by only a single saying, the analysis is forced to assume that they are unconnected. Anyone familiar with the sayings collections and the numerous possible associations between the sayings within them will realize that this is a considerable disadvantage. However, the problems involved in determining and understanding such links are formidable, perhaps insuperable.

These problems are illustrated clearly by a comparison between two recent and independent studies of the sayings in Prov. 26 by scholars who have attempted to find an explanatory structure. In the first of these, Kenneth Hoglund has studied 26. 1–12 as a 'literary unit' or 'pericope', which consists of five separate components, linked in different ways.[15] The first component, 1–3, is held together by verbal and structural links, and corresponds to the third, 6–8, where 6 is linked to 3, 7 to 2, and 8 to 1; this structure envelopes the second, central unit 4–5, a paradoxical pair of sayings. The fourth, 9–11, is internally linked, but 9 and 10 both refer back to 6; the fifth, 12, is a summary, and also refers back to 5. The unit as a whole is intended to create cumulatively a picture of the fool, and of his virtual inability to change his nature, though he is not so far gone as the man 'wise in his own eyes'.

Jutta Krispenz, on the other hand, in a book which deals with the sayings collections as a whole,[16] takes the main unit here to be 26. 1–16. This, she claims, consists of three 'strophes' (1–5, 6–12, 13–16); the last saying of each includes the expression 'wise in his own eyes'. The first two strophes are bipartite: 1–5 consists of two pairs (1–2, 4–5), with 3 attached to the first; 6–12 consists of a pair (11–12) preceded by a 'concentric' structure, where 6 corresponds to 10 and 7 to 9, so that 8 is emphasized. A link between 8 and 1 binds the two strophes together. The third strophe has only catchword linking in 14–16, while 13 is introductory. The first strophe is about the danger of becoming like a fool, and the danger to the fool of becoming 'wise in his own eyes'; the second picks up the theme of becoming foolish through contact with the fool, while the third deals with the sluggard, a hopeless case who is already wise in his own eyes. The unit as a whole is optimistic about the possibility of improvement for the fool, so long as he makes an effort.

Broadly speaking, then, Hoglund and Krispenz come to much the same conclusion about the overall meaning: since, however, they each rest their case heavily on v. 12, this is not surprising, and it hardly vindicates the approach. Of more significance are the differences between them in their analysis of the structure, which demonstrates the degree to which each has selected only some of the possible links. Since both perceive some sort of 'concentric' structure, though in different places, it can hardly even be said

---

[15] K. Hoglund, 'The Fool and the Wise in Dialogue', in K. Hoglund *et al.* (eds.), *The Listening Heart* (Sheffield, 1987), 161–80.

[16] J. Krispenz, *Spruchkompositionen im Buch Proverbia* (Frankfurt, 1989). See pp. 107 ff.

that they are looking for different things. Furthermore, the very selection of the units for consideration is essentially arbitrary: a case could certainly be made for links between vv. 1–2 and 25. 25, 26, a little before, and for links between 10 and 18 f. or 11 and 17, just after.

Nearest-neighbour analysis is by no means free of subjectivity, particularly in the area of determining thematic links, but it compares well in this respect with the approach taken by Krispenz and Hoglund. On the level of method, the problem is that there is no way of determining who is right and who is wrong about the structure. I myself am inclined to suspect that the sort of associations which they seek to explain result, at least in part, from a much simpler sort of redaction, in which the redactor casts back over his page for inspiration, or to give a general coherence to his work. If the redactor was in fact an author, creating sayings, then it is, perhaps, difficult to understand why he did not make his supposed point more clearly. On the other hand, if he was using sayings which were already in existence, as is generally (and probably rightly) assumed, I think that scholars who seek complicated structures are greatly underestimating the difficulties involved. The only clear example of sentence literature with a systematic arrangement of its material, consistently grouping by theme and drawing out paradoxes or contradictions, is the Demotic Papyrus Insinger (**xxii**): in this the structure is very much simpler. Even taking account only of nearest-neighbour links, it is a wonder that the redactors of the material in Proverbs achieved the degree of arrangement and co-ordination that they did. In general, then, I would suggest that straightforward association of sayings with those which have preceded them immediately, or shortly before, is probably to be viewed as at least the principal method of organizing the sayings. The very large number of nearest-neighbour links, and the possibility of an oral counterpart to the process, tell in favour of this. If there are larger and more complicated structures to be found, I suspect that we have no satisfactory criteria for identifying them at all, let alone beyond reasonable doubt.

(b) *Structures and Sources*

Having observed that Hoglund speaks of his structure as a 'pericope', it seems worth saying a few words about the question of sources, as it relates to the identification of structures within the collections. In the earlier analysis, we noted that changes in the formal characteristics of the collections might be used as evidence for the existence of sub-collections within them; since these changes are fairly subtle, I suggested that the sub-collections were probably independent collections (with different original redactors). Such distinctions within the text are a basic criterion in source criticism, and if a unit of material is broadly congruent with the material around it, this is a strong indication that it is not an independent source. Simply to show that such a unit forms a coherent structure is quite inadequate as a demonstration, even if the structure is analogous to that of another, complete text.

This is where an argument advanced by Glendon Bryce, and since accepted by some scholars, falls down badly.[17] Bryce argues that Prov. 25. 2–27 is a 'wisdom-book' in itself, and describes its structure using an approach similar to that of Krispenz and Hoglund, and open to similar criticisms. I do not intend to discuss that aspect of his article here. The structure which he finds consists of two major sections, each dealing with a different theme; they are preceded by a bipartite introduction and joined by a pattern of 'rubrics'. This structure is, he claims, paralleled by that of the Sehetepibre version of *The Loyalist Instruction* (vii). Since that work differs from his 'wisdom-book' in some important respects, not least because it is not sentence literature, Bryce also seeks a parallel in the *Kemit*, an Egyptian educational work which bears no resemblance to anything in Proverbs, but does contain miscellaneous short units.[18] The resemblance to either work is not close, and one must question the validity of analogies which depend upon the cross-breeding of two quite different works. Be that as it may, what Bryce quite fails to do is demonstrate any good reason why these verses should be regarded as a section distinct from the rest of the sub-collection within which they lie. In fact, as we have seen, the formal characteristics of Prov. 25. 2–27 appear to be very close indeed to those of the following chapters.

---

[17] G. E. Bryce, 'Another Wisdom-"Book" in Proverbs', *JBL* 91 (1972), 145–57.

[18] The *Kemit*, reconstructed from numerous fragments, seems to have been a compilation of exercise material for use in schools. It is not an 'instruction'. See especially H. Brunner, *Altägyptische Erziehung* (Wiesbaden, 1957), 83–5, 86–8.

(c) *Themes*

In all of the studies just discussed, and in a number of others,[19] the authors work on the assumption that thematic considerations are of great importance to the redactor. This is not unreasonable, but it is an assumption which needs more justification than it is normally given. After all, of all the literary forms found in the OT, the short sayings in these collections are probably the least suited to the discussion of complex ideas or the development of themes. This is an area which deserves discussion at much greater length than is possible here, but I shall try to point out some of the major problems which seem to be involved.

It is not generally possible to identify some single possible theme in an individual saying, even when the broad meaning and interrelationship of the elements is clear. This is because, as often noted, the point of such sayings may vary according to the context in which they are assumed to apply.[20] If we take each to be entirely separate, and view the collections as atomistic, then any judgement about the context must be based on assumptions about the original *Sitz im Leben*. On the other hand, if we take the concept of a collection seriously, we may try to view the sayings which are adjacent, the section in which it lies, or the collection itself as an interpretative context against which a saying may be understood. We could, of course, do this purely on a 'reader' level, but here I am concerned particularly with establishing the intention of the redactor.

Attempts to find a context in the collection as a whole, or in substantial sections of it, seem to be the least satisfactory. Essentially, when we are seeking thematic associations between different sayings, we are looking for the overlap between their different possible themes. If the sayings in question are a small group with broadly similar concerns, the association between them may be fairly specific; thus, as we have seen, the three sayings in 14. 6–8 may be associated by the appearance in each of a character who is lacking in wisdom. When, however, we consider a group in which the sayings are more diverse, and this is inevitably the case

[19] See especially O. Plöger, 'Zur Auslegung der Sentenzensammlungen des Proverbienbuches', in H. W. Wolff (ed.), *Probleme biblischer Theologie* (Munich, 1971), 402–16.

[20] This is to oversimplify. On the problem generally, see Carole Fontaine's *Traditional Sayings in the Old Testament* (Sheffield, 1982).

with large sections of the material, it becomes correspondingly difficult to find common ground, and it becomes less clear that the association is significant. Reverting to Hoglund's article for an example, we find that in passing he describes 25. 2–27 as dealing with 'matters of social relations'.[21] Actually, I am not sure how well vv. 2, 3, 13, 16, and 25 suit this, but even so, has anything useful really been said? This sort of description could readily fit almost any part of Proverbs, and, arguably, it says more about wisdom literature generally than about Prov. 25 in particular. More to the point, it seems unlikely either that the redactor set out to illustrate something so vague, or that it is important for an understanding of any of the sayings. In general it is possible to find some 'theme' which will cover almost any group of sayings, so long as one does not mind it being rather unspecific.

As with the structure, however, it may be more profitable to look at associative links between individual sayings than at larger structures or blocks. For instance, we could say that the sayings in 14. 35–15. 2 are all to do with the interaction of different people, or some such. This would, however, miss what seems to be a much more precise way of linking the sayings thematically. 14. 35 tells us that the king favours those of his servants who act wisely, but is angry with those who act reprehensibly; 15. 1 tells us that a soothing reply averts anger, while rough speech provokes it; finally, 15. 2 claims that the tongue of the wise gives(?) knowledge, but the mouths of fools foolishness. In other words, 15. 1 seems to be linked to the preceding saying by the theme of anger, and to the next saying by that of speech. This is not a thematic block, since the first and third sayings are not associated except via the second, but a thematic chain. The method is analagous to that used in the verbal links, but where the saying there may be linked to any word in the saying which precedes it, here the link is forged with one of the possible themes. For similar chains, see 12. 12–14 and 15. 31–3.

All this suggests that, even when a series is linked throughout by the same theme, the redactor is more interested in associating the sayings than in bringing out the proper meaning of each, as he understands it, through its position. Such a suggestion is wholly consonant with the redactional interest in verbal links and literal

---

[21] Hoglund, *The Listening Heart*, 162.

links. Again, though, I would not wish to claim that the arrangement or juxtaposition of sayings is never thematically significant: in, for example, 25. 4–5, there is clearly more than simple association at work. I am concerned merely to emphasize that we cannot start to make broad assumptions about the collections as a whole, and should not neglect explanations for the arrangement which are at once simpler and more interesting.

3. *The Sayings Collections: Conclusions*

Given the many difficulties, it is odd that so little discussion has been devoted to how we should approach the sayings collections. Where scholars have taken the trouble to justify their assumptions at all, it has usually been in a few lines. However, the issue is not an easy one, and my own remarks constitute no more than an introduction to some of the problems.

The examination of nearest-neighbour analysis undertaken in the first part of this chapter showed that this method gave results which conformed in certain important areas to previous conclusions reached by scholars on different grounds. Used in conjunction with other data, moreover, it seemed to be a useful way of approaching several aspects of the collections. Unfortunately, it is a method with some serious limitations also, and the most serious of these were discussed in the second part. Of course, the greatest objection to it, and one that Krispenz has raised against earlier assessments of such links, is that it may be simply the wrong way to approach material which is structured in much broader patterns.[22] However, attempts to discern these broader structural arrangements run into considerable difficulties, and are highly selective. Furthermore, they suggest a complicated explanation for phenomena which can be explained, on the whole, more simply.

Bound up with such attempts are assumptions that the redactor is concerned principally with providing a context within which themes may be treated, and against which the sayings may be understood. However, since we can describe a theme to suit almost any group of sayings, the identification of broad themes seems to say little of any significance about either the sayings or the collections. Moreover, among the few close thematic links

---

[22] Krispenz, *Spruchkompositionen*, esp. 9 ff.

which exist between adjacent sayings, there are some which suggest that theme was merely another associative method employed in the redaction, rather than a central concern.

In general, the analysis of the many links between adjacent sayings is probably the only reasonably controlled approach that we can take to the collections, whatever its drawbacks. It is not, however, merely a last resort: to my mind, the best explanation for the arrangement of the sayings is that associative links, especially but not exclusively between adjacent sayings, represent the usual method of arranging the sayings. I would, of course, allow that there are probably exceptions. If this is indeed the case, then the collections are, broadly, atomistic: an understanding of the individual sayings is neither dependent on, nor necessarily enhanced by, a consideration of their place in a collection. This is close to the position of McKane, as quoted at the beginning of this chapter. If the 'collection' is of limited use for an understanding of the sayings, it is, however, of the utmost importance for an understanding of wisdom literature, as will become clear in later chapters.

3
Proverbs and the Court

We may now turn to issues which more directly affect our understanding of the origins and nature of wisdom literature in Israel. This chapter and the next will look at evidence drawn principally from Proverbs itself, and will rely in part upon conclusions reached in the preliminary chapters. Chapters 5 and 6 will examine other biblical evidence from an exegetical viewpoint, while the last two chapters will consider more historical and circumstantial evidence. The first issue to be tackled is probably the most important: do the contents or presentation of material in any part of Proverbs suggest an origin or redaction within the royal court or bureaucracy? The various kinds of evidence are most conveniently considered under different headings, and I shall discuss each separately.

1. *The Superscriptions in Proverbs*

Three sections of Proverbs are attributed to King Solomon in their superscriptions (1. 1; 10. 1; 25. 1). In 25. 1*b* there is also a reference to the 'men of Hezekiah', while 31. 1 attributes what follows to a foreign king, Lemuel, or his mother. Such attributions are, however, to be treated with great caution, most especially when they involve Solomon. Ecclesiastes, the Song of Songs, the Wisdom of Solomon, and Pss. 72 and 127 are all attributed to Solomon, but it is most unlikely that he composed any of them.[1] In view of this, and despite a widespread inclination to associate the origins of wisdom with Solomon's reign, most scholars have resisted the temptation to take the Solomonic attributions in Proverbs seriously.[2] The pseudonymity of some foreign instructions

---

[1] Cf. C. H. Toy, *A Critical and Exegetical Commentary on the Book of Proverbs* (Edinburgh, 1899), pp. xix.

[2] Though see p. 213 of W. Baumgartner, 'The Wisdom Literature', in H. H. Rowley (ed.), *The Old Testament and Modern Study* (Oxford, 1951), 210–37.

presents, as we have seen, a possible parallel for the attribution of such literature to a famously wise personage from the distant past.[3] It may be that some familiar tradition was attached to the mysterious Lemuel.

If the ascriptions to Solomon are usually viewed with healthy scepticism, the same cannot be said of the very different Prov. 25. 1*b*. Not only have we no clear knowledge of any tradition linking Hezekiah with wisdom, but we cannot even begin to regard this as a pseudonymous ascription when it is not, apparently, an inscription at all. So R. B. Y. Scott, for instance, while rejecting the historicity of the ascriptions to Solomon, finds this reference to the men of Hezekiah historically significant: 'Since no tendentious purpose can be suspected in the mentioning of the otherwise unknown "men of Hezekiah", this is first-rate evidence that an organized literary movement existed at Hezekiah's court and under his patronage.'[4] This reference is, indeed, the principal evidence for Scott's effective shift of the Israelite 'enlightenment' to the reign of Hezekiah, when, he supposes, the Solomonic tradition arose as a projection back in time of a contemporary phenomenon.

If we compare the superscriptions to the different collections, certain similarities and cross-references become obvious. Firstly, two of them seemingly refer back to previous superscriptions: thus 25. 1 tells us that 'These also (*gam-'ēlleh*) are proverbs of Solomon', and 24. 23 that 'These also (*gam-'ēlleh*) are (sayings) of the wise.' They apparently assume the existence of 10. 1 (and 1. 1?) and 22. 17 respectively.[5] Further, the use of '*mišĕlê*', 'mashals', is restricted to the Solomonic ascriptions, 'words' being used elsewhere. This may suggest that the term '*mišĕlê šĕlōmōh*' is a cliché; there is no good reason, when all the instances are taken into account, to suppose that the phrase is a technical term for a certain type of saying.[6]

---

[3] See Ch. 1, sect. 1(b), above.

[4] R. B. Y. Scott, 'Solomon and the Beginnings of Wisdom in Israel', SVT 3 (1955), 262–79.

[5] 22. 17 is usually taken to be a title 'absorbed' into the text, rather as in 1. 1. See Fichtner in *BHS*, ad loc., and also the unnatural position of λόγοις σοφῶν at the beginning of the sentence in LXX.

[6] As suggested by Scott, 'Solomon and the Beginnings of Wisdom', 272 f.; cf. S. R. Driver, *Introduction to the Literature of the Old Testament*[9] (Edinburgh, 1913), 407. In 'Folk Proverbs of the Ancient Near East', *TRSC* 15 (1961), 47–56, Scott describes 'Proverbs of Solomon' as 'the bilinear couplet in poetic parallelism'.

The arrangement of titles is interesting in itself, and may suggest an artificial classification:

1. 1:	Mashals of Solomon . . .
10. 1:	Mashals of Solomon.
22. 17:	(Words of the wise).
24. 23:	Also of the wise.
25. 1:	Also mashals of Solomon . . .
30. 1:	Words of Agur.
31. 1:	Words of Lemuel . . .

1. 1 introduces the first section, and the book, with the longest description of Solomon; it is followed by a collection of mashals of Solomon, and then by a collection of words of the wise. Then come two collections, attributed to the wise and to Solomon respectively, and marked as additional to the preceding collections. Finally, there are two collections of 'words', attributed to Agur and to Lemuel's mother. The ascriptions do not cover all the collections isolated by modern scholars, and the neatness of their arrangement suggests that they form an essentially unified classification of the text. In that case they would not have belonged to the individual collections before those were brought together. It is tempting to speculate that the 'also' ascriptions mark the enlargement of an original collection. However, the evidence for all this is very slight, and we can reasonably go no further than to suggest that the broad consistency and interrelatedness of the basic ascriptions tell against their originality. At the very least, it is most unlikely that 24. 23 and 25. 1 can have stood in their present forms at the head of independent collections.

If there is a perceptible pattern of ascriptions in Proverbs, then the 'men of Hezekiah' in 25. 1*b* lie outside it. They are not described as authors, the basic ascription being to Solomon, but as having done something to the collection. The verb used for their activity is the hiphil form of *'tq*, which the LXX here translates by ᾽εξεγράψαντο, and the Vulgate by *transtulerunt*. The Vulgate implies an understanding of the verb as meaning 'transfer'; the Greek probably means 'copy' (for oneself?). If these versions reflect the original meaning of the Hebrew, and refer to transcription of the material, then 25. 1*b* is a unique and curious statement, the only OT reference to the transmission of a text. However, the meaning of the Hebrew was still debated by the rabbis,[7] and these translations may be no more than guesses to suit the context. Certainly, 'copy' or 'transcribe' accords badly with other OT uses of this form of *ʿtq*. These are in Gen. 12. 8; 26. 22 and Job 32. 15 where the use is intransitive and the sense 'move away', and in Job 9. 5, where the verb is used of 'removing' mountains (//'overthrow'). In all of these verses the basic sense is of movement or removal *away*, not forward,[8] and they give no support to Scott's suggestion that a meaning 'transmit' or 'transcribe' arose from a broader idea of 'bringing forward (from the past)'.[9] It is hard to see how 'abandon' or 'remove' could become 'copy' or 'pass on'. In short, the usual understanding of this verse, as a reference to transmission, is founded upon late, speculative interpretations, and requires that we postulate a special, technical meaning for the Hebrew verb, one which is quite inexplicable in terms of the normal usage. That is not an impossible procedure, but it is a shaky foundation for historical reconstruction.

For all that, Gressmann[10] and many subsequent scholars have, without qualms, used the verse as a historical datum. Indeed, not only have they accepted that the reference is to transmission, but they have assumed that the note is, unlike the ascriptions to Solomon, early and reliable. Such confidence has been founded in part on the lack of a clear, traditional association of Hezekiah with wisdom in the OT, and in part on the very specific nature of the verse. On the latter point, Toy long ago pointed out that 'still more definite statements are prefixed to certain obviously late psalms ascribed to David (see, for example, ψ 51–60) . . .'.[11] Specificity is certainly no argument for historicity, and if later exegetical tradition sought to place psalms in the appropriate period of David's life, it is interesting to wonder whether a similar process was at work here, seeking to associate with Hezekiah a collection of proverbs which was already linked with Solomon. Something comparable seems to have occurred in Isa. 38. 9, where a psalm

---

[7] Rabbinic suggestions include 'suppress', 'translate', 'consider'; cf. esp. Marcus Jastrow, *A Dictionary of the Targumim, the Talmud Babli and Yerushalmi, and the Midrashic Literature* (London and New York, 1903), ad loc., and the references there, particularly *Yalk. Prov.* 961. I know of no comparative philological evidence to suggest an early sense 'copy'.

[8] See esp. Job 32. 15: the words have deserted the speakers, not 'advanced from' them.   [9] Scott, 'Solomon and the Beginnings of Wisdom', p. 273 n. 2.

[10] Gressmann, 'Die neugefundene Lehre des Amen-em-ope'. See p. 286.

[11] Toy, *A Critical and Exegetical Commentary*, p. xx.

is inserted into the prose text and attributed to Hezekiah. While not on a par with the numerous attributions to Solomon, this might indicate that Hezekiah was another pious and important king to whom suitable literature might be attributed. At the very least, as the series of miracle and other stories associated with him in 2 Kgs. 18–20 and Isa. 36–8 show, Hezekiah was a king about whom tales were told. In view of this, it is at least arguable that Hezekiah appears in Prov. 25. 1 because some late tradition associated with him the series of sayings which follow that verse and concern the king.

Oesterley has, in fact, argued along those lines,[12] and if his evidence is not especially compelling, we must certainly accept that Prov. 25. 1 is not explicable only as a genuine historical notice. If a process of traditional exegesis was at work here, there may be a further extension of this exegesis visible in the LXX and Targum readings of 'friends' for 'men'.[13] The 'men of Hezekiah' are quite unspecified in the Hebrew, and the translators have, perhaps, seen a reference to the 'friends' of Prov. 25. 8, 9, 17, 18. Despite the claims built on this verse, incidentally, the 'men' cannot be assumed to have been scribes, or any professional servants of Hezekiah; similar OT usage does no more than suggest that they were in some way supporters of him, or under his patronage (cf. 1 Sam. 23. 3, 5).

In general, then, the ascriptions in Proverbs present many problems. Those to Solomon, as is generally agreed, probably reflect a traditional association of this king with wisdom: we shall discuss the date and accuracy of the tradition in a later chapter. The reference to the men of Hezekiah in 25. 1 is seemingly tacked on to an ascription to Solomon, which may in turn be a part of an overall system of ascriptions in Proverbs. It might have been intended to explain why the following section is separate from the first 'Solomonic' collection—because it was 'moved' or 'removed' under Hezekiah—or perhaps reflect some tradition about Hezekiah. Either of these explanations can claim more supporting evidence than can speculation that the clause is a simple, contemporary

---

[12] W. O. E. Oesterley, *The Book of Proverbs* (London, 1929), 219 f. Cf. Toy, *A Critical and Exegetical Commentary*, ad loc.

[13] See Fichtner in *BHS*, ad loc., and A. Baumgartner, *Etude critique sur l'état du texte du livre des proverbes d'après les principales traductions anciennes* (Leipzig, 1890), ad loc.

reference to the process of transmission. Nice though it would be to have some clear historical references in the sentence literature, it is wishful thinking to take this verse that way.

The attributions to 'the wise' have not been discussed here. If this is a technical term for scribes or officials, then they are possibly of significance. However, as I shall argue in Chapter 7, there is little evidence for such a meaning, and they may simply reflect a desire to mark the sections without attributing them to a named individual.

2. *Court and King Sayings in Proverbs*

In his last major study of wisdom, Gerhard von Rad acknowledged that the proportion of court-orientated sayings in Proverbs was very low:

In spite of our first definition of the *Sitz im Leben*, it is simply not possible to regard the book of Proverbs merely as a product of courtly knowledge and serving for the training of high officials . . . sentences from the fairly narrow world of court and high officials are, on the whole, only scantily represented. Thus the supposition emerges that the wise men of the court . . . also functioned as collectors of non-courtly teaching material and that wisdom was not by any means located only at court.[14]

This represents not so much a shift away from his earlier position, as a closer definition of the royal court's role in the formation of the wisdom literature. Thus, although it is in itself the origin of certain sayings, the court, according to von Rad, functions also as a collector of non-courtly material, associated with the middle classes and property owners.

This description of the court, as a centre for the collection and editing of sayings, is apparently based, at least in part, in Prov. 25. 1. I have already questioned the historical significance of this reference, but even if it were clearly authentic, it is hard to see how it could be used to support such a hypothesis. At best, the men of Hezekiah are said to have transcribed or copied the material, which is hardly the same as collecting or editing it. Nevertheless, the idea of the court as a centre of collection gives full weight to the fact that many of the sayings in Proverbs reflect

---

[14] G. von Rad, *Weisheit in Israel*. Extract from ET, p. 17; the original German was not available to me.

a specific interest in activities outside the royal court.[15] The theory demands, however, some sort of evidence to suggest that a lot of non-courtly material was collected in the court, rather than that a little courtly material was collected outside the court, and, indeed, that at least some of the material can reasonably be called 'courtly'. It is necessary to show, then, both that there is material in Proverbs which can only reasonably be attributed to court circles, and that there are redactional features in the collections which highlight this material.

Turning first to the sayings in Proverbs which concern kings and rulers, we find a certain unevenness both of distribution and of opinion. I include under this heading some thirty-two sayings: 8. 15; 14. 28, 35; 16. 10, 12, 13, 14, 15; 17. 7; 19. 12; 20. 2, 8, 26, 28; 21. 1; 22. 11, 29; 25. 2, 3, 4 f.; 28. 2, 15, 16; 29. 2, 4, 12, 14, 16, 26; 30. 29–31; 31. 4 f. Despite the connection of king sayings with Yahweh sayings in chs. 16 and 22, I assume here that all these sayings refer literally to the king or rulers: there is evidence, for example, the LXX substitution of 'Lord' for 'king' in 22. 11, that later exegetes interpreted some sayings as referring to God. If the sayings are arranged according to the customary divisions of the book, we find that twenty-five of the thirty-two lie in the sections 16. 1–22. 16 and 25–9. Furthermore, twenty-one of them are in 16. 10–15; 20. 2–28; 25. 2–5; 28–9, and are thus concentrated even within the sections. Of the other sections, only 10–14/15 has more than one saying, and both its sayings are in ch. 14, in close proximity to each other and perhaps in our 'grey area'.

As regards their opinion, all the sayings in chs. 28–9 express a conditional, if not entirely sceptical, view of kingship and rulers. Thus, for instance, while in 16. 10, and perhaps also 21. 1, the king is an inerrant instrument of the divine will, 29. 26 observes that 'Many seek the favour of a ruler, but from the Lord a man gets justice', and thus not only distances the king from God, but implicitly criticizes his judgement. Clearly, not all of the sayings can readily be categorized as optimistic or pessimistic about kingship in this way. Many, indeed, deal not so much with the nature of the king, as with the power he wields over others, and with the proper behaviour of individuals seeking to gain his favour

[15] Skladny, *Die ältesten Spruchsammlungen in Israel.* Such interests, though, need not reflect a variety of different origins: interest in an activity does not imply direct involvement in it. Cf. the Sumerian *Farmer's Instruction* (**xxxv**).

or avoid his wrath. Thus 14. 35; 16. 13, 14, 15; 19. 12; 20. 2; 22. 11, 29 are all concerned with the favour and anger of the king.

Given the variety of subject and opinion in all these sayings, it seems unlikely that they should be treated as a broad unity. On the basis of their favourable attitude to the king and/or their apparently specific application to those close to the king, I think that 14. 35; 16. 10, 12, 13, 14; 20. 2, 8, 26; 21. 1; 22. 11 and 25. 2, 3, 4 f. are the sayings most consistent with a court origin. In addition, other sayings with a more general applicability, such as 16. 15; 19. 12; and 20. 28, are at least compatible with such an origin. It is again noteworthy that a high proportion of these sayings lie within short sections: 16. 10–15; 20. 2–21. 1; and 25. 2–5.

If some of the king sayings are at least consistent with an origin in the royal court, it is still not clear that this was in fact where they originated. Some raise difficulties in terms of their content; thus, when 21. 1 declares that 'The king's heart is a stream of water in the hand of the Lord; he turns it wherever he will', we might choose to follow Skladny in seeing here an assertion of the distance between even the mightiest of men and God,[16] or McKane in seeing an assertion of the king's independence from advisers in matters of state.[17] Yet one interpretation suggests subordination of the king, and the other a belittling of his counsellors.

This sort of difficulty must force us to take seriously the possible objections to an origin in the Israelite court for the king sayings. The most obvious protest must be against the assumption that a king is interesting only to those directly around him. Most writers reject a court origin for those sayings which are broadly unfavourable to the king, and it is unreasonable, therefore, to accept such an origin automatically for those which are sympathetic to him: we can hardly presume that everyone except courtiers hated the king. F. W. Golka has argued recently along similar lines, claiming that king sayings may arise readily among the general population. He illustrates his argument with African folk-sayings, from which he adduces parallels, some more convincing than others, to the king sayings of Proverbs.[18] Such comparisons must be treated with

---

[16] Ibid. 29. [17] McKane, _Proverbs: A New Approach_, ad loc.

[18] F. W. Golka, 'Die Königs- und Hofsprüche und der Ursprung der israelitischen Weisheit', _VT_ 36 (1986), 13–36, and 'Die Flecken des Leoparden: Biblische und afrikanische Weisheit im Sprichwort', in R. Albertz _et al._ (eds), _Schöpfung und Befreiung_ (Stuttgart, 1989), 149–63.

due caution,[19] but Golka makes a valuable point and a valid protest.

A second presumption in need of challenge is that the sayings, if they originated in a royal court at all, must have originated in the *Israelite* royal court. On this point, let me begin by observing that king sayings are found not only in Proverbs, but also in texts which are generally reckoned post-exilic, and therefore post-monarchic. Qoh. 8. 2–4 and Sir. 7. 4 f., indeed, not only assume the existence of a king, but recommend behaviour in his presence. See also Qoh. 2. 12, the obscure 5. 9, and 10. 16, 17, 20; Sir. 10. 3, 10; 38. 2; 51. 6; Wisd. 6. 24; 11. 10; Tobit 12. 7, 11.

Gressmann suggests that such post-exilic king sayings reflect inertia in the tradition, a tendency to continue with what has gone before on the part of writers who are not so much authors as collectors.[20] It is probable that the later writers saw some more general application for the sayings, and Ecclesiastes may be maintaining its historical fiction, so one need not view their work as such a wholly effete and mechanical process. None the less, it does seem probable that they inherited the convention of including king sayings. In that case, we should consider the possibility that some of the early wisdom literature itself inherited such a convention from its sources. The king is a prominent theme in Egyptian instructions from the Middle kingdom, and certain motifs from those might be reflected in Proverbs. Thus Bryce points out specific similarities between assertions in Prov. 25. 2 f., and the description of the king of the Sehetepibre version of *The Loyalist Instruction* (**vii**), verso l. 12: 'He is Sia ('Perception') who is before hearts, his eyes seek out every body.'[21] In Prov. 16. 12; 20. 28 LXX; and 25. 4–5, we find an idea of the throne being supported by righteousness: Brunner has argued that this image goes back to Egyptian conceptions of the throne founded upon $m3't$[22] and there may be Egyptian influence on the nearby 16. 2; 21. 2 and 25. 21–3.

However, we have already noted the concentration of king

---

[19] Cf. p. 233 of R. N. Whybray, 'The Social World of the Wisdom Writers', in R. E. Clements (ed.), *The World of Ancient Israel* (Cambridge, 1989), 227–50.

[20] Gressmann, '*Die neugefundene Lehre des Amen-em-ope*', 287.

[21] Bryce, 'Another Wisdom-"Book" in Proverbs'. See p. 155.

[22] H. Brunner, 'Gerechtigkeit als Fundament des Thrones', *VT* 8 (1958), 426–28.

sayings, particularly within specific series, and parallels to this are of greater significance. In this respect the *Aramaic Sayings of Ahikar* (**li**) are especially important, since they include a very similar series of king sayings in ll. 100–8. These are of varying length, and deal with much the same subjects as are found in the biblical sayings, with a particular interest in the anger of the king. The series is twice interrupted by other sayings (ll. 105*a*, 106*b*), but is clearly a coherent unit of material. There are various other close parallels between *Ahikar* and the sentence literature of Proverbs, and, of the comparable works which are extant, it is probably the closest in terms of date, place, and language. In view of this, there are very good grounds for believing that the king sayings, and series of such sayings in Proverbs, reflect the imitation of a known convention. Since *Ahikar* has affinities with the Mesopotamian literature, it is also worth noting the group of sayings linked with *lugal* in Sumerian sayings collection 12 (**xxxvi**).

To sum up, then, king sayings occur infrequently in Proverbs, and are for the most part confined to short series of sayings. Of these relatively few sayings, only a very small number seem to be potential products of the royal court, and certain of those can be attributed to members of the court only with difficulty. Moreover, an interest in the king is not necessarily a prerogative of the court alone, and sayings which deal with the king may quite readily have originated outside the court. Finally, sayings which recommend particular behaviour in the presence of the king, and deal with the king himself, are found in OT wisdom literature dating from a period when there was neither king nor court in Israel. This not only indicates that such sayings might be found interesting by collectors of wisdom material outside court circles, but also draws attention to the possibility that, if these were vestiges of earlier wisdom, so might be the sayings in Proverbs. Parallels both to the sayings and to their presentation in series lend weight to this possibility.

Closely associated with the king sayings are those which deal specifically with proper behaviour in the royal court (as opposed to more general sayings about proper behaviour, which might originally have been intended for the court, but lack specific reference). Certain of the sayings which we have treated as king sayings are, in effect, also court sayings (e.g. 16. 14). The most striking sayings are found in chs. 23 and 25:

When you sit to dine with a ruler,
pay close attention to what is before you;
and take a knife to your throat
if you are a man of appetite.
Do not desire his delicacies,
for it is deceptive food.   (23. 1–3)

Do not advance yourself in the king's presence
and do not stand in the place of the great;
for it is better that one say, 'Come up here',
than that you be put lower in the presence of the prince.   (25. 6 f.)

By forbearance a ruler[23] may be persuaded,
and a gentle tongue will break a bone.   (25. 15)

The third saying is probably, however, merely a testament to the strength of a level temper, which may influence even the most powerful of men. The addressee in the other sayings is apparently the individual who might from time to time actually find himself in the presence of the king or, in the first, a man of importance. Other sayings, such as 24. 21 f.,[24] are less specific, and this is true of most of the sayings which deal with the anger and favour of the king.

Again, such sayings may have been derived originally from non-Israelite sources. The imagery of 25. 15, for instance, is close to that of a saying in *Ahikar* 105 f., although its sense is rather different: 'Gentle is the tongue of a k[ing], but it breaks the ribs of a dragon, like death which is [n]ot seen.'[25] There is a similar assertion about the strength of a king's words, in *Merikare* (iv) l. 32. The saying in Prov. 23. 1–3 lies, of course, in the section related to *Amenemope* (xiii), and corresponds to *Amenemope* 23. 13–18:

Do not eat food in the presence of a noble,
and then put your mouth before ‹him›.

[23] Some commentators, e.g. Toy, Oesterley, emend to 'one who is angry'; others, e.g. Gemser, translate as 'judge'.

[24] J. A. Emerton views 24. 21 as a direct address to a prince or king, pointing *wmlk* as a qal imperative and translating 'Fear Yahwe, my son, and thou wilt rule . . .'; cf. pp. 210 f. of 'Notes on Some Passages in the Book of Proverbs', *JTS* NS 20 (1969), 201–20.

[25] See J. M. Lindenberger, *The Aramaic Proverbs of Ahiqar* (Baltimore and London, 1983), 91. McKane, *Proverbs: A New Approach*, ad loc., points out that the expression is used differently in each case, but it is the metaphor of a soft tongue breaking bones, however understood, that constitutes the basis for comparison.

If you are sated, chew(?) falsely
take pleasure in your spittle.
Look at the bowl which is before you,
and let it serve your needs.[26]

Similar advice appears in the older instructions of *Kagemni* (**ii**)
and *Ptahhotep* (**iii**). Prov. 25.6 f. offers advice on seating onself in
the king's presence, and close parallels to this too are found in the
Egyptian literature (e.g. *Ptahhotep* ll. 220 ff.).

The ruler of Prov. 23. 1 is not necessarily to be identified with
the king, and this is nowhere the sense of the close Egyptian
parallels: rather, he is probably, like the *sr* of *Amenemope*, a
nobleman or senior official, someone more important than oneself.
In the broader context of the relationship between *Amenemope*
and Proverbs, it is interesting to note that there seems to be some
generalization away from the court. Thus, where *Amenemope* 27.
16 f. reads: 'As to a scribe who is experienced in his office, he will
find himself worthy(?) to be a courtier',[27] the equivalent Prov.
22. 29 says: 'Do you see a man skilful in his work? He will stand
before kings; he will not stand before obscure men.' The most
important point about the Egyptian sayings, however, is the strong
evidence they constitute against the courtier sayings in Proverbs
being original compositions of the Israelite court. This is true also
of more general sayings about the value of counsellors, such as 11.
14 and 15. 22, with which we may compare *Merikare* (**iv**) ll. 44 f.,
115 ff.

In short, then, the small number of king and court sayings in
Proverbs seem to imitate conventions, motifs, and actual sayings
from other, non-Israelite sources, and there is little sign of any
innovation here. To be sure, it is possible that they were borrowed
by or transmitted through the royal court, but there is little
evidence for the active composition of Israelite court wisdom. In
fact, it is just as likely that such sayings would have been of interest
to redactors who were not courtiers or state officials, and to much
of the Israelite population. In this respect, it is worth recalling
both that they were found interesting even by post-exilic writers,
and that Proverbs includes many sayings related to other specific

---

[26] This is a very difficult passage. I read *r-ḥȝt:f* in line 13, and *sȝ(w):k* in
l. 15. In line 16, *st ḏȝy ḥr m* is clearly corrupt, and must be corrected to *st sḏȝy
ḥr m* or *sḏȝy ḥr m*; in l. 17, *kȝy = gȝy*.

[27] *smr* is probably more precise than 'courtier', and is used in a number of titles.

situations or activities in which only a few, if any, readers would
have been involved.

An interesting study of the role played by king and court sayings
in Prov. 10–29 has been made by W. Lee Humphreys, who
examines internal evidence for linking the collections in this
section with the royal court and the education of courtiers.[28] Basic
to his approach is the belief that a 'motif of the wise courtier' can
be discerned in the Egyptian instructional literature, portraying
the ideal courtier whose life is devoted to the service of the king.
This motif embraces not only references to the king and court, but
also themes found in conjunction with such references in the
Egyptian literature. These subsidiary themes are not, Humphreys
notes, restricted in their application to the courtier alone, and are
of more limited evidential value. They include sayings about the
benefits of, for instance, good counsel and self-restraint.

After a brief discussion of his motif in Egyptian literature,
Humphreys examines as collections 10. 1–15. 33; 16. 1–22. 16; 22.
17–24. 34; 25–7; and 28–9, concluding that the motif plays a
prominent part only in 16. 1–22. 16 and 25. 2–27, which latter,
following Bryce, he takes to be an independent sub-collection.[29]
This conclusion about the distribution is, of course, similar to my
own above. The limitation of the theme in Proverbs is, Humphreys
argues, in part a result of the difference between the perceptions
in Israel and Egypt of the king's relationship to the deity. Finally,
his study leads him to conclude that the small proportion of 'wise-
courtier' sayings in Proverbs makes it probable that 'circles other
than a court educational centre played formative roles in the
middle stages of the development of the book.'[30]

However, like Skladny and others,[31] Humphreys views the
concentration of the sayings within the series 16. 1–15 and 20. 22–
21. 3 as significant. The placing of these series at the beginning
and near the end of a collection (16. 1–22. 16) may, he suggests,
indicate that this collection received its shape at the hands of those

[28] W. L. Humphreys, 'The Motif of the Wise Courtier in the Book of Proverbs',
in J. Gammie (ed.), *Israelite Wisdom: Theological and Literary Studies in Honor
of Samuel Terrien* (New York, 1978), 177–90. See also his 'The Motif of the Wise
Courtier in the Old Testament', dissertation (New York, 1970).

[29] See G. E. Bryce, 'Another Wisdom- "Book" in Proverbs', 145–57.

[30] Humphreys, 'The Motif of the Wise Courtier', 187.

[31] Skladny, *Die ältesten Spruchsammlungen in Israel*, 46. Cf. Boström, *Paranomasi
i den Äldre Hebreiska Maschallitteraturen*, 92 f.

concerned with the training of future courtiers. He further observes that the subsidiary themes associated with his wise-courtier motif play a significant role in this collection, in contrast to the previous collection, 10. 1–15. 33.

These series are indeed evidence of an interest in collecting together sayings which mention the king or Yahweh. As we have seen, such series may be a convention inherited from elsewhere, but we should also recall that Proverbs contains other series of sayings linked by a character, most importantly those which feature the fool and the sluggard in 26. 1–12, 13–16; not dissimilar is the concentration of more broadly linked righteous/wicked antitheses and sayings about speech in chs. 10–15 . So far as I am aware, nobody has ever ventured to suggest that an obvious interest in sluggards and fools is key evidence for the *Sitz im Leben* of Proverbs.

More importantly, even if we were to take these series as evidence for the redaction of king and court sayings at the royal court, it would still not be clear that they constitute evidence for the redaction of non-court sayings at the royal court. Their relationship to the sub-collection in 16(?)–22. 16 as a whole is crucial here: if they were deliberately positioned at key points in the collection, it would be reasonable to suggest that they reflect a major concern of the collector. However, their position in the collection is not, in fact, especially striking. They do not lie at the beginning and end, but at the (estimated) beginning and *near* the end, a miss which is as good as a mile. In fact, there is a great deal of material between 21. 3 and 22 . 16, while the beginning of ch. 16 seems firmly attached to the preceding verses. It will be recalled, of course, that there appears to be a 'grey area' in the middle of Prov. 10. 1–22. 16, the extent of which cannot be properly defined. Despite Humphreys' unsuccessful efforts to address this problem, it is clearly a considerable obstacle to any assumption that the series were important original features of the second sub-collection. It is simply not possible to show that the second sub-collection begins at 16. 1, and it very probably does not.

The end of ch. 15 and most of ch. 16 are made up of several unusually long verbal chains, of which the Yahweh and king series are just two. Within neither is there any strong thematic coherence, and if any train of thought is visible, it can hardly be said that either makes any point. Surely it takes more than the assembling of a few sayings which mention the king to indicate a special editorial purpose. In 20. 22–21. 3 There is no coherent series as such. Rather, 20. 22–4 are linked by 'Yahweh' and v. 24 then begins a short series linked literally (vv. 24–6). Verse 27 mentions Yahweh and v. 28 the king, but vv. 29 f. mention neither; there are no apparent links here. Finally, 21. 1–3 are Yahweh sayings, the first mentioning the king also. In other words, only three of the sayings mention the king, and the structure is explicable on other grounds. If we insist on finding some thematic significance in the redaction, then it is important to bear in mind that these series are as interested in Yahweh as in the king. Short of excising the Yahweh sayings as secondary (a tendency in scholarship which we shall discuss later), we simply cannot understand the series as merely courtly eulogies of the king.

All this leaves out 25. 2–7, which Humphreys sees as part of an independent work, following Bryce, and I, for reasons outlined earlier, do not. Here there clearly is a series of king sayings standing at the beginning of a collection, and the first three are certainly grand enough to indicate a special purpose, though the fourth spoils this a bit. This is the only series where we can even entertain the idea that special redactional interest is involved. However, this is the short sub-collection which also includes the fool and sluggard sayings, and there is a strong possibility that the redactor's interest is not so much in collecting king sayings as in forming series of sayings about a particular character.

3. *Conclusions*

Neither the ascriptions nor the court and king sayings in Proverbs are significant evidence for the composition or redaction of wisdom literature in and for the royal court. Were we to ask 'Is the Israelite wisdom literature interested in the king and the royal court?', then the answer would certainly be 'yes': both the early and the late, post-exilic wisdom literature demonstrate such an interest, although neither devote much space to it. The more relevant question is whether or not we find any material for which composition or redaction in the court must be supposed, and the answer to that question is 'no'. It is hard to maintain that only courtiers were interested in the court and king, were likely to find themselves in the presence of someone more powerful than themselves, or were required to be persuasive and to make a good impression. The use of similar sayings in post-exilic wisdom literature, moreover, and close parallels in non-Israelite texts, lend weight to the idea that such interest in the king and court as we do find was inherited by Israel through its adoption of foreign wisdom literature, that it is a convention of the genre, and that there is no need to posit a phase of composition at the court in order to explain its presence. Finally, the position of the relevant sayings cannot support any notion of a special redactional interest.

4
Was Early Wisdom Secular?

Discussion about early wisdom in Israel has been influenced for some years by the claim that it was a fundamentally secular tradition, in which theology played no part. This claim is associated especially with the work of William McKane,[1] although some similar ideas had been advanced earlier, most notably by Johannes Fichtner.[2] McKane does not claim that the 'wise men' must have been personally irreligious, but that piety was not 'a constituent part of the *ʿēṣā* which regulated their approach to statecraft'.[3] Wisdom was basically secular, a 'disciplined empiricism' in which religious idealism had no place, and the elements of which were drawn from a commitment to administration and government. This character led to bitter clashes with the prophetic tradition, until wisdom finally underwent a reinterpretation which brought it into line with Yahwistic piety, and led to the introduction of religious sayings into the originally secular wisdom literature. Clearly, if this view is correct, and if the earliest wisdom literature can be shown to have been concerned principally with statecraft and the administrative profession, then it constitutes very strong evidence for the opinion that wisdom literature arose within administrative circles.

McKane's opinions are, however, to be distinguished from those of many scholars who agree that the *Sitz im Leben* of early wisdom was in the royal administration. Von Rad, for instance, believes Yahwistic piety to have been inherent in wisdom from an early stage. Where McKane sees Prov. 16. 9; 19. 21; 20. 24; and 21. 30 f. as 'a rejoinder to the claims of old wisdom', von Rad sees them as a recognition by old wisdom of its own limits, when

---

[1] McKane, *Prophets and Wise Men; Proverbs: A New Approach.*
[2] J. Fichtner, 'Jesaja unter den Weisen'
[3] McKane, *Prophets and Wise Men,* 54.

confronted with the incalculable factor of divine intervention.[4] Where for McKane, moreover, the early wisdom tradition is geared to practical ends only, for von Rad it represents also an attempt to find man's place in the world. These two views derive from very different understandings of the wisdom literature, and in particular of the books of Proverbs.

The similarity between McKane's view and older, humanistic ideas about the Egyptian instructions may provoke some suspicion that, like those theories, it depends more on modern ideas than on the texts. McKane's own application of his results to contemporary concerns does nothing to quieten such doubts.[5] His theory cannot, however, be dismissed as simply anachronistic, and McKane has never strayed beyond the bounds of strict historical possibility. He does not attempt to view early wisdom as a sort of philosophical humanism, which would be quite improbable, but claims that it is a tradition of *Realpolitik*, which is eminently plausible. His ideas rest in part upon his interpretation of prophetic and other texts, but also find expression in an analysis of Proverbs. I shall examine this analysis first, alongside some similar arguments by other scholars, before turning to the other material, to which the discussion in my next chapter is also relevant.

1. *Yahwistic Reinterpretation in Proverbs*

In his commentary on Proverbs, McKane divides the individual sayings of the sentence literature into three classes: class A contains those sayings which he believes to be 'concerned with the education of the individual for a successful and harmonious life', set in the framework of old wisdom. Class B contains those concerned with the community, and C those characterized by 'the presence of God-language or by other items of vocabulary expressive of a moralism which derives from Yahwistic piety'.[6] From this, he goes on to argue that the third class is to be seen as a later, Yahwistic reinterpretation of the empirical and non-religious old

[4] See e.g. von Rad, *Weisheit in Israel*, ch. 6.
[5] See McKane, *Prophets and Wise Men*, 113–30, and the introduction to the reissue of 1983 (pp. 9–14).
[6] McKane, *Proverbs: A New Approach*, 10–22.

wisdom represented in Class A. Thus, a perception of interpretative activity in the literature is taken to support the notion of development from a secular to a religious viewpoint within the tradition.

As evidence of such reinterpretation, McKane points to different attitudes and usages in the sentences of the A and C classes. The positive uses of *mĕzimmôt* in 8. 12*b*; 14, 17*b*, and of *taḥbûlôt* in 11. 14*a*,, as compared to the pejorative use of these terms in the 'C class' 12. 2*b* and 12. 5 respectively, are cited as instances of such reinterpretation. More generally, McKane points to 19. 21; 20. 24; and 21. 30, as Yahwistic condemnations of early wisdom's intellectual aspirations, a development which he finds also in chs. 1–9. The 'fountain of life' is no longer the instruction of the wise, as claimed in 13. 14, but the fear of Yahweh, according to 14. 27. Where 17. 8; 18. 16; and 21. 14 indicate the advantages of bribery, it is loftily condemned by 15. 27 and 17. 23.

These observations show, at the very least, the element of variety present in the sentence literature, but there are methodological problems involved in using them as evidence for reinterpretation. Though I broadly agree with McKane that the sayings collections may be regarded as atomistic, this does not mean that their existence should be disregarded altogether. Presumably McKane believes the collections to be later than the composition of the 'reinterpretative' sayings; otherwise, we would be looking at the insertion of such sayings into a text, and structural features would indeed be important. In that case, the coexistence of the early, secular sayings, and the later, reinterpretative sayings needs some explanation: why did the redactor not simply omit those sayings with which he, as a late, and presumably therefore 'Yahwistic' wise man, disagreed? The collections may not be integrated wholes, but there is no good reason to suppose that they were simply catch-alls for whatever sayings the collectors happened to know.

Furthermore, McKane's own classification is imposed upon the material, not drawn from it, and rests on presuppositions about the development of wisdom, which are then justified with reference to the classification. This argument is not only subjective, but alarmingly circular. For example, 15. 27 condemns bribery, and is thus classed as a C sentence; 17. 8; 18. 16; and 21. 14 all acknowledge the expediency of bribery and are thus class A.

Clearly there are two different points of view here, but the
different views have been used as the criterion for classification of
the sentences: they can hardly, then, be used themselves as
evidence of the distinction between the classes. That would be to
use an assumption to prove itself. In this instance the problem is
highlighted by the fact that 15. 27 may, on other grounds, be
related to sentences which McKane classifies as A or B: the use
of root *BṢʿ* (cf. 28. 16 'B'), the unusual expression *ʿōkēr bêtô* (cf.
11. 29 'A'), and the condemnation of greed (which McKane
attributes to class A, e.g. 13. 11, and to Egyptian literature). Pre-
empting the next section, we may note, incidentally, that the
taking of bribes to corrupt justice is already condemned in
Amenemope (21. 1 ff.): it is hardly, then, necessarily late and
Yahwistic.

Such methodological considerations apart, problems are raised
by McKane's specific examples of reinterpretation. Certainly
mězimmôt is used pejoratively in Prov. 12. 2 and 24. 8; it is also
used in this way in Job (21. 27), Jeremiah (11. 15), and certain
psalms (10. 2, 4; 21. 12; 37. 7; 139. 20). A more positive sense is
found in Prov. 1. 4; 2. 11; 3. 21; 5. 2; 8. 12; and 14. 17 (if MT is
amended in accordance with LXX),[7] but also, again, in Job (42.
2) and in Jeremiah (23. 20; 30. 24; 51. 11), where it is used of
Yahweh's purposes. If it is McKane's contention that the use of
both a positive and a pejorative sense for the term in Proverbs is
evidence of later reinterpretation, the same must, logically, be
held to be true of the examples in Job and Jeremiah, where both
senses are found also. It is manifestly simpler to assume that the
term could be used in either sense contemporaneously, perhaps
deriving its moral content from its context. Something similar is
probably true also of *taḥbûlôt*, which is only once found in a
pejorative sense (12. 5), when the sense is not inherent, but
derives from the adjacent 'wicked'.[8]

Setting aside the verses which are cited by McKane as evidence
of a Yahwistic condemnation of the aspirations of early wisdom
(Prov. 16. 9, etc.), we may turn finally to the apparent substitution

---

[7] See D. Winton Thomas, 'Textual and Philological Notes on Some Passages in
the Book of Proverbs', SVT 3 (1955), 280–92, esp. 286.

[8] For some similar criticisms, see pp. 320 f. of F. M. Wilson, 'Sacred and
Profane? The Yahwistic Redaction of Proverbs Reconsidered', in K. G. Hoglund
et al. (eds.), *The Listening Heart* (Sheffield, 1987), 313–34.

in 14. 27 of 'the fear of Yahweh' for the instruction of the wise in
13. 14. This point has been picked up and enlarged upon by R. B.
Y. Scott, whose analysis leads him to support McKane on this
issue.[9] Scott finds a number of variants in which, he argues,
specifically religious terminology has been introduced into an
earlier saying. The most noteworthy groups of such sayings are:

1. 13. 14*a*; 16. 22*a*; 10. 11*a*; 14. 27*a*   *4.* 10. 15a=18. 11*a*; 18. 10
2. 16. 8; 15. 16.   *5.* 27. 21; 17. 3
3. 28. 21; 18. 5; 17. 15

Reasonably, Scott argues that 'these examples suggest that
couplets using "religious" or "wisdom" terms sometimes were
composed on the basis of traditional sayings in which these notes
were lacking.' In other words, it is suggested that 'religious'
wisdom in some way recycled older, 'secular' sayings. Yet Scott
has himself noted a very great number of variants, most of which
show no introduction of religious terminology (e.g. 10. 1, cf. 15.
20). Moreover, 'religious' variants are found on sayings which are
already 'religious' (e.g. 16. 2, cf. 21. 2). Surely the multiplication
of variants on sayings is not to be attributed to systematic
reinterpretation, but is rather a feature of the composition,
transmission, and collection of sayings. A large number of such
variants are found in the Israelite and the non–Israelite sources:
Prov. 27. 3, for example, has counterparts not only in Sir. 22.
14 f., but also, in varied forms, in the versions of *Ahikar* (Aramaic
111 f., Syriac 45 f.). In some instances, variation may be due
simply to the popularity of a particular simile or figure of speech,
and the 'fountain of life' examples may be one such. There
seems no good reason to take 'religious' variants as a special
case, and to isolate them as an interpretative stage. Perhaps some
were deliberate variations, but this is a long way from saying that
they exemplify later, Yahwistic developments in the wisdom
tradition.

In general, then, the observations of McKane and Scott shed
much light upon the variety within, and vitality of the literature.
They do not, however, constitute evidence of a historical dimen-
sion to this variety. That is to say, they do not in themselves imply

---

[9] R. B. Y. Scott, 'Wise and Foolish, Righteous and Wicked', SVT 23 (1972),
146–65.

the reinterpretation of an early, wholly secular wisdom by a later, Yahwistic wisdom. Evidence that 'secular' and 'religious' sayings belonged to different groups at different times cannot be adduced from these observations.

A different approach to the problem has been made, albeit rather tentatively, by R. N. Whybray, who takes far greater account of the present arrangement of the material.[10] In contrast to that of McKane, his is explicitly a study of redaction and addition within the collections. Whybray chooses to examine the 'Yahweh sayings' in 10. 1–22. 16, that is, those which mention the divine name. He emphasizes that this is for the sake of convenience, and is not meant to imply that they form an exclusive 'religious' group. The concentration of such sayings, alongside 'royal' sayings, in 15. 33–16. 9, he argues, indicates a deliberate intention to set a theological kernel in the centre of the book, while more than half the other Yahweh sayings appear to reinterpret one or more adjacent sayings, with only three standing as single verses unconnected to their context or to other Yahweh sayings. He concludes, therefore, that the arrangement of sayings 'was made in order to reinterpret older "secular wisdom sayings by the juxtaposition or inclusion in the group of Yahweh-sayings which assert the absolute primacy of Yahweh, his righteous will, his omniscience, his active and personal intervention in human affairs.'[11] Many of those sayings which McKane places in his class C are not, however, from the same stage of development as the Yahweh sayings, but rather represent an intermediate theological stage, in which righteousness is its own reward, and the source of moral consequence is not, therefore, explicitly divine.

The most obvious problem here is the transferral of the argument from a redactional to a historical context: even if Whybray is correct in detecting an editorial tendency to reinterpret material by the juxtaposition and insertion of Yahweh sayings, this implies only that an editor felt his material needed reinterpretation. It cannot subsequently be assumed that the material represented 'old' wisdom, and the editor a later, Yahwistic wisdom, unless it

[10] R. N. Whybray, 'Yahweh-Sayings and their Contexts in Proverbs 10¹–22¹⁶', in M. Gilbert (ed.), *La Sagesse de l'Ancien Testament* (Louvain, 1979), 153–65. In his earlier *Wisdom in Proverbs* Whybray had already argued for Yahwistic reinterpretation in the passages concerning the figure of Wisdom in Prov. 1–9.

[11] Whybray, 'Yahweh-Sayings', 165.

be presupposed that the wisdom tradition underwent a linear development from secularism to Yahwism, remaining at every stage entirely coherent and unified. Further, Whybray undertakes to examine the Yahweh sayings as sayings which can be separated from others by the objective criterion of the use of the divine name. Yet this is not really so objective as it sounds, since it becomes clear that Whybray believes all but a couple of these sayings to belong together as a group. His choice of the criterion of the divine name in fact contains another presupposition, that the presence of the divine name makes a sentence fundamentally different from sentences where it is absent, and fundamentally similar to other sentences where it is present. Such an assumption requires justification from another source, and Whybray seeks this in what he perceives to be a distinctive use of the Yahweh sayings. As I shall argue below, however, the placing of the Yahweh sayings in their context appears distinctive only because the Yahweh sayings alone have been studied in this respect. If the use of the sayings is not distinctive, the whole schema collapses.

Whybray's analysis can be usefully compared with that of Skehan in this area, already mentioned in an earlier chapter.[12] Skehan recalls that the number of proverbs in 10. 1–22. 16 corresponds to the numerical value of the Hebrew name 'Solomon' in the superscription (375), and that the second half of the material differs from the first in its strikingly lower proportion of antithetical sayings. He suggests that this shift away from antithetical sayings in fact occurs after 14. 26, noting that around a quarter of the verses from there to the end of ch. 15 lack antithetical parallelism, and that these verses mark for the first time a much greater concentration on Yahweh, and an interest in the king. Skehan argues, therefore, that between 14. 26 and 16. 15 one may discern the work of an editor seeking to join two collections of roughly the same size, one composed predominantly of antithetical sayings, and expanding these collections to bring the total length up to his target of 375 sayings. The central, editorial section contains a high proportion of the duplicates and variants found in the work as a whole, and Skehan believes these to have been composed *ad hoc* to round out the work. Also included among the expansions are sayings about hearing, about Yahweh, and about the king.

---

[12] Skehan, 'A Single Editor for the Whole Book of Proverbs'.

Thus Skehan and Whybray are essentially in agreement that the central section of 10. 1–22. 16 is editorial, but their views on the nature and extent of the editorial work are very different. For Whybray, the central section is deliberately positioned to emphasize certain religious ideas, which are found also in editorial insertions throughout the work; for Skehan, the central section is essentially padding, a necessary addition to make up numbers.

Skehan's conclusions are, of course, similar to those reached in the 'nearest-neighbour' analysis undertaken in Chapter 2, although he goes further in seeking to define the nature and extent of the central section, my 'grey area'. Whybray does not discuss the problems raised by the sudden switch from antithetical parallelism, and thus does not confront the obstacle it presents to his own theory. If, as Whybray suggests, the Yahweh sayings are essentially secondary to the material in which they are embedded, it is surely improbable that they should follow the same structural patterns as that material. Yet some 73 per cent of the Yahweh sayings in chs. 10–14 are antithetical, as compared to 50 per cent in ch. 15 and 23.5 per cent in 16. 1–22. 16. In other words, the Yahweh sayings also display a dramatic shift from the antithetical to the non-antithetical, and the figures compare well with those of 88.7 per cent, 67 per cent, and 23 per cent for all the sayings, especially in view of the small numbers involved. Unless we assume conscious, but not consistent, imitation of the style by the editor, this fact must raise considerable doubts about the secondary but unified nature of the Yahweh sayings. If the two parts were originally separate collections, the secondary insertions must have taken place independently in each, and it is difficult to maintain that the insertions in each are related to each other and also to the central section.

It is, incidentally, interesting to look in this connection at the seventeen non-antithetical sayings of chs. 10–14, which we earlier suggested might well be later additions to the basic sub-collection. Only three of these are Yahweh sayings (10. 22; 14. 26, 27), and, indeed, only seven are described by McKane as class C sayings. Again, this is broadly comparable with the 36 per cent class C sayings which McKane finds in these chapters as a whole. Clearly, the only group of sayings for the secondary nature of which a strong case can be put on formal grounds, is not a

Yahwistic layer but consists of much the same mixture as the sub-collection itself.

Whybray's argument that the Yahweh sayings appear in most instances to correct or modify other sayings is itself questionable. He isolates twenty-five Yahweh sayings outside the 'kernel', which he believes to be clear reinterpretations of adjacent sayings (10. 3, 22, 27, 29; 11. 20; 12. 2, 22; 14. 2; 15. 3, 8, 9, 11, 16; 16. 20, 33; 17. 3; 18. 10; 19. 21; 20. 10, 12, 22, 23, 24, 27; 22. 12), and eight other possibles (11. 1; 15. 25, 26, 29; 19. 3; 22. 2, 4, 14). None of the latter eight seems particularly convincing. The basic twenty-five represent a little over half the Yahweh sayings outside the kernel. The problem here is to determine the extent to which the juxtaposition of Yahweh sayings and non-Yahweh sayings results from a deliberate attempt to modify the meaning of the latter, rather than from principles of arrangement used more generally in the text for the positioning of sayings. In other words, does, say, 10. 3 follow 10. 2 for a reason which is qualitatively different from the reason that 10. 5 follows 10. 4?

In his discussion of 10. 3, Whybray notes that it

picks up the vocabulary of verse 2, with the terms *ṣaddīq*, 'righteous', and *rᵉšā'īm*, 'wicked men' . . . The general sense of these two sayings is very similar: the wicked man's greed will not be allowed to go unchecked, while the righteous man will be preserved from starvation. The difference between them lies in the definition of the source of the moral power which will ensure that this occurs: in verse 2 it is his own righteousness which will protect the righteous man, whereas in verse 3 it is Yahweh who will do so.[13]

Certainly the theme here is similar, but so also are the vocabulary and the structure: both verses begin with *lō'* plus verb, and both have a chiastic arrangement. If we look further on, we find that verse 4 is also linked formally with verse 3, having a chiastic arrangement itself, and strikingly, a similar singular/plural antithesis (a type of link not picked up in our earlier analysis of verbal/literal and thematic links). Its thematic link, however, is with the next verse, verse 5, which also deals with laziness, but lacks the structural similarity, replacing chiasmus with a bold juxtaposition of nouns and alliteration; the use of the 'sons' imagery provides a

---

[13] Whybray, 'Yahweh-Sayings', 163.

link with verse 1, and with other passages in Proverbs. In other words, these verses show the associative linking typical of the sentence literature, and it is entirely reasonable to suppose that verse 3 is placed next to verse 2 because of its verbal, thematic, and structural similarities to that verse, just as it is probably followed by verse 4 because of the structural similarities with that verse. There is, therefore, no reason to believe that the position of the verse represents deliberate insertion to make a theological point: such a claim is not, after all, made for the juxtaposition of verses 4 and 5. On a different note, we may well ask why some Yahwistic editor decided to place his saying here, where its theme does not entirely match that of the previous verse, while 13. 25, for example, which is much closer in its imagery, is left entirely uncorrected.

To take another example, this time from the 'possible' list, 15. 29 has no real thematic connection with its context, but is linked to 15. 28 by the righteous/wicked antithesis, and with the series 15. 30–2 by the use of root *ŠMᶜ*. Again, these links provide a more convincing explanation for the position of the verse than does the supposition of Yahwistic insertion. I cannot cover all the examples here, but it should be clear that juxtaposition for the purpose of reinterpretation is hardly the only plausible explanation for the juxtaposition of the sayings. Of course it is not improbable that some verses are positioned to modify or elucidate their neighbours: that is, perhaps, part of the point of arranging materials thematically; however, there is no evidence of such modification as a consistent and secondary process. This is an issue which I have examined in general terms above.

None of these attempts by McKane, Scott, and Whybray succeeds, then, in demonstrating a reinterpretation of an early secular wisdom by a later, Yahwistic wisdom. That is not, logically, to say that such a reinterpretation did not happen, but rather that the particular approaches are unsuccessful. Is it probable, however, that such a process occurred? The answer to this question must be sought in other material.

2. *The Non-Israelite Sources*

If the description of early Israelite wisdom as 'secular' implied a lack of any reference to God, it would also imply a substantial divergence from the comparable foreign material, which makes frequent reference to the divine. However, this is not what McKane and others take as their criterion of secularism, and the Egyptian instructions have themselves been characterized as 'secular' or 'pragmatic': indeed, McKane himself asserts that the moral instruction of these texts is grounded not in piety but in power. I shall discuss that claim shortly. First, however, we may note that there is a contradiction involved in accepting 'god sayings' as integral to the material in, say, *Amenemope*, while rejecting them as secondary in the Israelite material. Is there a qualitative difference between the sayings in each book sufficiently great to justify this difference in treatment?

In some important cases, there is no clear difference perceptible, and, indeed, the parallels are close enough to suggest foreign influence upon Proverbs. So, for example, Prov. 16. 9; 19. 21; 20. 24; and 21. 30 f., which contrast the power and success of divine and human action, and which McKane views as 'a rejoinder to the claims of old wisdom', find counterparts in several, non-Israelite sources, including *Amenemope* (**xiii**), where we find, for example, 'The words which men say are one thing, but that which the god does, another.'[14] McKane recognizes the difficulty of his position, noting the parallels to 16. 1 in *Ahikar* (**li**) and to 16. 9 in *Amenemope*, yet he places both these verses in his class C: 'I would maintain this thesis of a Yahwistic reinterpretation, even though thoughts not dissimilar to vv. 1 and 9 are found in extra-Israelite wisdom.'[15] Yet it surely strains credulity to claim that Israelite wisdom, in imposing a Yahwistic reinterpretation upon its earlier, secular manifestation, quite coincidentally chose to express this reinterpretation in sentiments so very similar to those of non-Israelite wisdom. Given the close relationship between *Amenemope* and Proverbs, moreover, it is tantamount to suggesting that Israelite wisdom originally rejected the sentiments before later, coincidentally, re-expressing them. In making such a suggestion, incidentally, McKane is contradicting the logic of his own claims about the instruction literature, where the existence of formal parallels is used to deny the development of the form independently within Israel. It is surely simpler to conclude that

[14] *Amenemope* 19. 16 f. This translation, which takes *rwy3ty* to indicate difference, goes back to Sethe, and is adopted by most commentators.

[15] McKane, *Proverbs: A New Approach*, 495.

early wisdom accepted such statements about the relationship of
human and divine actions from foreign sources, along with so
much else. It should be recalled, we may add, that the verses
under consideration here are not merely examples of McKane's
class C, but are used by him as important evidence for both the
viewpoint and the very existence of such a class.

To take another example from *Amenemope*, 9. 5 ff. corresponds
to an idea found several times in Proverbs:

> Better is poverty in the hand of the god
> than riches in a storehouse;
> Better is bread, when the heart is happy,
> than riches with grief.[16]

This we may compare most directly with Prov. 15. 16 f.:

> Better is a little with the fear of the Lord
> than great treasure and trouble with it.
> Better is a dinner of herbs where love is
> than a fatted ox and hatred with it.

Amenemope 16. 11 ff. is similar, as are Prov. 16. 8; 28. 6; and
Ps. 37. 16. In view of the juxtaposition of the 'god' and 'non-god'
sayings in the Egyptian, it would be hard to justify any assumption
that the similar juxtaposition in the Hebrew indicates Yahwistic
reinterpretation by means of a variant. Further, as Bryce notes,
Prov. 15. 16 has strong verbal links with the Egyptian, and is
unlikely, therefore, to be a late variant of the next verse.[17]

It is possible to multiply examples,[18] but I think the important
point to bear in mind is that where Proverbs draws upon non-
Israelite traditions, it is drawing upon traditions which are themselves grounded in the religious beliefs of other nations. The
Egyptian texts, for instance, operate against a background of
m3ˁt: they assume a social and cosmic order which has been
perfect since the creation, and is maintained by gods, kings, and
men. Thus, as Frankfort has argued, the success of the individual
indicates his 'attunement' to *m3ˁt*, and advice on how to succeed

---

[16] Taking *šnn* as 'grief' or 'vexation' with most commentators, as a good parallel
to *ḥ3ty ndm* in the previous line. Alternatively, it is derived from *šni*, and means
'strife'.   [17] Bryce, *A Legacy of Wisdom*, 71 ff.
[18] Numerous other correspondences have been noted by H. D. Preuss in 'Das
Gottesbild der älteren Weisheit Israels', SVT 23 (1972), 117–45.

is, in effect, advice on how to behave in accord with *m3ʿt*. To suppose that such advice is wholly secular is, therefore, fallacious, and Frankfort characterizes such supposition as the 'Pragmatic Misinterpretation'.[19] By the New Kingdom in Egypt, we must, moreover, reckon with the development of an intense personal piety, as reflected in *Amenemope*. Again, the Mesopotamian texts show a strong interest in religion and divine action. None of the non-Israelite works, then, gives any reason to suppose that Israelite wisdom was 'secular'; rather the opposite. Their correspondence with the Hebrew texts, moreover, is frequently very precise, despite McKane's extraordinary complaint that criticisms based on the non-Israelite material are too general.[20]

3. *The Righteous and the Wise*

Even among the 'religious' sayings more characteristic of Israelite than of non-Israelite wisdom, it is usually difficult to assume an origin which is specifically Yahwistic. Pre-eminent among the sayings assigned by McKane to his class C, for example, are those which contrast the righteous with the wicked. McKane says that he finds it 'hard to resist the conclusion that the antithesis of *ṣaddīq* and *rāšāʿ* is a dogmatic classification and that it is expressive of a premise of Yahwistic piety, namely, the doctrine of theodicy.'[21] Certainly these sayings are marked out by their number and distribution, and it is possible that they are the vehicle for a specific body of ideas. It is not at all clear, however, that those ideas are either late or specifically Yahwistic.

The most important objection to McKane's assessment of the sayings is the appearance of the righteous and wicked in the *Aramaic Ahikar* (li) (*ṣdyq* in lines 126, 128, 173, and probably 167, *ršyʿ* in line 171, and *ršyʾn* in 168). Very similar ideas seem to underlie the sayings in this text, where the righteous are again assured of divine protection, and punishment is promised for the wicked. The most striking parallel is in lines 168–9a, which follow an exhortation to support the righteous: '[. . .] of the wicked will be swept away in the day of storm, and its gates will fall into ruin;

---

[19] H. Frankfort, *Ancient Egyptian Religion* (New York, 1948).
[20] See McKane, *Proverbs: A New Approach*, 16, and p. 10 in the 1983 reissue of *Prophets and Wise Men*.   [21] McKane, *Proverbs: A New Approach*, 420.

for the spoil [. . .]'.[22] Compare Prov. 10. 26 and 12. 7: 'When the storm has passed, the wicked is no more, but the righteous is established for ever'; 'The wicked are overthrown and are no more, but the house of the righteous will stand'; and also the similar 12. 12 and 14. 11. Though the form of the Aramaic saying is somewhat different, the imagery is so similar that some relationship with the biblical sayings seems overwhelmingly probable. I cannot, myself, resist the conclusion that the righteous and wicked sayings in Proverbs represent a type of saying known also outside Israel: their origin is unlikely to have been in late Yahwistic piety.

In connection with these sayings, it is interesting to note that on the only two occasions when the noun *ḥkmh*, 'wisdom', appears in the mass of West Semitic inscriptions collected by Donner and Röllig,[23] it is in association with *ṣdq(h)*, 'righteousness'. Thus in the late eighth- or early seventh-century bilingual inscription of Azitawadda, from Karatepe in S. Anatolia, the ruler declares that 'every king treated me as a father on account of my righteousness and on account of my wisdom and on account of the goodness of my heart' (*KAI* 26 A (I) ll. 12 f.). On the late eighth-century statue from Zenjirli, set up for Panammuwa II, it is said that 'on account of his wisdom and on account of his righteousness, he grasped the hem of the robe of his lord, the king of Assyria' (*KAI* 215 l. 11). One should not make too much of these texts, one in Phoenician, the other in Aramaic, and neither from Palestine. Nevertheless, unless this is an extraordinary coincidence, it does seem possible that the terms 'wisdom' and 'righteousness' were regularly associated in the eighth/seventh centuries: another obstacle to any idea of 'righteousness' as a late, Yahwistic entrant to the vocabulary of wisdom.

4. *Prophets and Wise Men*

Finally, we may turn specifically to the central thesis of McKane's book *Prophets and Wise Men*. There it is argued that the reflection of wisdom in other traditions in the Old Testament demonstrates its secular nature and separation from the prophetic tradition. In

---

[22] See Lindenberger, *The Aramaic Proverbs of Ahiqar*, 171.
[23] H. Donner and W. Röllig, *Kanaanäische und arämaische Inschriften* (Wiesbaden, 1962–4).

this study of non-wisdom, mainly prophetic, texts, McKane's theory seeks the external validation of which it is clearly in need. Much of the material which he discusses is to be examined in the next chapter and I do not wish to pre-empt my conclusions there. Let us for the moment, then, accept McKane's view that there was a class of 'wise men' in Israel, associated with the wisdom literature, but set aside his internal evidence from Proverbs for secular wisdom, as being unproven or false: on the basis of non-wisdom passages, does he make a good case for a secular wisdom tradition?

McKane's analysis of the biblical texts begins in his fourth chapter, with a study of 2 Sam. 16. 23 and related verses in the Succession Narrative. These verses, he argues, demonstrate the existence of two distinct systems of guidance, depending on human counsel and the word of God respectively, held in an uneasy balance. When in 14. 20 the wise woman of Tekoa compares the wisdom of David with that of the messenger of God (cf. 19. 28 (ET 27)), 'David's wisdom and the wisdom of the *mal'āk* of God are assumed to be two separate and distinctive procedures, the one relying on human reason and the other on a divine revelation communicated by the *mal'āk* of God.'[24] Of 16. 23, where an editorial note claims that the counsel of Ahithophel was like that of the oracle of God, McKane writes: 'Taken at its face value the verse means that there are two parallel and unconnected systems of reliable guidance in matters of state.'[25] Thus it implies that, 'the *dābār* of God and *'ēṣā* are equal partners in statecraft.'[26] This argument seems to lack weight. Each of the verses, in its context, clearly seeks to emphasize the wisdom of Ahithophel or David, and does so by comparison with the 'ideal' guidance of God (this is particularly clear in 14. 20 and 19. 28, where the speakers appear to be employing flattery). The human wisdom is not equated with divine guidance, but we can no more speak of the verses indicating two systems of guidance than we can of 'brave as a lion' implying two systems of bravery. The verses are interested in asserting parity of efficacy, not in questions of difference in type, and cannot be used as evidence for McKane's conclusion.

In the subsequent chapters, McKane examines a great deal of

---

[24] McKane, *Prophets and Wise Men*, 59.   [25] Ibid. 55.   [26] Ibid. 60.

material from the prophetic literature, and it is with this examination that we come to the heart of his study. Most important for the present discussion is a series of passages, which McKane describes as 'The Attack on Old Wisdom': Isa. 5. 19–24; 10. 13 ff.; 19. 11–13; 29. 14–16; 30. 1–5; 31. 1–3; Jer. 49. 7; and Ezek. 28. 2 ff. Their key feature is an attack on human presumption, and a declaration that the power of God is vastly greater than that of men and nations. For McKane this is, of course, an attack on the pretensions of secular wisdom, but if, as seems likely, assertions on the 'Man proposes, God disposes' type were actually an important part of wisdom from earliest times, it is difficult to see how the passages can be an informed attack on wisdom *per se*.

At times, indeed, the polemic is clearly against people who are wholly alien to the spirit of the wisdom literature: Isa. 5. 19–24, for example (probably to be taken with the similar woe-sayings of vv. 8 and 11, at least), condemns the consolidation of large estates, perpetual drunkenness, decadent feasting, and the corruption of justice. It is hard to reconcile the image of these greedy, corrupt, and drunken sensualists with the description of the wise men given by McKane, let alone with the impression given by Proverbs. It is quite inaccurate to remark, as does McKane, that wisdom approves the sort of bribery condemned here: Prov. 19. 6 and 21. 14 mention only the use of 'presents' to win favour generally, and 'open doors' (probably the meaning in 17. 8 also), while the corruption of justice and oppression of the poor are roundly condemned in Egyptian and Israelite wisdom. It is most probable that Isa. 5 is an attack not on wise men, but on corrupt rulers generally. If the men attacked in any of the passages cited were 'wise men', and certainly some believed themselves to be wise in some way, they were not representative of the wisdom tradition. Seeing a prophetic attack on wisdom here is like viewing Jeremiah's attack on false prophets as an attack on prophecy. At most we can say that the wisdom tradition and prophecy were united in their disdain for those who placed too great a value upon their own abilities, who were 'wise in their own eyes', and neglected to take account of the action of God. In no one of McKane's examples, nor in their cumulative effect, is there any evidence to support the idea of a sustained conflict between the 'inspired' prophetic tradition and a 'secular' wisdom tradition.

5. *Conclusions*

The theory that early Israelite wisdom was a secular tradition has been examined in some depth, and found wanting in almost every respect. The internal evidence of Proverbs cited by McKane and others is, I have argued, largely illusory, while the Egyptian and other non-Israelite evidence suggests that wisdom literature conventionally incorporated religious elements long before it reached Israel, if, indeed, it ever lacked them. It is not so difficult to believe that there existed individuals who emphasized human ability at the expense of ignoring divine action altogether. It may be that such individuals provoked the prophetic attacks examined by McKane, and it is conceivable, though not demonstrable, that they might have identified themselves with some tradition embodied in the wisdom literature. To take them, however, as representatives of wisdom, let alone as guides to the nature of wisdom, would be to fly in the face of compelling evidence to the contrary.

5
The Wise in the Old Testament

We have touched on the issue of 'wise men' and their importance in William McKane's portrayal of a secular wisdom tradition. More generally, though, scholars have long assumed that a specific class of 'wise men' is referred to in the Old Testament, and have associated this class with the state bureaucracy, or some part of it, on the one hand, and with the wisdom literature on the other. The administrative association is asserted on the basis of particular texts in which 'wise men' appear, while the association with the wisdom literature rests principally upon the very description of these men as 'wise'. Of course the root *HKM* is used widely in the OT, and in many places it clearly does not refer either to state administrators or to the wisdom literature. It is reasonable, therefore, to view any such usage as special or technical, containing some implication beyond the broader sense of intelligence or skill.[1] After first outlining the range of uses attested in the OT, I wish in this chapter to examine the references to 'wise men', and to ask whether they are indeed references to a single class. If so, is this class associated with the state administration, and does this description itself imply some connection with the wisdom literature?

1. Common Uses of 'Wisdom'

In most cases it is clear that *HKM* lacks any really 'technical' sense. So in Exod. 1. 10 and 2 Sam. 13. 3, the primary sense is of shrewd calculation, with no ethical or professional implication; this is probably the case also in 1 Kgs. 2. 6, 9, where the context is, however, more political. At the same time, the root is used of

---

[1] W. McKane, in his review of R. N. Whybray, *The Intellectual Tradition in the Old Testament,* in *JSS* 20 (1975), 243–48, argues that the establishment of a technical usage is unimportant, but his own work constantly presupposes such a usage.

the skill shown by, and inherent in artisans (Exod. 28. 3; 31. 3, 6; 35. 25, 26, 31, 35; 36. 1, 2, 4; 1 Kgs. 7. 14; 1 Chr. 22. 15 (ET 14); 28. 21; 2 Chr. 2. 6 (ET 7), 12 f. (ET 13 f.); Ps. 58. 6; Isa. 40. 20; Jer. 10. 9; Ezek. 27. 8 f.). This 'skill' is most notably the skill of the artisans who work on priestly robes, the sanctuary, and the temple, and is viewed in Exod. 35 f. as divinely inspired, although it is also the skill of those who make idols. The use of *HKM* for artistic skill is mainly late, but it clearly embraces the ideas of intelligence and ability which underlie other uses, and should not be regarded as a fundamentally different idea.

Similar is the use of *HKM* for 'skill in government'. Joshua is endowed with such wisdom (Deut. 34. 9 (P)), it is flatteringly attributed to David (2 Sam. 14. 20), and it is claimed by the kings of Assyria (Isa. 10. 13) and Tyre (Ezek. 28). In a curious expression, Ezra is said to possess the wisdom of his God, which is probably to be understood in the same sort of way, as is the selection of leaders for Israel on the basis of their wisdom, understanding, and knowledge, in Deut. 1. 13, 15. It is this sort of 'governmental' wisdom which Solomon requests, and is granted, in 1 Kgs. 3: 'an understanding mind to govern your people, that I may discern between good and evil'.

Closely related to this is wisdom in a forensic sense, the ability to judge, which Solomon again possesses, and which is implied in Deut. 16. 19 (perhaps a proverb). Such ideas of government and judgement are probably embodied in the idea of divine wisdom, which is found in the Ugaritic texts (e.g. *CTA* 4. iv. 41), and is a characteristic of gods, or perhaps specifically of El, according to Ezek. 28. 2. The idea of artisanship may be present as well, in the particular association of Yahweh's wisdom with the creation (see especially Prov. 8. 22–31, also Ps. 104. 24; Jer. 10. 12; 51. 15). Wisdom is, however, associated with other divine action (Isa. 31. 2), and is a gift which God may grant to individuals or to the nation (Isa. 33. 6).

HKM is used of Israel, both in a negative way to express its lack of sense as a lack of wisdom (Deut. 32. 6, 9; cf. Hos. 13. 13), or its skill in doing evil (Jer. 4. 22), and in a positive way, where the wisdom of Israel lies in its possession of Yahweh's statutes (Deut. 4. 6). The remnant of the nation, the 'shoot from the stump of Jesse', will be endowed with the spirit of wisdom (Isa. 11. 2). 'Wise' is used of other nations in Isa. 47. 10; Jer. 49. 7; and Zech. 9. 2.

In none of these cases does the term have any literary connotation, and only in two sources is such a connotation found outside the wisdom literature itself: in the story of Solomon's wisdom, and in the book of Daniel, where Daniel and his companions are said to have been skilful in 'letters and wisdom' (1. 17). There is possibly some similar idea in the reference to famous wise men in the former (1 Kgs. 5. 11: ET 4. 31), but the reference is obscure.[2]

2. *The Succession Narrative*

'Wisdom' has a range of closely related applications, which have different nuances but fundamentally the same basic sense of intelligence, good judgement, and skill. It does not always have an ethical or religious implication, but may on occasion be regarded as a gift from God, to be used or abused (Ezek. 28. 17). Since the qualities implied by 'wise' might be thought to have been useful, if not requisite, for a counsellor or official in the Israelite bureaucracy, it is all the more astonishing that it is never explicitly used to describe any of the numerous Israelite scribes and counsellors who appear in the OT. Thus Ahithophel, David's renegade counsellor, is never called 'wise', though the term is far from unusual in the Succession Narrative, and though McKane devotes an entire chapter of his book *Prophets and Wise Men* to him as the archetypal royal counsellor and wise man; nor is his rival Hushai. Indeed, the 'wise' individuals in this narrative are, for the most part, very clearly not royal counsellors.

The only possible candidate here for the description 'wise' counsellor, in any official sense, is Jonadab, though as David's nephew he is a member of the royal family, and there is no indication that he holds any official post.[3] Jonadab is hard done by in modern scholarship: the RSV turns the description of him as 'wise' into 'crafty' (2 Sam 13. 3), and Whybray regards it as

---

[2] Solomon is described as being wiser than Ethan the Ezrahite and Heman, Calcol, and Darda, the sons of Mahol. Ethan, Heman, Calcol, and Dara (*sic*) are listed in 1 Chr. 2. 6 as sons of Zerah, the son of Judah and Tamar. This suggests that 'Ezrahite' might be a corruption of Zerahite (cf. Num. 26. 20), but Heman and Ethan are both called 'Ezrahites' in the titles to Pss. 88 and 89. Mahol is unknown. There is clearly considerable confusion in the tradition.

[3] Whether or not the 'King's friend' was the title of an official, it seems unlikely that Jonadab, as his 'friend' held some position as an adviser to Amnon, contra A. Van Selms, 'The Origin of the Title "the King's Friend"', *JNES* 16 (1957), 118–23.

'probably ironical in intention'.[4] Yet when he reappears in 13. 30 ff., he is clearly not a villain, but gives sensible advice to the king, and prevents a panic. To be strictly fair to him, then, Jonadab's advice to his lovesick friend and cousin Amnon goes no further than to suggest a way in which he can be alone with Tamar and gain her sympathy: Amnon's rape of his sister seems to be his own idea. Be that as it may, Jonadab is called 'wise' in connection with this advice, which is non-professional and ultimately disastrous, and not later when he gives sensible and perceptive advice to the king.

The only other man who is called 'wise' here is David himself, in 14. 20. In this case the description may indeed be a little ironical, since the king has just been duped, and not for the first time in the narrative. Anyway, as the king, David is clearly neither scribe nor counsellor. The character who calls him 'wise' is a woman, one of two in the narrative who are themselves described as 'wise'. This 'wise woman of Tekoa' has been brought to Jerusalem by Joab, David's general, and at his behest presents David with a false case for judgement, turns the king's own ruling against him, and persuades him to permit the return of Absalom, who is in exile (this, again, results in disaster).

The details of the exchange are obscured by confusion in the text; more importantly, the role of the woman is a matter of some dispute. G. G. Nicol has argued that the strong emphasis placed on the wisdom of the woman has led to a neglect of the wisdom of Joab, who achieves his objective 'by commissioning her to act and speak precisely according to his own careful direction'.[5] J. Hoftijzer, on the other hand, maintains, surely correctly, that the woman is not portrayed merely as a puppet of Joab, but that, when she extracts from the king a sworn judgement (14. 11), in place of his initial vague statement, she is responding to circumstances which could hardly have been foreseen.[6] Anyway, it is certainly not the wisdom of Joab that is involved in ch. 20, when another wise woman, this time from Abel, confronts him from the wall as he besieges that city. When this woman learns that he is only after the fugitive Sheba, she 'goes to all the people in her wisdom', and the rebel's head is shortly thereafter thrown out to Joab.

---

[4] Whybray, *The Intellectual Tradition in the Old Testament*, 90.

[5] G. G. Nicol, 'The Wisdom of Joab and the Wise Woman of Tekoa', *St. Th.* 36 (1982), 97–104.

[6] J. Hoftijzer, 'David and the Tekoite Woman', *VT* 20 (1970), 419–44.

C. V. Camp[7] compares the stratagem of the woman of Tekoa with the prophetic use of 'juridical parables' (cf. 2 Sam. 12. 1–15; 1 Kgs. 20. 38–43), and the challenge from the wall by the woman of Abel with the exchanges across city walls by military leaders in 2 Sam. 2. 18–23, 24–8 and 2 Kgs. 18. 17–36. From this she concludes that wise women were customarily granted a kind of authority similar to that of prophets and military leaders. The basis of this authority, she suggests, lay ultimately in the joint responsibility of the mother and father for the education of a child, which is to be linked with early Yahwistic egalitarianism, and in a more general concept of motherhood. This hypothesis rests, however, on a wholly unjustified leap from the realm of literary comparison to that of historical conclusion. The 'juridical' parable, moreover, is a literary type, known outside Israel,[8] while the parley across the wall with Joab resembles the parallels only slightly in all but setting. The deductions about maternal education have been discussed earlier.

Hoftijzer has observed that the fundamental difference between Nathan's parable in 2 Sam. 12. and that of the woman of Tekoa lies in the woman's *lack* of power and immunity. Both the wise women in the narrative lack the authority to cajole or command: they have no political or religious power, and they employ shrewdness and persuasiveness as their only tools. This is apparently what constitutes the wisdom of the woman of Abel, when she 'goes to all the people in her wisdom'. The other main female characters in the Succession Narrative (Bathsheba and Tamar) are entirely passive, catalysts for the disasters which ensue from the lust they arouse; the 'wise women', on the other hand, are active characters who play a positive role in the course of events. As Eissfeldt has observed, they manipulate powerful men into the settlement of a matter.[9]

It is hard to say whether 'wise', when applied to these women, has any significance beyond this general one of shrewdness and persuasiveness. Some slight link with literary wisdom is suggested

[7] C. V. Camp, 'The Wise Women of 2 Samuel: A Role Model for Women in Early Israel', *CBQ* 43 (1981), 14–29. See also her *Wisdom and the Feminine in the Book of Proverbs* (Sheffield, 1985), 120.

[8] For an Egyptian narrative parallel to the 'parable', see the story of Horus and Seth (Pap. Chester Beatty I, recto) 6. 7 ff.

[9] O. Eissfeldt, *Einleitung in das Alte Testament*[3] (Tübingen, 1964), 15; ET *Introduction to the Old Testament* (Oxford, 1965), 12.

by their use of sayings which are seemingly traditional or proverbial (14. 14; 20. 18). Eissfeldt assumes that these women must have had some tradition or training, and Brenner connects them with 'either a profession or else a social institution which was forgotten later on'.[10] Nicol suggests that they must be understood in the light of Jer. 9. 16 (ET 17), where the 'wise women' are seemingly associated with mourning rites. Possibly the description is stressed in the narrative for purely literary purposes, to highlight the symmetry created by placing a 'wise woman' episode at each end of the story of the rebellion, and the delightful contrast they make, on both occasions, with the stolid Joab. In any case, they are clearly not royal officials, although their wisdom is not of a sort inappropriate to such officials. The author of the Succession Narrative clearly feels no reluctance to use the term 'wise', and apparently understands it in a quite conventional way. If we are to assume that he was aware of a special association between the term and the counsellors of the royal court, his failure to use it of Ahithophel and Hushai, both pre-eminently counsellors, becomes a little puzzling. Something similar, indeed, might be said of the OT as a whole.

3. 'Wise Men' Texts

Wisdom is evidently not a quality confined to men: women possess it or are associated with it not only in Proverbs and the Succession Narrative, but also elsewhere as artisans and advisors (Judg. 5. 29). In the last few pages we have seen *ḤKM* used in many other contexts and of many other individuals where there is no question of the reference being to state officials. We have seen that it is possible to speak of a particular association between 'wisdom' and such areas as artisanship and leadership, but that such association never seems to give the term a new, technical sense. As we turn now to the handful of passages in which such a sense has been found by some scholars, it is important to bear in mind both the free and wide usage elsewhere, and the relative paucity of these passages.

(a) *Foreign Wise Men*

Let us begin with passages which refer to 'wise men' outside Israel. Isa. 19. 11 f. declares that:

---

[10] A. Brenner, *The Israelite Woman* (Sheffield, 1985), 44.

Utterly foolish are the nobles of Zoan,
the wise counsellors of Pharaoh give stupid counsel.
How can you say to Pharaoh,
'I am a son of wise men, a son of kings of old'?
Where then are your wise men?
Let them tell you and make known
what the Lord of Hosts has purposed against Egypt.

The characters in whom we are interested here are the 'wise counsellors' and 'wise men': who are they, and are they identical? The answer to the second question would appear to be negative: 'wise counsellors' here is parallel to 'nobles of Zoan' (= Tanis), but the first 'wise men' to 'kings of old'. Moreover, 'where then?', *'ayyām 'ēpô'*, is an expression implying that something does not exist (cf. Judg. 9. 38; Job 17. 15), and it is reasonable to assume that the second reference to 'wise men' also indicates the 'ancient kings', since the 'wise counsellors' certainly do exist. The author of this late addition to the book is declaring that the Egyptian counsellors, whom he ironically dubs wise, give stupid counsel, and this makes their claim to be the descendants of ancient wise kings seem ridiculous; if these ancient kings, unlike their descendants, really were wise, maybe Pharaoh should ask *them* what Yahweh has purposed! This is the only interpretation of the passage which makes any sense of 'Where then are your wise men?': these wise men who might give proper counsel cannot be the counsellors who are already there and giving bad counsel.

As we have said, the counsellors are called 'wise' ironically, in contrast to the stupidity of their counsel; this is shown by the somewhat contrived structure of the clause:

wise–counsellors–pharaoh–counsel–stupid

'Wise' is not part of a cliché, 'wise counsellors', but of a stylized chiastic clause in which it corresponds to, and is contrasted with 'stupid'. To sum up, then, this passage at least shows the use of 'wise' to describe counsellors, albeit non-Israelite ones, and the application of 'wisdom' to giving political advice. The unqualified use of 'wise men', however, is in a reference not to professional counsellors, but to ancient kings.

Egyptian 'wise men' crop up again in Gen. 41. 8 and Exod. 7. 11. In the former, they are summoned, along with the *ḥarṭummê miṣrayim*, to determine the meaning of Pharaoh's dream. They are the wise men and magicians 'of Egypt', and there is no reason to suppose that they are attached to the court: that Pharaoh has to 'send and call' for them suggests, perhaps, that they were not. In the second passage, wise men are again 'called for', this time along with 'sorcerers', to match Aaron's transformation of his stick into a snake. The wise men and sorcerers are collectively called the *ḥarṭummê miṣrayim* here: it is generally acknowledged that *ḥarṭom* is derived ultimately from the Egyptian title *ḥry-ḥb(t) ḥry-tp*, the 'chief ritual book carrier'. Whatever the OT writers understood by the term, its use here to describe both 'wise men' and 'sorcerers' implies that the two are of the same 'magical' ilk. In both passages, indeed, the 'wisdom' required is magical or mantic, and the wise are presumably men skilled in the arcane arts: they are not professional counsellors. The 'wise men' of Babylon who appear in the Aramaic portions of Daniel (e.g. 2. 12 ff.; 4. 3: ET 4. 6) are certainly diviners.

Foreign wise men feature also in the story of Esther, where the seven nobles 'who saw the king's face and sat first in the kingdom' are described as 'wise men knowing the times' (Esther 1. 13), and are consulted by the Persian king on a matter of law. Their 'knowledge of the times' probably does not indicate skill in divination,[11] but a grasp of politics (cf. 1 Chr. 12. 33), and their role is perhaps to be identified with that of the seven Persians who are 'counsellors' to the king in Ezra 7. 14. They are, anyway, clearly considered to be the highest officials and most intimate courtiers of the king.[12] What is less clear is that 'wise' is used as a technical term here, since much of the verse is taken up with emphasizing the ability of these men in legal matters. There is no reason at all to exclude a more general sense of the term, which, as we have seen, is used elsewhere in the OT of political and forensic ability. The verse, then, does not preclude an understanding of 'wise' in a technical sense here, but nor is it evidence for such usage. The other occurrence of 'wise men' in Esther is at 6. 13, where Haman's wise men are either identical with his friends of the previous verse, or, more probably, a simple textual error (cf. *BHS*, ad loc.).

[11] Contra H.-P. Müller, 'Magisch-mantische Weisheit und die Gestalt Daniels', *UF* I (1969), 79–94, esp. 80.

[12] On the possible relationship between these men, the 'six helpers' of Darius, and the later great families of Iran, see R. N. Frye, *The Heritage of Persia*[2] (London, 1976), 106.

Textual problems also surround the 'wise men' of the nations in Jer. 10. 7. As MT stands, the 'wise' appear to be the idols of the next verse: the reading of Theodotion, 'kings' for 'kingdoms', which would make 'wise men' parallel with 'kings', is attractive. The passage in vv. 5–8 interrupts the flow of the oracle, and is omitted in LXX, whose text is supported here[13] by 4QJer[b]. There are, therefore, excellent grounds for regarding it as a late addition. In view of these difficulties, it is not easy to identify the 'wise' of v. 7: they are perhaps kings, idols, or wise men in a general sense. There are certainly no grounds for assuming that they are officials, or a special group of any kind.

The 'wise men' of Edom who are threatened with destruction in Obad. 8 are not clearly specified. The noun lacks an article and stands in parallel with 'understanding', which suggests that the oracle is threatening the removal of wisdom, rather than a specific group, from a nation traditionally associated with wisdom. It is interesting to compare Jer. 49. 7 ff., where the loss of wisdom is part of the shameful destruction of Edom, and where reference to state officials would seem quite inappropriate. In Jer. 50. 35 and 51. 57, however, the matter is rather different. In these passages the 'wise men' of Babylon are included in lists of groups, and on both occasions follow the *śārîm*, the nobles or senior officials. There can be little doubt that they are intended to be a group of some sort here. The first list runs: inhabitants, nobles, wise men, diviners, warriors, (horses, chariots), foreign troops, treasures, waters.[14] The second: nobles, wise men, governors, prefects, warriors. From the second list it seems probable that the association of 'wise men' is not just with diviners in the first, as the usage in Daniel might suggest, but with the *śārîm* too; it is also clear that the lists do not contain synonyms for the same class, and that the 'wise men' and *śārîm* are not, therefore, identical. Who are they, then? The second list is very consciously a list of foreign officials: *peḥāh*, 'governor', and *segen*, 'prefect', are both loan-words from the Assyrian. It does not seem likely, therefore, that the author is merely applying to Babylon a term with which he is familiar from Israel. The two passages may show a 'technical' usage of

---

[13] See F. M. Cross, *The Ancient Library of Qumran* (London, 1958), 139.

[14] On the horses and chariots, see *BHS* apparatus, ad loc. Here and in Isa. 44. 25 (below), *bārîm* (cf. Akkad. *bārû*) is plausibly to be read for MT *badîm*; cf. C. R. North, *The Second Isaiah* (Oxford, 1964), 144.

'wise men' applied at a late date to a group in Babylon, but we cannot identify that group with any certainty, nor assume that they are scribes or counsellors.

Of the passages which speak of wise men in a non-Israelite context, then, only the Aramaic portions in Daniel and the oracle against Babylon in Jeremiah appear to demonstrate a technical use of the term. In the former it is used of diviners: this is possibly the sense in the latter also. Clearly, neither can be used to prove the use of the term in pre-exilic Israel to describe a particular Israelite class. Though in Jer. 50. 35; 51. 57; Isa. 19. 11 f.; and Esther 1. 13 there is some association with *śārîm*, the term used in 1 Kgs. 4. 2 of high officials (whom I shall discuss in a later chapter), there is certainly no equation with them of a group of 'wise men'.

(b) *Israelite Wise Men*

What, then, of the use of the terms in an Israelite context? In Isa. 29. 13 f. Yahweh declares that, since Israel's worship has become mechanical, and not heartfelt, he will again work wonders, 'and the wisdom of their wise men will fail, and the discernment of their discerning men will hide away.' Some scholars have seen behind this a reference to historical relations between Israel and Egypt;[15] McKane seems to make an implausible division of the material, so that v. 14 is linked not with v. 13, but with vv. 15 f.[16] Yet the passage is not to do with the punishment of conspiracy and politics, but with the restoration of the religion:

> Because this people draw near with their mouth
> and honour me with their lips,
> though their hearts are far from me,
> and their fear of me a commandment of men
> learned by rote,
> Therefore, behold, I shall again work wonders with
> this people, working wonders,
> and there will fail the wisdom of their wise and
> the discernment of their discerners will hide away.

The complacency of the people, and the degeneration of their religious observance into mere lip-service are the cause

---

[15] See e.g. O. Kaiser, *Der Prophet Jesaja: Kap.* 13–39 (Göttingen, 1973), ad loc.; ET *Isaiah* 13–39² (London, 1980).

[16] McKane, *Prophets and Wise Men*, 70.

of Yahweh's complaint: the people no longer 'fear' him because
they feel awe, but because they are told to. So, he declares,
he is going to work extraordinary wonders. The wise and
discerning are not a group, or groups,[17] who have corrupted the
people and are to be punished: the final line is emphasizing the
miraculous nature of the events to come. Confronted with these
events, even the most intelligent will be dumbfounded: the miracles
are to be 'mind-boggling'. The hithp. of *sātar* is used elsewhere
only in Isa. 45. 15, of God hiding himself away, and in 1 Sam. 23.
19; 26. 1; and the title of Ps. 54, of David hiding from the forces
of Saul. The verb used with wisdom, *'ābad*, is used for the 'failing'
of courage in Jer. 4. 9, and some such sense is probably intended
here. The imagery, then, is of the retreat of human intelligence in
the face of what it cannot comprehend. To be sure, there may be
some implication in these verses that human intelligence has been
allowed to play too great a role in the national religion, but there
is no indication of any reference to a specific group.

In Isa. 5. 21 the prophet declares: 'Woe to those who are wise
in their own eyes and discerning in their own sight.' The context
is a series of exclamations in which he attacks those who call for
speedy divine action despite their own iniquities: those who
confuse good and evil, those who are wise in their own eyes, and
those who are mighty in their drinking but corrupt in their
dispensation of justice (Isa. 5. 18–23). McKane sees here an attack
on a class of officials who wish to substitute human intelligence for
piety; the expression 'wise in one's own eyes' is an expression used
by 'the wise' themselves, which the prophet is turning against
them.[18] Certainly this idiom is one favoured by the wisdom
literature to express a false conceit in one's own intelligence (cf.
Prov. 26. 5, 12, 16; 28. 11), with some implication of hubris (Prov.
3. 7). Yet it is clearly dangerous to suppose that the use of the
phrase in Isaiah must be an *ironic* borrowing from that literature,
since the prophet seems to be using it in precisely the same way
that it is used there. The attack is a general one upon a corrupt

---

[17] Whybray, *The Intellectual Tradition in the Old Testament*, 19, points out that
if we are to take the 'wise' as a group here, we must logically take the 'discerning'
to be a group also. This is a fairly good example of Whybray's approach to the
search for 'technical' usage, which is valid within limits, although it is easy to
understand McKane's impatience with it.

[18] McKane, *Prophets and Wise Men*, 66.

and iniquitous establishment, which attempts to justify itself and its corruption, and there is no reason to suppose that the target is a group which is called, or calls itself, 'the wise'.

Even more improbable is the claim that we should understand the 'wisdom' of God in Isa. 31. 2 to be set against the 'false' wisdom of the nation's leaders. If they did claim wisdom, in the sense of a political intelligence overriding religious claims, there is no actual mention of it here. 'Wise men', on the other hand, are indeed mentioned in Isa. 44. 25, alongside diviners, and in contrast to prophets. Clearly, what unites these groups is not some particular social or political status, but their giving of advice and guidance without reference to the divine 'word'. Deutero-Isaiah shows antipathy toward such people, but neither the context nor the date of the passage allows the assumption that 'wise men' here are a specific group within government.

The key texts within Jeremiah have each provoked considerable discussion, but there is really no more reference to a class of wise men in this book than we found in Isaiah. In Jer. 8. 8 f. the prophet asks:

> How is it that you say, 'Wise are we,
> and *tôrāh* of Yahweh is with us'?
> yet, behold, into falsehood has the false pen
> of the scribes turned it.[19]
> Wise men will be shamed, shattered, and taken;
> behold, they reject the word of Yahweh,
> and what wisdom is there in them?

The context here is somewhat confused by the apparent insertion of a later addition in vv. 10*b*–12; the previous verses are aimed at the nation in general (8. 5). The structure of vv. 8 f. is, however, a little clearer. The first verse begins with the quotation of something said by the prophet's hearers: the quotation appears to finish before the asseverative *'ākēn*, 'yet', in 8*b*, which introduces the prophet's own comment. The change to the third person in 8*b* appears to tell against the identification of the scribes mentioned there with those who are claiming to be wise in 8*a*, since the latter are addressed in the second person. The 'wise men' in v. 9, whose punishment is to ensue from the intolerable situation, may be the addressees, the scribes, or a third, as yet unnamed group. The last

---

[19] Cf. *BHS* apparatus, ad loc.

is improbable, and the link formed by 'wise' probably indicates that the prophet is describing the people quoted in 8*b*. The prophet's hearers, then, are claiming to be wise and to possess *tôrāh* of Yahweh; the prophet protests that this *tôrāh* has been corrupted by the scribes, and prophesies that those who call themselves wise will be destroyed, since they are in fact rejecting the divine word, and their wisdom is therefore unreal.

The important problem, then, is the identification of the addressees, who call themselves wise but have rejected the Word. Who would associate possession of divine *tôrāh* with the possession of wisdom? McKane is forced to suppose that these verses represent a fundamental change in the nature of the 'wise men', from a wholly secular, political group, to one which is concerned with legal piety, since they accord ill with his previous descriptions of the wise man as *Realpolitiker*.[20]

General associations of wisdom with *tôrāh* are found in Pss. 19. 8 (ET 7); 119, but the most probable reference is to the Deuteronomic claim in Deut. 4. 6, that the possession of the Law makes Israel a 'wise' nation. Deut. 4 not only expresses the idea of wisdom through law, but prohibits tampering with this law, the crime of which the scribes are here accused (cf. Jer. 5. 31). The impression that the audience addressed is not a specific group, but the people as a whole, is reinforced not only by the context, but also by the accusation that they have rejected (*mā'āsû*) the word of Yahweh: rejection by the people is a prophetic cliché (cf. Amos 2. 4; Isa. 5. 24; 30. 12; Jer. 6. 19; Ezek. 20. 24. See also Lev. 26. 15 and 2 Kgs. 17. 15); the only individual described as doing so in these terms is Saul, the king.

To sum up, then, there are good reasons to suppose that Jeremiah's address is to the people generally, who claim that they are wise because they possess divine instruction. The prophet attacks this complacency, averring that the instruction which they possess has been corrupted by the scribes, and does not truly represent the divine Word. The 'wise' people are actually, therefore, rebelling against the Word, and will be destroyed, since their wisdom is illusory. It may be inferred from the final question that the prophet does not disagree that possession of divine instruction may constitute wisdom, but he claims that the written *tôrāh*,

[20] McKane, *Prophets and Wise Men*, 102–12.

whatever we may understand that to have been, is not the true
Word of God. If we insist on identifying a group of 'the wise' here,
it cannot be a group of secular, politically orientated, scribes, but
must be either a group of 'wise men' separate from the usual
hypothetical group, as Lindblom suggests,[21] or a radical development of that latter group, as McKane would have it. Either
solution, by multiplying groups or stages of groups puts an
intolerable burden on a theory which is hard pressed to prove the
existence of even a single such group or stage.

Jer. 9. 22 f. (ET 23 f.) has the prophet declare:

> Let not a wise man boast of his wisdom,
> and let not a mighty man boast of his might;
> let not a wealthy man boast of his wealth,
> but let the boaster boast of this:
> understanding and knowing me.
> For I am Yahweh who does *ḥesed*,
> justice and righteousness on the earth,
> for in these things I delight.
>
> Utterance of Yahweh.

As Whybray has pointed out, it is highly unlikely that we should
view the 'wise man' here as representative of a particular professional group, as McKane would have it.[22] The mighty man
might conceivably be a professional soldier, but are we really to
suppose that Israelite society included a group of 'professional'
rich men?[23] The characters here are chosen not as representatives
of professions, but as men who possess three different sorts of
human power—intellectual, physical, and economic, of which they
might be inclined to boast. The only thing, declares the prophet,
which is worth boasting about, is true knowledge of God.

Something similar is true of Jer. 18. 18:

And they said, 'Come, let us make plans against Jeremiah, for *tôrāh* will
not perish from a priest, nor *'ēṣāh* from a wise man, nor *dābār* from a
prophet. Come, let us smite him with the tongue, and pay no attention
to any of his words.'

For McKane, the wise man here is 'the representative of the
political establishment and the prophet and priest of the religious

[21] J. Lindblom, 'Wisdom in the Old Testament Prophets', SVT 3 (1960),
192–204.   [22] Cf. *Prophets and Wise Men*, 90.
[23] Whybray, *The Intellectual Tradition in the Old Testament*, 21 f.

establishment and Jeremiah's opponents accuse him of trying to undermine both.'[24] This interpretation is not uncommon, although many others have been proposed for this difficult passage, the obscurity of which arises from the lack of a direct narrative context.[25] Underlying many interpretations is the idea that the words of the protagonists reflect their objection to Jeremiah's teaching, and that they have somehow been provoked by a prophecy of the cessation of instruction from the priest, counsel from the wise man, and word from the prophet. What, then, would such a prophecy actually have meant? Priest and prophet are found together regularly in Jeremiah, and elsewhere, as representatives of the religious establishment, which is why it is tempting to see this as a mere extension to include another group. Yet there is no statement here of the dissolution of the religious and political establishments: it is not the priest, wise man, and prophet themselves who are threatened with extinction, but their pronouncements. It is these pronouncements, in fact, which form the link between them: the priest's instruction in the law, the wise man's counsel, and the prophet's word represent the totality of the nation's guidance. If all these were to perish, the nation would be left utterly by itself and cut off from God, as was Saul in an earlier age.

This is clearly the sense of a very similar saying in Ezek. 7. 26, where the nation, in the midst of calamity, seeks 'a vision from the prophet, but the law perishes from the priest and counsel from the elders'. This leaves the nation paralysed with despair and terror, incapable of defending itself. The people are abandoned by God and bereft of guidance and comfort; left alone thus, they are unable to cope. The close similarity of wording suggests some relationship between the passages in Jeremiah and Ezekiel, but there is a crucial difference: where Jeremiah reads 'wise man',

---

[24] McKane, *Prophets and Wise Men*, p. 128. n. 1.

[25] In W. Rudolph, *Jeremia*[2] (Tübingen, 1958), 114, the various interpretations are classified as three types. The first two take 18*b*, in different ways, to indicate the authority or backing of the conspirators, the third takes it as a reference to a prophecy by Jeremiah. My own interpretation falls under the third heading, but differs from that of e.g. Lindblom, in that I do not understand the prophecy as one of doom upon certain groups, but as a prediction of the cessation of divine guidance as mediated by those who fulfil certain roles. Whybray regards 18*b* as a proverbial saying, which expresses contempt for the continual chatter of prophets and others: this does not satisfactorily explain the context of the saying in Ezekiel.

Ezekiel has 'elders'. What this shows is not some replacement of the 'wise man' by the 'elder' in the post-exilic period:[26] the only evidence at all for the technical use of 'wise' is, as is becoming clear, in the exilic and post-exilic periods. The significance of the change lies in its demonstration of the relative unimportance of the terminology. Counsel can come from 'wise men', 'elders', call them what you will: their importance is as the source of counsel.

The most plausible interpretation of Jer. 18. 18, then, is as a denial by Jeremiah's opponents that the nation's sources of guidance will, as he has apparently prophesied, fail; that is, a denial that God is going to turn his back on, and abandon, Israel. Perhaps, in that case, we do not altogether lack a context for the piece: the previous verse, 18. 17, is a prophecy that God will, in the day of Israel's calamity, turn his back on her. In the next oracle from God, he promises that he will 'make empty the counsel of Judah and Jerusalem'. We have on our side, it seems, the opinion of the book's redactor. This, the similar passage in Ezekiel, and the sense of the verse itself, all tell in favour of regarding Jer. 18. 18 as a reference to a prophecy of the abandonment of Israel and the cessation of guidance there. It is their unwillingness to accept that Yahweh might abandon his people which leads his hearers to reject Jeremiah; although they can bear to hear about Yahweh's anger and judgement, the idea that he might abandon them altogether is provocative beyond endurance.

If this is indeed the proper interpretation of this difficult verse, then its relevance to the understanding of wisdom lies in its placing 'counsel' alongside the priestly *tôrāh* and the prophetic word as a source of divine guidance for the nation. This should only be a source of astonishment to the reader imbued with the idea that wisdom is a wholly secular tradition. We have seen in the pages above that, on the contrary, wisdom is associated with God and with divine inspiration on a number of occasions. The religious significance of 'counsel' more specifically has been described by de Boer.[27] It is their role as sources of divine guidance, not as representatives of the establishment, which unites the priest, the wise man, and the prophet in Jer. 18. 18. The verse does not,

---

[26] See col. 77 Fichtner, 'Jesaja unter den Weisen'. ET in Crenshaw (ed.), *Studies in Ancient Israelite Wisdom*, 42.

[27] P. A. H. de Boer, 'The Counsellor', SVT 3 (1960), 42–71.

therefore, constitute evidence for the existence of a class of wise men representative of the secular or political establishment.

(c) *Wise men: Conclusions*

The only use of 'wise' as a technical term for royal officials, other than diviners, seems to be in late references to Babylonians, and it may be that they too are to be regarded as diviners. It is never used as a technical term for a class of Israelites, and although 'wise' is found on a number of occasions in association with foreign royal officials or counsellors, no official Israelite counsellor is ever explicitly called wise. Of the texts which we studied above, none required that we posit the existence of a class of 'wise men' defined in terms of their professional function, while our interpretation of many precluded such an idea. Indeed the use of 'wise men' to describe a variety of individuals could only have been a source of confusion if it were conventionally understood in Israel to indicate a specific class.

A final point which should be made is that we do possess lists of important groups in Israel in 2 Kgs. 24. 15 f.; Neh. 9. 32; Isa. 3. 1–3; 9. 14 (ET 15); Jer. 1. 18; 2. 8, 26; 4. 9; 8. 1; 13. 13; 32. 32; 34. 19; Mic. 3. 11; Zeph. 3. 3 f. If 'wise' really was a term especially associated with royal officials, and if 'wise men' was a normal term for an important group within the Israelite establishment, it is truly remarkable not only that 'wise' is never used to describe a royal counsellor or official in Israel, but that the 'wise men' do not appear in any of these lists. It is surely more reasonable to conclude that no such technical use existed, at least until the term was used of Babylonians in the exilic and post-exilic periods. The only truly technical use of the term in an earlier time seems to have been in references to foreign diviners and magicians.

3. *General Conclusions*

The usage of 'wise' in the Old Testament cannot be used to determine the setting of the tradition represented in the wisdom literature. In the first place, it shows no particular connection with the literary tradition: the importance of the term *ḤKM* in the wisdom literature does not mean that the wisdom tradition acquired some sort of exclusive proprietorship over it. There is no reason to believe that an Israelite who heard the word would connect it immediately with the literary tradition. Even were there evidence, then, of a group of officials known as 'wise men', this would in itself give no cause to assume that they were connected with the wisdom tradition. As it is, the evidence for the existence of such a group is quite inadequate. In several instances, the interpretation of passages by certain scholars seems to have been so influenced by the assumption that such a group did exist, that the content of the passage itself has been all but ignored. This points to something which will become more obvious as we go on: the consensus that wisdom emerged from a scribal and educational tradition has profoundly affected the exegesis of many important passages outside the wisdom literature itself.

6

Joseph

The patriarchs of Genesis bear little resemblance to the anonymous heroes of Proverbs, and the complex prose narrative of the Joseph story in Gen. 37–50 is hardly reminiscent of anything in the wisdom literature. Nevertheless, since the publication of an article on Joseph by Gerhard von Rad in 1953, the Joseph Narrative has been regarded by many scholars as a manifestation of early wisdom with close links to Proverbs.[1] If this is true, then the narrative is of the greatest value for an understanding of wisdom, and it has played a significant part in many discussions of the subject.

It is important that von Rad's claims about the narrative be properly understood. Subsequent studies of other texts have made 'wisdom influence' a familiar subject over the last few decades; von Rad, however, does not describe the Joseph Narrative as a text 'influenced' by the wisdom tradition, but as a wisdom text itself. For him, the story was composed to embody the educational ideals of the wise men, whom he supposes to have been active in the royal court under the early monarchy. On the one hand, the character of Joseph is depicted in such a way as to exemplify their ideals of behaviour, while on the other, the underlying theological presuppositions of the work are identical to those of the wisdom literature. In this chapter I shall examine, therefore, both the characterization of Joseph and the theology of the narrative.

1. The Characterization of Joseph

The figure of Joseph himself is the most important element in von Rad's description of the narrative as 'a didactic wisdom story'. He

[1] G. von Rad, 'Josephsgeschichte und ältere Chokma; cf. also his *Die Josephsgeschichte* (Neukirchen, 1954), and his commentary, *Das erste Buch Mose, Genesis* (Göttingen, 1956), ET *Genesis: A Commentary* (London, 1959). Von Rad's opinions have been supported by many scholars. See e.g. R. de Vaux, *Histoire ancienne d'Israël*, I (Paris, 1971), 281 f., ET *The Early History of Israel*, I (London, 1978), 296, and C. T. Fritsch 'God Was With Him', *Interpretation*, 9 (1955), 21–34.

contends that the character and behaviour of Joseph are a blue-
print for the young man aspiring to power in the royal court, that
he is an idealized figure conforming to the model wise man, as
described in Hebrew and Egyptian wisdom literature. This ideal
character is founded on the fear of Yahweh, and built up in the
'hard school of humiliation'. Joseph displays it in his behaviour
towards Potiphar's wife, in his shrewd counselling of Pharaoh, and
in his forbearance from revenge upon his brothers. In his relationship with these brothers he shows extraordinary control over his
emotions, and an ability to 'keep silence'. In more general terms,
Joseph is a young man 'of the finest education and breeding,
of godliness and experience in the ways of the world'; he
conforms to the ideal of a man, 'who, through his breeding,
modesty, learning, congeniality and self-control, has attained a
noble character'.

Certain objections to this assessment present themselves at
once. We may reasonably ask, for example, what leads von Rad
to attribute a fine education to Joseph, who is, after all, merely a
shepherd boy in ch. 37; furthermore '*Weltgewandheit*', 'experience
in the ways of the world', is a wholly subjective impression, with
no specific justification from the text. For evidence of Joseph's
great self-control, moreover, he cites, remarkably, 42. 24; 43. 30 f.;
and 45. 1, all instances in which Joseph is seen to lose control.
Certainly these passages demonstrate the depth of Joseph's emo-
tion, and perhaps the pressure to which he is subjected, but they
hardly affirm his self-control. Crenshaw has rightly remarked that
'the failure of Joseph to control his emotions must not be overlooked',[2] and Redford demanded:[3] 'How can we apply a term like
"self-controlled" to a man who becomes violently angry one
minute, runs out to cry the next, and finally breaks down completely
when he can no longer continue the sham?'[4]

---

[2] See pp. 135 ff. of J. L. Crenshaw, 'Method in Determining Wisdom Influence
upon "Historical" Literature', *JBL* 88 (1969), 129–42.

[3] See pp. 100 ff. of D. B. Redford, *A Study of the Biblical Story of Joseph*, SVT
20 (1970).

[4] H.-C. Schmitt, in *Die nichtpriesterliche Josephsgeschichte* (Berlin, 1980), 158 ff.,
argues that Jospeh's weeping in 43. 30 and 50. 1 are wholly compatible with
wisdom ideals of closeness within the family (cf. Sir. 38. 16 ff.). W. L. Humphreys,
Joseph and his Family (Columbia, sc, 1988), 144, believes that Joseph's self-control
is shown by his lack of anger at the forgetfulness of the butler; this argument from
silence, however, carries little conviction. The issue is a red herring: impassibility

Other aspects of von Rad's picture of Joseph are, if not quite so puzzling, at least based on interpretations of the text which are clearly open to challenge. Thus, the idea that in chs. 42–4 Joseph is somehow testing his brothers, outlined more fully in von Rad's commentary on Genesis,[5] is one which presents considerable difficulties. Given the considerable anguish and humiliation which Joseph inflicts upon his brothers, it is hard to believe that there is no element of punishment present, and this is never denied in the narrative. Joseph's tale-bearing[6] (cf. Prov. 11. 13), his indiscreet revelation of his dreams, and his false accusations against his brothers (cf. Prov. 12. 17 ff.), are all of importance in the story, and in the portrayal of Joseph, but are hardly in accord with the ethical ideals of the wisdom literature. It cannot be denied that we should expect in a didactic, idealizing text not only a more lucid, but also a more consistent idealization.

Of Joseph's rise to power, von Rad writes: 'Joseph is an administrator, and he became one by demonstrating a double skill to Pharaoh: speaking publicly and giving counsel. But that is just what the wisdom teachers continually insist upon.' I shall not discuss at this point the reasons for Joseph's elevation, although it should be evident that there is more than his courtly abilities involved. What is more important is that the Joseph Narrative does not in the least depict the hero's rise as the inevitable promotion of an able counsellor through the ranks of bureaucracy: Joseph arrives at the court as the result of a unique chain of

is greatly overemphasized by von Rad as an attribute of the wise man, and it is, equally, an element plainly lacking in the narrative. Note, incidentally, that the term used of Joseph's controlling himself (43. 31; 45. 1), *'āpaq* (hithp.), is used nowhere in the wisdom literature.

[5] Von Rad, *Das Erste Buch Mose*, ad loc.

[6] See also Prov. 10. 18, where the same term, *dibbāh*, is used. J. Peck, in his 'Note on Genesis 37: 2 and Joseph's Character', *ET* 82 (1970/71), 342 f., has proposed that the 3 pl. suffix on *dibbāh* in 37. 2 should be taken as a subjective genitive, and the clause rendered 'Joseph brought their [his brothers'] slanders against him to his father'. *Dibbāh* always bears an unpleasant connotation, and Peck finds the idea of Joseph as a slanderer incompatible with the subsequent characterization. His rendering is possible (cf. GK § 135 *m*), but since the ambiguity is syntactical, his survey of other examples of *dibbāh* with suffixes is as irrelevant as his references to the LXX. In fact, the LXX of 37. 2 does not translate the suffix at all (contra LSJ *sub* καταφέρω: αὐτῶν here qualifies τὸν πατέρα), and probably took the genitive as objective: this is the more natural understanding, since *bô'* (hiph.) does not mean 'report', and there is no 'against him' in the Hebrew.

circumstances, summoned from prison to interpret the Pharaoh's dreams. There is nothing in ch. 41 to suggest that Joseph is elevated as a result of his rhetorical ability or persuasiveness.[7] The situation is inimitable, and, praiseworthy though Joseph may be, it is difficult to see all this as a path to be followed by aspiring royal advisers.

Finally, and perhaps most fundamentally, von Rad's attempts to compare Joseph's behaviour and character with the ideals of the wisdom literature rely too much on apparent, rather than real, correspondences. The clearest and most important example of this is his claim that Joseph's 'keeping silence' with his brothers corresponds to the teaching of passages in Proverbs (e.g. 10. 19; 12. 23) and in the Egyptian instructions. Joseph's silence in the story consists wholly of his decision not to reveal his real identity to his brothers: it is not a physical silence or a discreet manner. Even leaving aside Joseph's garrulousness in ch. 37, at every subsequent meeting prior to his self-exposure, he is shown interrogating, accusing or, sometimes, reassuring his brothers, once (44. 15) boasting to them of his supposed abilities. It is not at all this sort of deception and self-concealment which the wisdom literature and Egyptian instructions have in mind.

G. W. Coats has presented an important development of von Rad's theory, which takes account of and eliminates certain of these difficulties.[8] Coats argues that chs. 39–41 are to be taken as a separate 'kernel', and are to be characterized as a 'political legend', similar to that of Solomon in 1 Kgs. 3. 5–8:

The purpose of a legend would be to paint an ideal figure as a model for edification of subsequent generations. As an ideal the legendary principal can appear faultless, almost superhuman, at least more than a little unrealistic . . . In both cases the legendary heroes exemplify the proper use of power by an administrator already in office.[9]

For Coats, the Joseph of this kernel 'seems totally different from the presentation of the same figure in Gen. 37. In crisis situations,

[7] When Humphreys, *Joseph and his Family*, 143, observes that Joseph's interpretation and advice carried immediate conviction, and must therefore have been persuasively phrased, we must pause to ponder what would have happened to the rest of the story had he not been believed. Narrative constraints are at work here, not deliberate implications.

[8] G. W. Coats, 'The Joseph Story and Ancient Wisdom: A Reappraisal', *CBQ* 35 (1973), 285–97, and *From Canaan to Egypt* (Washington, DC, 1976).

[9] Coats, 'The Joseph Story and Ancient Wisdom', 290.

in despair and poverty, in power at all levels, he is the image of
a well-disciplined leader, an ideal administrator of a powerful
office.'[10] For Coats also, then, Joseph is an idealized figure,
although now his exercise of power, rather than his attainment of
it, is the model for emulation. By separating the Joseph of chs.
39–41 from the shepherd boy of ch. 37, and from the arbitrary
tyrant of the later chapters, whom he believes to have been a
deliberate contrast, Coats is able to overcome many of the
problems of von Rad's theory. Yet it is still no easier to perceive
any real didactic purpose. When he concludes that: 'The young
man who rises through the ranks to a position of power knows
from the ideal pattern, the legendary Joseph, that discretion and
wisdom are essential', the reader is surely moved to wonder
whether this whole, sophisticated story could really have been
written to illustrate such a jejune truism. This is hardly didacticism
in any meaningful sense.

The chief obstacle to any hypothesis about the character of
Joseph in chs. 39–41 is that Joseph in these chapters is a rather
pale figure, whose behaviour is described in general terms, and
whose administrative successes are ascribed not to his own ability,
but to divine intervention (39. 3, 5, 21, 23; cf. also 40. 8; 41. 16).
A great proportion of these chapters, furthermore, is given over
to descriptions of dream-interpretations, which are related in far
greater detail than Joseph's administrative activities. The only
point at which we can make any real judgement of Joseph's
behaviour while he is in a position of responsibility, is in his
response to the advances of Potiphar's wife, and much is therefore
made of this by Coats.[11]

Of this story von Rad had commented that, 'The narrative in
Gen. xxxix reads like a story composed *ad hoc* to illustrate the
admonitions of the wise', citing passages from Proverbs and *Any*
(**xii**) which warn against 'strange' and married women. Coats
accepts this correspondence, as does B. S. Childs, who remarks
that 'Joseph reveals the ultimate in self-control and repulses the
advances of Potiphar's wife because of his fear of God . . .'.[12]
Coats, however, argues that the basis of Joseph's refusal is his

---

[10] Coats, *From Canaan to Egypt*, 32.

[11] Redford, *The Biblical Story of Joseph*, excludes the narrative as secondary,
which is possible but unproven.

[12] B. S. Childs, 'The Birth of Moses', *JBL* 84 (1965), 109–22.

responsibility towards his master, while Childs apparently asserts a basis in obedience to God (as does Crenshaw). Essentially, then, two points of contact with the wisdom tradition are claimed for this story: the first that it corresponds to the wisdom literature's warnings against loose women, the second that Joseph's refusal shows him to be following wisdom precepts, either religious or ethical.

For the attitude of the OT wisdom literature to strange women, von Rad cites Prov. 22. 14 and 23. 27 f., to which we may add 2. 16–19; 5. 1–14; 6. 20–35; 7. 1–27; 9. 13–18; and 30. 20. Of these, the last is probably to be distinguished from the rest, referring as it does merely to the disingenuousness of the adulteress. The other passages warn against the seductions and temptations of loose women, perceiving them as a trap. Frequently they warn that the result of succumbing to such temptations is death, the path to Sheol. In 6. 24–35, dishonour and the seriousness of the punishment are emphasized. It seems probable that, on one level at least, the 'death' in these passages is a reference to the fatal punishment for adultery, be it through judicial sentence of death or through personal vengeance; this aspect is found also in the Egyptian material.[13] For Prov. 1–9 there may also be, as we have seen, some symbolic significance. The emphasis, then, is not upon the moral issues involved in adultery, but upon the difficulty of resisting the temptation and the dangerous consequences of succumbing to it. Again, we have already noted that Prov. 1–9 seems to lay great emphasis upon the power of the woman to attract through speech analogous to the call of Wisdom.

In contrast to the voluptuous seductions by *femmes fatales* in the wisdom literature, the attempt by Potiphar's wife to seduce Joseph, although frequently repeated, is rather perfunctory. Joseph's refusal bears no resemblance to anything in the passages from Proverbs. He speaks of how good his master has been to him, and how he has given him everything except his wife: 'How then can I do this great wickedness, and sin against God?' Here *hārā'āh haggĕdōlāh* is not simply the sin of adultery. Joseph argues not on the grounds of some inherent sinfulness in adultery, but that to take Potiphar's wife, when he has been given everything else, would be wrong.

---

[13] The motif is common in Egyptian instructions: see, e.g., *Any* 3. 13 f.; *'Onchsheshonqy* 23. 6 ff. makes explicit the fatal consequences.

Coats describes this motive as a matter of 'Joseph's responsibility to his master', Westermann and Gunkel as a 'breach of trust', but neither of these descriptions is adequate. Joseph has no 'responsibility', in terms of what Coats calls 'a proper order for administration', to avoid sleeping with his master's wife. Rather, Joseph's refusal appeals to the ethical wrongness, in more general terms, of taking from a man the only thing which he has not given. Joseph's reply shows none of the self-interest which characterizes the remarks of the proverbial literature on the subject of adultery. Whether we understand the 'sin against God' to be a description of the ethical basis for refusal, or a second, religious basis, it too is an expression quite unknown in the wisdom exhortations against adultery. Beyond the topic itself, it is, indeed, difficult to find any correspondence between the story here and the wisdom passages cited.[14] The point should also be made, incidentally, that it is a strange didacticism indeed which promises a prison sentence as the reward for virtue!

Von Rad's claim that the story reads like an *ad hoc* composition must, moreover, be judged in the context of the numerous parallels to the central motif.[15] The Egyptian tale of the two brothers, Anubis/Anpu and Bata, has often been cited as a close parallel, indeed, a possible source for the story in Gen. 39, and a similar story is told in the *Iliad*, where Anteia attempts to seduce Bellerophon.[16] Of other, later parallels, we may note in particular the stories of Peleus, Hippolytus, and Tenes.[17] In early Jewish literature we find the tale of Susannah, the wife of Joakim, accused by two elders whom she has spurned, where, of course, the sexes

---

[14] The anonymity of Potiphar's wife is not a similarity: such anonymity marks much of this narrative, and also the early chapters of Exodus. Names are, of course, rare in Proverbs, but there is no reason to suppose that anonymity *per se* is a feature of wisdom-literature style.

[15] I omit here the more broadly parallel tales of the fury of women scorned, such as that of Gilgamesh and Ishtar. On parallels to the story in Gen. 39, see D. Irvin in section III. 3 of J. H. Hayes and J. M. Miller (eds.), *Israelite and Judean History* (London, 1977), esp. 185–8, and J. D. Yohannan (ed.), *Joseph and Potiphar's Wife in World Literature* (New York, 1968).

[16] *Iliad* vi. 155 ff. The tale of the Two Brothers is translated in M. Lichtheim, *Ancient Egyptian Literature*, ii (Berkeley, Calif., Los Angeles, and London, 1976), 203–11.

[17] For Peleus, see Apollodorus, iii. The best known version of the story of Hippolytus is that of Euripides. For Tenes, see Plutarch, *Quaest. Graec.* 28 (= *Mor.* 350 d–f).

are reversed, but the motif the same.[18] None of these stories has any apparent origin in the wisdom tradition. The prevalence of the motif makes it improbable that Gen. 39 was composed especially to illustrate wisdom teachings about adultery, and it shows no significant variations from the theme which might indicate that it has been adapted to such a purpose.

If neither the story of Potiphar's wife nor Joseph's behaviour in that story seem to demonstrate any close relationship with the wisdom tradition, then Coats's theory begins to lack credibility. It is difficult to find any other point in these chapters where Joseph's behaviour, while he is in a position of responsibility, serves as a possible model for emulation. The Joseph Narrative, moreover, is not at all interested in the ethics of power: where the wisdom literature looks at the correct use of power, it emphasizes above all the importance of honesty (cf. Prov. 17. 8; 29. 4) and justice (cf. Prov. 16. 10, 12; 29. 14). If the Joseph Narrative, or at least chs. 39–41, is indeed intended to exemplify and teach wisdom ideals for administration, the omission of these key wisdom concepts is astonishing.

W. L. Humphreys has presented an argument similar to those of von Rad and Coats, although he is inclined to see wisdom influence rather than a primary wisdom purpose in the Joseph Narrative.[19] Like Coats, he treats chs. 39–41 as a separate unit, and believes that the portrayal of Joseph in these chapters is based on wisdom models of the ideal courtier.[20] Much of the evidence which he adduces is similar to that discussed above, although his approach is generally more cautious. The main emphasis in the argument is upon Joseph's courtliness, and his service to the king as an administrator: Humphreys' new contribution in this area is his treatment of 47. 13–26, which he believes to be a continuation of 39–41. He denies that the primary purpose of this passage is aetiological, and claims that it is intended to portray the advantage to the king of Joseph's actions as a great administrator.

But is this really the intention? Even if we bear in mind Childs's

---

[18] In Susannah, the legal consequences are clearly drawn out, as is the fact that adultery is a 'sin in the sight of the Lord'. The story is hardly, however, about a 'strange woman', and influence from the wisdom literature seems unlikely.

[19] Humphreys, *Joseph and his Family*, 135 ff.

[20] This builds on his earlier work, 'A Life-Style for Diaspora: A Study in the Tales of Esther and Daniel', *JBL* 92 (1973), 211–23, and 'The Motif of the Wise Courtier in the Book of Proverbs', in Gammie (ed.), *Israelite Wisdom*, 177–90.

conclusion, that the formula 'to this day' is generally a secondary redactional remark, intended to confirm an independent tradition,[21] the passage still appears to be, in essence, an attempt to explain the situation which was perceived to exist in Egypt. This is clear not least from v. 22, which details the exception of priestly land. That the passage is secondary is accepted by most commentators, on the grounds of its intrusiveness, style, and vocabulary.[22] Further, it shows signs of disunity: vv. 13–15a include Canaan, which is absent in subsequent verses, while the intention of the measures changes abruptly in v. 23, from the relief of starvation to the provision of seed for resowing, presumably after the famine. In any case, were the intention here to demonstrate Joseph's ability, we should expect to find him initiating all the action; but in vv. 18–20, the steps he takes, which enable the 'land reforms' and are particularly critical, are all suggested by the Egyptians themselves.

If, then, there is no reason to suppose that the narrative is attempting to idealize Joseph's behaviour, does it at least identify him as a 'wise man' by having him declare in 42. 18 that he 'fears God'? Describing Joseph's 'ideal' character, von Rad comments that, 'The foundation and starting point for this educational aspiration is the "fear of God", which Joseph professes; "fear of God" is quite simply obedience in respect of the commands of God (Prov. i. 7, xv. 33; Gen. xlii. 18).'[23] The expression 'fear God' is common in the wisdom literature but is by no means exclusive to it, and its presence alone cannot be taken to indicate wisdom influence; the meaning, in the context of 42. 18, must be the prime consideration:

Joseph said to them on the third day, 'Do this and live: I fear God. If you are honest men, let one of your brothers be bound in your prison . . .'

The clause 'I fear God' follows the double imperative clause without any connecting particle, but is probably causal:[24] it cannot be taken with the subsequent conditional sentence, and as a wholly

[21] B. S. Childs, 'A Study of the Formula "Until This Day"', *JBL* 82 (1963), 279–92, esp. 289.

[22] For details and references, see C. Westermann, *Genesis, iii. Genesis 37–50* (Neukirchen, 1982); ET *Genesis 37–50: A Commentary* (London, 1986), ad loc.

[23] Von Rad, 'Josephsgeschichte und ältere Chokma', 122.

[24] See GK § 158 a.

independent sentence it would interrupt the command and make
no sense. The clause must, then, refer to the promise implicit in
the second imperative, which serves as the apodosis of a condition.
The unusual word-order of the Hebrew, which places 'God' at the
beginning of the clause, might suggest that Joseph is emphasizing
here his own allegiance to the same God as the brothers, but,
again, that by itself makes little sense unless it is meant to imply
something more. Von Rad understands the expression to indicate
obedience to the divine law, but this is surely inappropriate here.
Rather, the context requires that the clause be in some way an
affirmation of the promise that the brothers will live if they obey
Joseph's command, and of Joseph's fairness and reliability in this
matter.

It would be wrong to force this meaning on the clause simply
because it is appropriate to the context, but there is some evidence
to suggest that the expression 'fear God' may have the general
connotation of honesty, reliability, and straight-dealing. Thus, in
Exod. 18. 21 Jethro advises Moses to 'choose able men from all
the people, such as fear God, men who are trustworthy and who
hate a bribe'. In Neh. 7. 2 responsibility is given to a man because
he is *'îš 'ĕmet wĕyārē' 'et-hā'ĕlōhîm*. In Deut. 25. 17 ff., the
criticism of Amalek, who 'did not fear God', is not of his
paganism, but of his unfair attack upon a weakened Israel. In Job
1. 1, 8 and Prov. 3. 7, the term appears to have at least some
ethical content. We should not suppose that in any of these
instances the term has taken on a completely new meaning,
independent of its religious sense, but in each it appears to be used
with the connotation of reliability and fairness uppermost. This is
surely also the content of the expression on Joseph's lips: he is
telling his brothers, 'do this and live, for I am a fair and reliable
man.' Whether or not we choose to understand it in this sense, it
would be perverse to regard the verse as a declaration of the basis
of Joseph's general character and behaviour, or as a simple
revelation of his religious faith.

Any association with the passages cited by von Rad from
Proverbs is difficult. 'The fear of Yahweh is the beginning of
knowledge' (Prov. 1. 7) and 'The fear of Yahweh is instruction in
wisdom' (Prov. 15. 33) represent a use of the expression and an
association of ideas which are, perhaps, characteristic of the
wisdom literature. This is not how the term is used in the Joseph

Narrative, and there is no particular reason to associate Gen. 42.
18 with the wisdom literature rather than with any of the other
OT literature which uses the term.

To conclude, then, we have found no reason to suppose that
the character and behaviour of Joseph in the Joseph Narrative are
intended to represent and teach the ideals for behaviour which are
to be found in the wisdom literature. Where it is not actually
contradictory to such ideals, the behaviour of Joseph is either too
generally or too specifically described to serve as a model for
emulation. Where there is some opportunity to compare the
attitudes of the Joseph Narrative and the wisdom literature to a
specific situation, as in the tale of Potiphar's wife and in that of
the administration of Egypt by Joseph, the concerns and emphases
of the wisdom literature appear to be wholly lacking.

2. *Joseph and God*

Although von Rad barely mentions them in his 1953 article, it is
the three pairs of dreams in the Joseph Narrative which, more than
anything, give it its distinctive nature. They are not expressions of
a dream-science in Israel, but, like dreams in some other ancient
stories, serve a narrative purpose.[25] They do, however, raise
important questions about the narrator's understanding of divine
action in the world, and about the nature of Joseph's abilities.
Granted that it is his interpretation of Pharaoh's dreams which
presents Joseph with his opportunity to advance to a position of
power, can we regard this interpretation as an expression of
educated wisdom, or is it something more akin to inspiration? Do
the dreams in the narrative, moreover, imply an understanding of
God as a hidden power, whose purposes are inscrutable, and agree
in this respect with other indications in the story?

There can be little doubt that Joseph's ability to interpret
dreams is regarded as God-given. In 40. 8, responding to the
complaint of the butler and baker that there is no one to interpret
their dreams, Joseph asks, *'hălô' lē'lōhîm pitronîm?'* ('Do interpretations not belong to God?'), while in 41. 16 he apparently
disclaims any independent ability to interpret Pharaoh's dreams:
'biľādāy 'ĕlōhîm ya'ăneh 'et-šĕlôm par'ōh' (on the meaning of

---

[25] See my 'Joseph, Dreams and Wisdom', M. Phil. thesis (Oxford, 1989).

which, see below). That Pharaoh accepts the source of the
interpretation as divine is shown by his remarks in 41. 38 f. It
seems too strong, incidentally, to call Joseph's response in 40. 8
'completely polemic', and to claim that 'the interpretation of
dreams is not a human art but a charisma which God can grant',[26]
nor is this the emphasis of 41. 16. There is no attack on human
presumption in these sayings, but rather a claim in the former that
professional interpretation is not a necessity, since God may
communicate interpretation to whomsoever he pleases,[27] and an
affirmation in the latter that Joseph enjoys divine aid in his
interpretation, and should not be perceived simply as a professional interpreter of dreams.

If the interpretation is from God, the role of Joseph in the
process is unclear. 41. 16 has generally been taken to be a
complete disavowal of any part in it by Joseph, *bilʿādāy* being
taken in the sense 'No, not I', an exclamation to be taken
separately from the following clause.[28] The existence of such a
meaning is, however, questionable.[29] Moreover, the text here is
difficult: the Samaritan and LXX texts (cf. also the Syriac) have
read *bilʿādāy* without the first-person suffix, and vocalized *yʿnh* as
a niphal, with an indefinite subject. They also read a negative
before the verb, and thus render: 'Without God (it) cannot be
answered . . .'. If these versions reflect the original reading, then
Joseph is stating that divine aid is necessary for the interpretation,
and perhaps thus explaining the failure of the wise men of the
court. If we retain the MT reading we should translate *bilʿādāy* as
'besides me', or 'not just I but'.[30] Joseph is affirming the basis of
his interpretation, rather than that he has no part in it.[31]

---

[26] Von Rad, *Das erste Buch Mose*, ad loc.
[27] Westermann, *Genesis 37–50*, ad loc.
[28] e.g. by Westermann, ibid. ad loc.
[29] This use is found by commentators only here and in Gen. 14. 24, where it is
usually taken to mean 'not for myself', but is surely to be repointed without the
suffix: 'I have sworn . . . I shall take nothing . . . *except* what the young men have
eaten' (cf. LXX πλὴν ʿῶν; Vulg. *exceptis his*).
[30] The simple form of the preposition means 'besides' in Isa. 45. 6, and probably
also in Job 34. 32 and Gen. 14. 24 (see n. 29). This is the usual sense of the more
common form with prefixed *min*. Both forms may also mean 'without the approval
of', as in Gen. 41. 44, but that seems inappropriate here.
[31] The last part of v. 16 is also very difficult. Contra Westermann, the accusative
particle is never used after *ʿānāh* to indicate the answer given, but generally for
the person answered, while the sense of the construct 'peace of Pharaoh' is unclear.

It is interesting to compare this with 41. 38, where Joseph is described as having the 'Spirit of God' in him. We find elsewhere in the OT various roles for the spirit: it comes upon men and makes them prophesy (e.g., Isa. 45. 6), gives them wisdom (Isa. 11. 2), or anoints them for special tasks (e.g. Isa. 61. 1). The technical term for prophetic inspiration (with *ʿal*) is not used here, although some similar idea is undoubtedly present; a closer image is that of Exod. 31. 3; 35. 31, where the spirit fills men and gives them a particular ability. 'Charisma' is probably a misleading term in this context: Joseph is portrayed as one with whom God communicates, and whom he enables, not as a charismatic prophet. It is this divine assistance which distinguishes Joseph from the 'wise men' of Egypt.

That Joseph has somehow been enabled by God is confirmed in the next verse (41. 39), which picks up the suggestion in v. 33, that Pharaoh choose a man *'nābôn wĕḥākām'*, to govern Egypt during the coming crisis. This verse cannot be taken to mean that Pharaoh supposed Joseph's interpretation, or God's revelation to him, to have demonstrated a quality which Joseph already possessed, since Joseph's 'discernment and wisdom' in some sense follow the revelation.[32] This point is important: 41. 39 is not claiming that Joseph has shown himself more wise than the wise men of the court by interpreting the dream. Rather, the revelation to Joseph by God of what is to come makes Joseph uniquely qualified to superintend the task ahead. This is the content of *nābôn wĕḥākām*, which implies just government with divine aid.[33] The description of Joseph cannot be taken as an assertion that he displayed 'wisdom' by interpreting the dreams.

---

[32] W. J. P. Boyd, 'Notes on the Secondary Meanings of *'ḤR'*, *JTS* NS 12 (1961), 54–6, lists eight examples of *'aḥărê* with causal force, including this verse, and several with concessive. Of these, however, only three (Judg. 11. 36; 19. 23; 2 Sam. 19. 31 (ET 30)) seem to have a sense which is primarily causal, and all of these use *'aḥărê 'ăšer* + perf., rather than the more usual *'aḥărê* + inf. cs., which is found here. In all cases, as Boyd notes, the temporal element remains important, and in no instance does the subordinate clause serve to *confirm* the main clause, rather than provide the motive or circumstances for it.

[33] Thus Solomon in 1 Kgs. 3. 12 is given by God a 'discerning and wise heart' to govern justly; in Deut. 4. 6 Israel is to be called a 'wise and discerning people' for its proximity to God and the righteousness of its statutes. The two words are found separately and in parallel frequently in the wisdom literature, where they have a more general application. In combination, they appear to be a cliché describing the ideal quality for righteousness and fairness in government and judgement. There is no implication of ability in organization or counselling: Joseph is being described as fit to govern justly.

In the patriarchal narratives, God often communicates through dreams and visions, and these occasionally consist of non-symbolic images.[34] However, they are not enigmatic, and the meaning of the divine communication is always clear. In the Joseph Narrative, on the other hand, divine communication is portrayed as clear only once, in 46. 2–4;[35] elsewhere it is through symbolic dreams, even when the meaning of the dreams is clear to all, as in ch. 37. Far more, then, than in the material which precedes the Joseph Narrative in Genesis, divine action is portrayed as subtle and enigmatic.[36] Does this, however, imply that the narrative rests on a theology particularly close to that displayed in the wisdom literature?

The divine plan for the salvation of Israel is revealed and enacted through the dreams. Joseph's own dreams in ch. 37 are a divine promise of his future elevation; at the same time they motivate the attempt on his life by his brothers, which results in his transportation to Egypt. Joseph's imprisonment is necessary in order that he meet the butler, and interpret his dreams, so that when Pharaoh needs an interpreter, Joseph and his ability are known by someone at court. Finally, Joseph's interpretation of Pharaoh's dreams results in his elevation. By the time he confronts his brothers with his real identity, Joseph is obviously aware of the way in which events have been arranged by God. Thus in 45. 5 ff. he is able to tell those brothers that God had sent him ahead to preserve life, and so 'it was not you who sent me here, but God; and he has appointed me a father to Pharaoh, and lord of all his house and ruler over all the land of Egypt.' Again, in 50. 19 f. he reassures them: 'Do not be afraid, for am I in the place of God?

---

[34] See the E section of Jacob's dream at Bethel (Gen. 28. 11 f.) and the J section of his dream of the flocks (31. 10, 12*b*). Note also how the stars are integrated into the vision of Abraham in 15. 1 ff.

[35] The theophany to Jacob serves to reaffirm the divine promises but also to cancel the previous prohibition against travelling to Egypt in 26. 1–5. This may indicate that the passage is a redactional device intended to overcome this apparent inconsistency (cf. Redford, *The Biblical Story of Joseph*, 20 ff.). It is possible that the curious episode in 37. 15 f. is also a theophany (cf. H. Holzinger, *Genesis* (Freiburg, 1898), 225), reminiscent as it is of the anonymous 'men' in Gen. 18, 32. 24 ff. If so, it is not clearly indicated as such.

[36] This portrayal of God alters radically in the blessings of chs. 48–9, where the concern is with later tribal history. These chapters place the narrative in a salvation-historical context, but, as almost all commentators agree, are not to be regarded as part of the narrative proper.

You planned evil against me, but God planned it for good, to bring about the present preservation of many people.'

These verses represent Joseph's explanation for the vicissitudes of his life, but they are not climaxes to the story, nor the exposition of a moral, and they must be taken in their context.[37] In 45. 5 ff. Joseph is urging his brothers not to reproach themselves for their past actions towards him, which were a part of God's plan: as they were unwitting agents of this plan, no guilt should be imputed to them. In 50. 19 f., Joseph again identifies their actions as a part of this divine plan: although their motives were in themselves bad, the brothers were unconsciously agents for good. Since God has used them in this way, Joseph explains, to seek bloody vengeance upon them would be to usurp God's position, to reject the way in which God has arranged matters. The motives of the brothers are not irrelevant: the dreams of future superiority sent by God to Joseph inspired the malicious actions of the brothers, which led eventually to Joseph's elevation and thence to the preservation of their own and others' lives. There is no gulf between the plans of the brothers and the divine plan, since their motives and consequent actions were a part of that divine plan from the start.

Von Rad sees in these sayings a connection with early wisdom ideas of the divine economy,[38] comparing with them Prov. 16. 9; 19. 21; 20. 24; 21. 30 ff. and *Amenemope* 19. 16, which each express an antithesis between the human action in the first clause and the divine activity in the second. They are thus similar in both form and content to the saying, 'You planned evil against me, but God planned it for good' in 50. 20. He suggests that this saying may be an adapted '*Weisheitsspruch*'. Such passages in the wisdom literature are not, however, concerned with the role of human activities within the divine plan, but rather with the limit set upon human endeavours by the overriding divine action:

> Many are the plans in the mind of a man,
> > but (it is) the purpose of Yahweh which will be
> established.
>
> (Prov. 19. 21)

> The god is in his success,
> the man is in his failure;

[37] Cf. Westermann, *Genesis* 37–50, ad loc.
[38] Von Rad, 'Josephsgeschichte und ältere Chokma', 124 ff.

The words which men say are one thing,
That which the god does, another.

(*Amenemope* 19. 14 ff.)[39]

The sentiment expressed in such sayings is clearly quite different from that of the sayings in the Joseph Narrative. Whereas in the latter, human actions and motives are a part of the divine plan, in the wisdom literature they are set over against it, and the wisdom sayings contrast the impotence and frustration of human endeavour with the infallibility of divine action. In the Joseph Narrative, God is portrayed as manipulating human desires and behaviour in accordance with his plan; in the wisdom sayings the divine activity is disconnected from human aspirations, and sets their parameter. In short, the Joseph Narrative integrates human and divine efforts, while the wisdom sayings contrast them. The thought expressed in these sayings, then, is not that which underlies the narrative, and Joseph's declarations are, consequently, most unlikely to have been 'adapted' from them.

If the ideas in the Joseph Narrative find no real echo in the wisdom literature, they are not, at least, unparalleled in the OT. The Succession Narrative appears to presuppose a similar type of divine action and control, and this is a factor in Whybray's 1968 description of it as 'a dramatization of proverbial wisdom'.[40] The theology of this narrative was discussed by von Rad himself in 1944, when he argued that 2 Sam. 11. 27; 12. 24; and 17. 14 are the key passages expressing the narrator's conception of divine activity in history:

he evidently thought of it as something hidden and certainly not confined to sensational events which stand out from all other occurrences . . . Rather he depicts a succession of occurrences in which the chain of inherent cause and effect is firmly knit up—so firmly indeed that human eye discerns no point at which God could have put in his hand. Yet secretly it is he who has brought all to pass; all the threads are in his hands; his activity embraces the great political events no less than the hidden counsels of human hearts. All human affairs are the sphere of God's providential working.[41]

---

[39] Taking *rwyȝty* to indicate difference, following Sethe and most subsequent commentators.   [40] R. N. Whybray, *The Succession Narrative* (London, 1968).
[41] G. von Rad, 'Der Anfang der Geschichtsschreibung im alten Israel', *AK* 32 (1944), 1–42; ET in *The Problem of the Hexateuch and other Essays* (Edinburgh, 1965), 166–204. Cited from ET p. 201 (Germ. p. 39).

Von Rad does not argue that the theology of the Succession Narrative is wisdom theology, even though it is evident that the theological ideas expressed are very close to those of the Joseph Narrative, since he believes the Joseph Narrative, unlike the Succession Narrative, to be 'devoid of any specifically theological interest in redemptive history'.[42] This distinction is, however, hard to maintain: the Joseph Narrative is arguably all about an act of divine salvation, and, if anything, it appears to have a greater interest in salvation history than does the Succession Narrative. The theological presuppositions of the Joseph Narrative and of the Succession Narrative, moreover, are not especially unusual. There are many places in the OT where some idea of unconscious submission to divine control is implicit, and many, indeed, where it is explicit. This idea is found with regard to Assyria and Cyrus in Isaiah (10. 5 ff.; 45. 1 ff.); we must assume also that the divine movement of the nations in Amos 9. 7 was without their knowledge. In Deut. 2. 30 ff., Sihon clearly attacks the Israelites with a view to harming them, but his attack is actually divinely inspired, providing as it does an excuse for the Israelites to annihilate the population of Heshbon and occupy its land. In 1 Sam. 25. 32 ff. the actions of Abigail, which prevent David from incurring guilt by the slaughter of Nabal, are attributed retrospectively to divine action. Comments about divine action in affairs of state are common in 1 and 2 Kgs., e.g. 1 Kgs. 15. 4, 29 f.; 16. 1 f., 18. In Exod. 7. 3 f., God explicitly hardens Pharaoh's heart for his own purposes. We need not multiply examples. Divine action is assumed in the OT, and the very idea of causation involves this assumption (cf. Amos 3. 3–6). The ideas of divine action found in the Joseph Narrative and the Succession Narrative reflect common Israelite beliefs about divine action in history.

What makes the two narratives distinctive in this respect is not the theological idea itself, but the literary treatment of it. The account of the divine action is minimized, with the result that suspense is heightened and a greater degree of realism achieved. The importance of the divine role is also, paradoxically, emphasized by this treatment. There is nothing, however, to suggest that the exhibition of this role is the primary intention of either narrative, or that the role reflects any belief which is specific to wisdom.

[42] See the comments of Whybray, *The Succession Narrative*, p. 78 n. 42.

As with the character of Joseph, then, there seems, on the face of it, to be little reason to associate the religious ideas and portrayal of God in the Joseph Narrative with the wisdom literature. There is no feeling in the Joseph Narrative that God's purpose is inscrutable—at least a part of it is revealed in the very first chapter—although the particular role in the plan of some of the characters is only understood by them in retrospect. Much less is there any of the bleak despair inspired in wisdom writers by the hiddenness of God: as we have seen, God's presence is felt throughout, and the characters, rightly or wrongly, attribute the turn of events to him (as in, e.g. 42. 21 f.). Certainly the absence or rarity of direct divine theophanies leaves the Joseph Narrative less grandly miraculous than some parts of the patriarchal narratives. Yet divine action in the salvation of the nation has not been displaced by some gritty wisdom realism, but has been masterfully understated, and imbued with a new subtlety and ambiguity. The distinctiveness of the Joseph Narrative in respect of its portrayal of God is essentially one of presentation rather than of presupposition.

3. *Conclusion*

The strength of von Rad's claim, that the Joseph Narrative was a product of the wisdom tradition, lay in the accumulation of numerous supposed correspondences with the Israelite and Egyptian wisdom literature. Our examination of this evidence has, however, shown it to be weak at every point, and neither in its presentation of Joseph, nor in its theological ideas have we found good reason to suppose that the Joseph Narrative depends on the ideas of the wisdom literature, let alone that it was intended to embody and teach them. In the final analysis, all that is left to connect the narrative with the wisdom literature is the appearance in it of the expressions 'wise and discreet' and 'fear the Lord'. As we have seen, however, neither of these is used in any sense which is peculiar to the wisdom literature, and though both are found more frequently in the wisdom literature than elsewhere, it is only the coincidence of the two falling in the same text that is striking. In any case, none of this adds up to the Joseph Narrative being a 'didactic wisdom text': there is really no reason to assume that the narrative was written to embody wisdom ideas and ideals, that Joseph is depicted as an archetypal wise man, or that we can, therefore, employ it as evidence for the nature of early wisdom.

7
Wisdom and the Reign of Solomon

A. SOLOMON AND WISDOM: GENERAL CONSIDERATIONS

Many modern interpreters are inclined to accept that the traditional association of Solomon with wisdom reflects a historical fact—the origins of literary wisdom in Israel during the reign of Solomon. Indeed, many go further, and claim that the biblical account of Solomon's reign preserves evidence of his close links with Egypt and of his administrative innovations, from which we may make deductions about the origins of wisdom in Israel. This issue goes to the heart of the classic 'Solomonic Enlightenment' hypothesis, and in examining it there are two fundamental questions: how historically reliable are the biblical traditions about Solomon's reign, and what can be deduced from those traditions about the origins and nature of wisdom literature in Israel?

R. B. Y. Scott distinguishes three different stages in the development of the OT descriptions of Solomon, in each of which his wisdom is understood somewhat differently. Thus in 1 Kgs. 2. 1–2, 5–9, and 5. 15–26 (ET 1–12), the original narratives were concerned only with Solomon's 'wisdom', or 'skill', in government. The editorial 5. 26 (ET 12), the rewritten dream story in 3. 4–15, and the appended story of the two mothers in 3. 16–28, all reflect an interest in forensic 'wisdom' on the part of the Deuteronomistic editor, and a more general interest in the ability to distinguish right from wrong. Finally, in 5. 9–14 (ET 4. 29–34); 10. 1–10, 13, 23 f., a post-exilic tradition, perhaps founded on the promise to Solomon of wisdom in 3. 12 ff., understands wisdom as intellectual brilliance and encyclopaedic knowledge. On the basis of Prov. 25. 1, with its mention of Hezekiah, Scott concludes that literary wisdom actually flourished in the eighth century, when a tradition of Solomon's wealth and wisdom was cultivated for political reasons. The elaborate descriptions of Solomon's proverbs and sayings are later developments of this tradition. Whatever the other evidence for a connection between Solomon and the origins of literary wisdom, 'the ostensible biblical evidence for this in the first Book of Kings is post-exilic in date and legendary in character.'[1]

For his late dating of the passages which involve wisdom of a literary type, Scott presents arguments based on textual considerations and on the vocabulary. If these do not clinch the matter, they are at least, broadly persuasive,[2] and it is worth recalling that our earlier survey found references to 'literary' wisdom only here and in Daniel. Of more doubtful value are his conclusions regarding the earlier development of the tradition. It is not clear that there is a strong distinction to be made between governmental and forensic wisdom, or that one can readily discern a linear development over time in the usage of *ḤKM*. At the same time, the difficulties which surround Prov. 25. 1 make it a poor basis for some 'Hezekian Enlightenment'; Scott's other evidence for this, involving presumed nationalism and the presence of 'wise men' in Hezekiah's court, is unconvincing.

A wholly different attitude to the material is taken by Albrecht Alt, who has famously suggested that the description of Solomon's sayings in 1 Kgs. 5. 13 (ET 4. 33) shows that he drew on ancient onomastic lists, themselves a manifestation of 'nature wisdom'.[3] 1 Kgs. 5. 13 claims that Solomon 'spoke of trees, from the cedar that is in Lebanon to the hyssop that grows out of the wall; he spoke also of beasts, and of birds, and of reptiles and of fish.' Alt compares in particular the *Onomasticon of Amenemope*, which probably dates from around 1100 BC, and is a list of 610 items, beginning with cosmological phenomena, then moving on to humans, towns, buildings, land, and agricultural products, listing different types of each. The earlier *Ramesseum Onomasticon* (*c.*1786–1633 BC) provides a somewhat closer parallel, in that it actually deals with plants and animals.

---

[1] Scott, 'Solomon and the Beginnings of Wisdom, 279.

[2] Scott's textual evidence demonstrates the fluidity of the text at a late period, but not that the passages in question are themselves late. His arguments for late vocabulary are as persuasive as such arguments ever are, but against the late usage, one might set e.g. the idiom for 'like the sand on the seashore' in 5. 9, which is only worded this way in Gen. 22. 17; Josh. 11. 4; and 1 Sam. 13. 5.

[3] A. Alt, 'Die Weisheit Salomos', *Th. LZ* 76 (1951), cols. 139–44; ET in J. L. Crenshaw (ed.), *Studies in Ancient Israelite Wisdom* (New York, 1976), 102–12.

Alt argues that these onomastica are evidence for the existence in the ancient Near East of a 'nature wisdom', which found its expression in a science of lists, and which strove to comprehend all that exists. The Solomonic wisdom described is a development from, or adaptation of this nature wisdom, and thus 1 Kgs. 5. 13 is evidence of the adoption of Egyptian wisdom by Solomon. These conclusions, however, have to be regarded with considerable scepticism. The nature and purpose of the onomastica have been much discussed, and the idea that their primary intention is the encyclopaedic coverage of the world is now widely rejected.[4] Although the introduction to the *Onomasticon of Amenemope* claims that it will teach 'all things that exist', the restricted scope of the list belies this claim, and the introduction cannot be taken seriously as a declaration of the work's purpose.[5] Michael Fox has pointed out that:

There is no science of lists in Egypt in any significant sense. There are only lists, lists of all sorts, with varied contents and principles of organization—medical, zoological, religious, geographical and more. There is nothing to suggest that the creation of lists was considered a single enterprise, as if geographical lists and lists of body parts were in some way intended to contribute to a common purpose of expanding and organizing the body of shared knowledge.[6]

Since, moreover, the scope of the foreign onomastica is not restricted to nature and to non-human affairs, 'nature wisdom' is in all ways a misleading description of these texts.

The most important obstacle to linking the sayings described in 1 Kgs. 5. 13 with the onomastica, however, is the character of the sayings themselves. Since Solomon's recitations are unlikely to have been merely tedious listings of species, Alt supposes that he

[4] On the Egyptian onomastica, see generally A. H. Gardiner, *Ancient Egyptian Onomastica* (London, 1947); H. Grapow and W. Westendorf, *Handbuch der Orientalistik*, I. I. 2 (Leiden, 1970), 219–25. On the examples from the Late Period: U. Kaplony-Heckel, 'Schüler und Schulwesen in der ägyptischen Spätzeit', *SAK* 1 (1974), 227–46. On the significance of the lists for biblical interpretation: M. V. Fox, 'Egyptian Onomastica and Biblical Wisdom', *VT* 36 (1986), 302–10.

[5] Gardiner, *Ancient Egyptian Onomastica*, describes the introduction as 'wordy and pretentious' (p. 1), and 'bombastic' (p. 35); cf. H. Brunner, *Altägyptische Erziehung* (Wiesbaden, 1957), 93, and Fox, 'Egyptian Onomastica', 303, who compares it to a book blurb.

[6] Fox, 'Egyptian Onomastica', 308 f. For a fuller description of the types of list, see Grapow and Westendorf, *Handbuch der Orientalisk*.

expanded the enumerations into series of proverbs about the things which had traditionally been enumerated: in other words, that he borrowed the contents but rejected the form of the lists. Since the form is the distinctive feature of these lists, it is hardly possible to say that Alt has established any connection at all. In the end, his argument rests on little more than that there are Egyptian lists featuring plants and animals, amongst many other things, while plant and animal sayings are attributed to Solomon.[7]

Do these sayings attributed to Solomon in themselves suggest an interest in 'nature wisdom'? Alt claims that the OT wisdom literature has no interest in the character of plants and animals, except in so far as they illustrate truths which are important for human life, and this is the starting point for his suggestion that the sayings attributed to Solomon are quite unlike the extant Israelite wisdom sayings. Actually, there is to be found in later Israelite wisdom an interest in nature which has no apparent connection with Egypt (e.g. Qoh. 1. 5–9), but why should we anyway assume that Solomon's sayings were about the character of the plants and animals? There is absolutely nothing in 1 Kgs. 5. 13 which prevents us understanding the sayings attributed to Solomon as fables or proverbs of a type attested in the OT (e.g. Prov. 30. 18–31; Judg. 9. 7–15), in Mesopotamian wisdom, and in *Ahikar* (li). The connection which Alt suggests cannot, then, be upheld: the concept of a nature wisdom in the onomastica is illusory, while the sayings attributed to Solomon are quite readily, and certainly more naturally, understood as fables or animal/plant proverbs.[8]

Most arguments for Egyptian influence on Solomon are more circumstantial than this, pointing to the prosperity of Solomon's reign, and to his good relations with Egypt. Such conditions, it is argued, would have permitted the establishment of a sophisticated administration and allowed the development of an educational system and intelligentsia. His close ties with Egypt would, moreover, have inclined Solomon and his subjects to look in that direction for inspiration, administrative and literary. Certainly the auspices were good for the consolidation of the Israelite state

---

[7] P. J. Nel, *The Structure and Ethos of the Wisdom Admonitions in Proverbs* (Berlin, 1982), 12, is even more literal-minded than Alt in his interpretation, seeing Solomon's sayings as a systematic classification of species.

[8] The sayings were taken to be fables by some earlier scholars: see e.g. p. 282 of H. Gressmann, 'Die neugefundene lehre des Amen-em-ope'.

under Solomon, with David's defeat of neighbouring enemies, and with the relative weakness of the major powers at that time. The biblical picture of Solomon's wealth may indeed reflect the fact that this was a period of prosperity for the nation. However, as is well known, the biblical picture is not entirely coherent.

Was Solomon's reign really so settled, content, and organized? David's reign was marked by civil war and conquest: Solomon may have inherited with his kingdom not only the existing rivalries and factional disputes, but also a vast number of subjects who had only recently been subjugated. His death was followed by the separation of the kingdom, and this is attributed in the OT account to resentment of his tyranny; the schism demonstrates also that there can have been no diminution in the bitterness between North and South found already under David (2 Sam. 20). As for the development of the state, archaeology has supplied evidence for the building of massive fortifications by Solomon, but nothing to suggest any more general programme of works or prosperity in the nation as a whole. In a recent survey and analysis of the archaeo-logical evidence, indeed, David Jamieson-Drake has concluded that the exercise of power through a centralized administration began long after Solomon.[9] So, when Eric Heaton tells us that 'The transformation of an ancient tribal society into a sophisticated national state within less than a century is itself a phenomenon sufficiently remarkable to merit investigation',[10] it must also, on all the evidence, merit doubt.

We find a certain ambiguity also in the biblical account of Solomon's relations with Egypt. On the one hand, they are indeed portrayed as being so cordial that he is given the hand in marriage of an Egyptian princess, with territory as a dowry; Israel sub-sequently engages in trade with Egypt (1 Kgs. 3. 1; 7. 8; 9. 16; 10. 28; 11. 1). On the other hand, it is in Egypt that Solomon's enemies Hadad and Jeroboam find protection (11. 14 ff., 40), and only a few years after Solomon's death, it is the Egyptians who ransack Jerusalem, ruled at that time by Solomon's son (1 Kgs. 14. 25 f.). Again, I do not wish to go into the intricate historical questions raised by these events, but it is obvious that the biblical text is hardly a sound basis for averring either that Solomon's rule

[9] D. W. Jamieson-Drake, *Scribes and Schools in Monarchic Judah* (Sheffield, 1991).

[10] E. W. Heaton, *Solomon's New Men* (London, 1974), 11.

was a settled and happy time for Israel, or that his relations with Egypt were entirely cordial. More importantly, and this is frequently overlooked, the account of Solomon's reign suggests quite clearly that his orientation was towards the North, and his relations with Hiram dominate the story. If we are to suppose that Solomon looked outside Palestine for cultural and administrative inspiration, this is surely, on the face of it, the direction in which he would have looked.

So far, we have assumed that the account of Solomon's reign is a broadly accurate reflection of the historical facts. This is a big assumption to make, however, about a text which is clearly composite, and frequently hyperbolic in its tone. Further, Solomon's reign was charged with political and religious significance for later Israel: it was, after all, the last reign during which the nation was united, at least nominally, and the time at which the first Temple was built. This must provoke some suspicion that the account has been coloured by nostalgia and by later political and religious ideology, and that it should only be used with considerable reservations as a historical source. In sum, then, the reliability of the account is open to question, but even when it is accepted in its entirety, those sections which praise Solomon are balanced by those which hint at unrest and tyranny. Only on the basis of a highly selective use of the material can it be claimed, without strong qualification, that Solomon's reign was settled and prosperous, and that his relations with Egypt were consistently cordial. The idea that he transformed Israel into a 'sophisticated national state', furthermore, has little grounding in the biblical, and none in the archaeological evidence. That there were some official posts and administrative mechanisms is most probable, and we shall examine these in the following pages: they cannot, however, be assumed to represent some complex national administration, are few in number, and seem mainly to predate Solomon.

B. EGYPT AND THE ESTABLISHMENT OF THE STATE ADMINISTRATION

1. *The Solomonic State Officials*

If the more general evidence for the reign of Solomon is somewhat ambiguous, there is one area, at least, in which scholars have seen a very precise correspondence with Egyptian practices. Over the past fifty years, the idea that Solomon may be shown to have imitated certain Egyptian administrative institutions has gained considerable ground, and is now amongst the most frequently cited evidence for Egyptian influence on Solomon's reign. Such imitation is viewed by many as the mechanism through which Egyptian wisdom entered Israel. For the rest of this chapter, therefore, I want to look at this issue in some detail, and in particular at the work of Tryggve Mettinger.

Mettinger, whose book was published in 1971,[11] was not the first scholar to suggest that certain of the official posts listed in 2 Sam. 8. 15–18 (// 1 Chr. 18. 14–17); 2 Sam. 20. 23–6; and 1 Kgs. 4. 1–6 were based on Egyptian prototypes, and much of the ground had been covered by previous studies, most notably those of de Vaux and Begrich.[12] Nevertheless, he differs from the opinions of both these scholars on several important issues, and it is his work which is most commonly associated with the idea. Mettinger himself sees the hypothesis of a Solomonic Enlightenment as corroborative evidence for his proposal that Egyptian prototypes underlie some of the most important governmental posts in Solomon's Israel. My concern here, is, of course, with the other side of the coin, the corroboration given to the Enlightenment and similar hypotheses by Mettinger, and I shall, therefore, concentrate on his other evidence.

Of the six official posts which he examines, Mettinger believes three to have been based on Egyptian prototypes: the *sôpēr*, the *mazkîr* and the official *'ăšer 'al-habbāyit*, whom he describes as the 'Royal Secretary', 'Royal Herald' and 'House-Minister' respectively. I shall examine these individually, but shall omit discussion of a fourth, the 'Friend of the King', for whom Mettinger finds the possibility of an Egyptian origin attractive, since he himself acknowledges the absence of any solid evidence.

[11] T. N. D. Mettinger, *Solomonic State Officials* (Lund, 1971). I am aware of no comprehensive study of the Egyptian officials during the Third Intermediate Period. For the Middle and New Kingdom evidence, see W. Helck, *Zur Verwaltung des mittleren und neuen Reichs* (Leiden, 1958); an index was issued at Leiden in 1975.

[12] R. de Vaux, 'Titres et fonctionnaires égyptiens à la cour de David et de Salomon', *RB* 48 (1939), 394–405; reprinted in his *Bible et Orient* (Paris, 1967), 139–201. J. Begrich, 'Sōfēr und Mazkīr. Ein Beitrag zur inneren Geschichte des davidisch-salomonischen Großreiches und des Königreiches Juda', *ZAW* 58 (1940), 1–29.

(a) *The sôpēr*

Unlike de Vaux and Begrich, who compared the 'scribe' here with the Egyptian *sš-nsw*, a rank title rather than a specific post, at least under the New Kingdom,[13] Mettinger finds an Egyptian prototype in the *sš šᶜt n nsw*, the 'royal letter-writer'. This Egyptian official is described as 'the head of the royal secretariat', from which the foreign and domestic correspondence of the king originated. The post was held by one individual at a time, who, in the Wilbour Papyrus at least, was known by his title alone, unlike his subordinates, whose names were used. For the activities of the Israelite *sôpēr*, Mettinger considers various passages. In 2 Kgs. 12. 11 and 22. 3, the royal secretaries of Jehoash and Josiah each share responsibility for the money raised for the restoration of the Temple; in 2 Kgs. 18. 18, Shebna, the *sôpēr*, is one of the officials who come out to meet the Rabshakeh, and in 19. 2 he is subsequently among those sent to see Isaiah. The story of Baruch's reading in the Temple and its consequences (Jer. 36) suggests, Mettinger believes, that Gemariah and Elishama were each *sôpēr* at the same time. Finally, after a lengthy discussion of the likely existence of royal annals, Mettinger claims that these were the responsibility of the *sôpēr*, apparently on the grounds that they must have been kept by some court official, and the *sôpēr* seems most appropriate for the job.

It is sometimes difficult to see how Mettinger's conclusions follow from his evidence. In summarizing the role of the *sôpēr*, he concludes both that the official was a '"writer" *par excellence* and from the beginning responsible for the royal correspondence',[14] and that he was responsible for the writing of royal annals. Yet he produces no substantial evidence for either of these claims. The passages which he examines show the *sôpēr* controlling money, acting as a royal delegate, and discussing matters of import with other officials; nowhere in the OT do we find any reference to his dealing with the royal correspondence or annals, nor is there any text which can lead us to that inference. Apparently, the basis for

---

[13] See Mettinger, *Solomonic State Officials*, p. 46 n. 5, and D. B. Redford in n. 4 (pp. 142 ff.) of his 'Studies in Relations between Palestine and Egypt during the First Millennium BC, I. The Taxation System of Solomon', in J. W. Wevers and D. B. Redford (eds.), *Studies on the Ancient Palestinian World Presented to Professor F. V. Winnett* (Toronto, 1972), 141–56.

[14] Mettinger, *Solomonic State Officials*, 42.

these conclusions is simply the suitability of such functions for someone whose title is linguistically connected with writing. In fact, even this connection is somewhat dubious: McKane and others have posited links with the Akkadian *šāpirum,*[15] and it is possible that the Akkadian root is a better guide to the sense of the title than the Hebrew *SPR,* the primary sense of which is, by the way, counting rather than writing. Taken as a denominative form, *sôpēr* may be connected with writing; it cannot, however, be claimed that the link with writing is necessarily implicit in the word, and one might recall the apparently military sense which it has in Judg. 5. 14. Without even this etymological prop, it is hard to see how Mettinger feels so confident that the *sôpēr* was a '"writer" *par excellence*'. Furthermore, even if his title were clearly associated with writing, it is not certain that this would indicate the functions of the official: over even a short time, the literal sense or etymology of titles can become notoriously misleading, as any British 'Knight Commander of the Bath', or Scottish 'writer', indeed, would happily testify.

Mettinger goes on to conclude that the function of the Egyptian *sš-šᶜt n nsw* 'corresponds so closely to what was true of the royal secretary in Israel that one is almost forced to conclude that we have here the prototype of the Israelite office'.[16] Yet not only has Mettinger produced no evidence to suggest that the Israelite *sôpēr* was head of a royal secretariat, or that he dealt with the royal correspondence, but he freely acknowledges the existence of two secretaries together under Solomon, and possibly also under Jehoiakim, while stressing that the Egyptian office was held by only one man at a time. Even were we to allow all Mettinger's claims about the functions of the *sôpēr,* it is not clear that these imply any correspondence between the Israelite and Egyptian posts close enough to make imitation any more than a possibility: such slight evidence can hardly 'force' us to conclude anything.

However, a further element is introduced into the argument when Mettinger takes up the theory of Cody, that the Egyptian title *sš-šᶜt,* in an altered form, lies behind the confusion surrounding the name of David's *sôpēr.*[17] In 2 Sam. 8. 17 we are told

---

[15] See McKane, *Prophets and Wise Men,* 25 ff. and references.
[16] Mettinger, *Solomonic State Officials,* 48.
[17] A. Cody, 'Le Titre égyptien et le nom propre du scribe de David', *RB* 72 (1965), 381–93.

that 'Seraiah was secretary', in 2 Sam. 20. 25 that 'Sheva was secretary', and in 1 Kgs. 4. 3 that 'Elihoreph and Ahijah the sons of Shisha were secretaries'. The parallel to the first of these in 1 Chr. 18. 16 gives the name as Shavsha, while the kethib in the second reads *šy'* for the qere *šw'*. Wide variation is found also in the LXX texts. On the reasonable assumption that the references are all to a single man, Cody argues that he was known at the time of David by his title *sš-s‘t*, which was rendered *šš'* in Hebrew, vocalized as *šašī'*. This title came, in the course of time, to be supplanted by the native term *sôpēr*, the foreign title being remembered in certain circles, but not fully understood. Thus 2 Sam. 8. 17 gives the correct personal name of the individual, with his Hebrew title, but when the (less authentic) list in ch. 20 was composed, the Egyptian title was used, furnished either from popular memory or from a list of titles: in either case, it was probably taken to be a name rather than a title. The preservation of the original pronunciation in oral tradition led eventually to the writing of the *yodh* when *matres lectionis* were introduced; the *shin* dropped out through textual corruption, and *šš'* thus became *šy'*, while in 1 Kgs. 4. 3, the *yodh* and the second *shin* were transposed, to give *šyš'*. The Chronicler adopted the form of 1 Kgs. 4, but the *yodh* was confused with *waw* when written in the square alphabet: the form *šwš'* thus emerged, and ultimately influenced, by way of the LXX, the Qere reading *šw'* in 2 Sam. 20. 25. These proposed changes are set out in Diagram 3.

There is no textual support for the second stage, which Cody hypothesizes from the supposed vocalization. Moreover, at 2 Sam. 20. 25, the LXX versions, including the Lucianic recension (important for the reconstruction of the Old Greek in this 'Kaige' section) suggest the existence of a form *šwš(')* in their *Vorlage*. This reading is supported also by some texts of the Targum, and

Diagram 3. Cody's theory.

2 Sam. 20. 25 K	1 Kgs. 4. 3	1 Chr. 18. 16	2 Sam. 20. 25 Q
1. šš'	šš'		
2. ššy'	ššy'		
3. šy'	šyš' ⟶	šyš'	(šy')
4.		šwš' —(LXX)⟶ šw'	

by Josephus *Ant.* 7. 293.[18] There is no reason to suppose that this reading is based on that of the Chronicler, nor, indeed, to suppose that the Chronicler's is based on 1 Kgs. 4. There are simpler explanations available for the facts. So, for example, the original form may have been *šwš*, in which case the development might be explained on the basis of a loss of a *shin* through haplography in 2 Sam. 20. 25, with *yodh/waw* confusions in the kethib of that verse and in 1 Kgs. 4. 3, where the LXX readings with *beta* may suggest an original *waw*. Alternatively, the basic form may have been *šš*, as Cody supposes, but with two rival vocalizations appearing, in which case the only textual corruption would be the loss of the *shin*. Other possibilities exist, but it must be concluded that Cody's suggestion, while not impossible, has little to commend it on text-critical grounds.

None the less, Cody is starting not from the problem of the interrelationship of these forms, but from the problem that the form *šryh* in 2 Sam. 8. 17 is not easily reconciled with any of them. The general inclination of commentators has been to reject this form altogether,[19] and the readings Σασα of LXX[LMN], Ασα of LXX[B] and Σισαν of Josephus, *Ant.* 7. 110, may all attest to a Hebrew manuscript tradition which read *šš* in 2 Sam. 8. 17: they do not follow the transliterations used in the other verses, which tells against their being simple harmonizations, Furthermore, for the other names and titles the Chronicler follows this list meticulously, with a single deliberate change (probably for dogmatic reasons) at the end; yet Cody supposes that he preferred the witness of the lists in 2 Sam. 20 and 1 Kgs. 4, even though they differed from each other, in this single instance.

For the confusion of this very title with the name of its bearer, Cody cites the postscript to the Amarna letter EA 316, which begins: 'To Šaḫšiḫašiḫa, of [my lord: me]ssage of Pu-Ba'la . . .' (ll. 16 f.)[20] Albright has explained the first name as the Egyptian

[18] Compare C. F. Burney, *Notes on the Hebrew Text of the Books of Kings* (Oxford, 1903), 38 f.

[19] This is the view of Burney, ibid. See also e.g. J. Wellhausen, *Der Text der Bücher Samuelis* (Göttingen, 1871), 177, and S. R. Driver, *Notes on the Hebrew Text and the Topography of the Books of Samuel*[2] (Oxford, 1913), 283. For a more recent discussion of the text-critical issues, see P. K. McCarter, *II Samuel* (Garden City, NY, 1984), esp. 433.

[20] I translate from Moran's French edition, but leave the first name, which he translates as 'scribe' on the basis of Albright's argument. See W. L. Moran, *Les*

title *sš-š't*, written here with a person determinative.[21] Yet this possible confusion on the part of Pu-ba'la about the title of a foreign official, if such it be, is hardly a true analogy to confusion on the part of the Israelites about a title used in their own court, even if it was a funny, foreign sort of title. Finally, both Cody and Mettinger cite *Wen-Amon* ii. 68, where reference is made to the *sš-š't* of the king of Byblos, who brings refreshments to Wen-Amon, as evidence for the familiarity of the title in Canaan. If this is simply the author's use of a familiar title for the benefit of his Egyptian readership, then the passage clearly proves nothing of the sort. If, on the other hand, the title was actually used in Byblos, this would appear to undermine any idea that Israel must have borrowed it directly from Egypt.

On balance, it seems easier to accept the contradictory traditions about the name of David's official than the immense and indigestible complexities of Cody's argument, with its failure to give any satisfactory answer to the basic question it raises: who were these circles who chose to remember an official by his title, (a title which underwent, we may remark, a tremendous phonetic transformation during its short trip from Egypt), yet forgot that it was a title? Or alternatively, if a list of officials giving only titles influenced our texts, why was this influence exerted in just this one case? Such explanations for the confusion of the title and the name do not really ring true, and they give us no good reason to suspend our disbelief for so much else of the argument.

Finally, it has been suggested that the names of David's *sôpēr* and his sons are themselves Egyptian, or reflect underlying Egyptian forms. There is nothing inherently improbable about this, but there is a danger of forcing the evidence. Thus, Mettinger takes the father's name to have been Seraiah, which is known elsewhere from the OT as a Hebrew name, but he suggests that this may reflect the conflation of an Egyptian name with a familiar Hebrew one. He gives as possibilities a number of Egyptian names from Ranke's lists (Ranke, i. 316. 23, 317. 4–6).[22] However, according to the *corrigenda* in Ranke, ii, page 388, the first of

---

Lettres d'El-Amarna (Paris, 1987), 540. A revised version is now available in English: *The Amarna Letters* (Baltimore and London, 1992); see p. 348.

[21] W. F. Albright, 'Cuneiform Material for Egyptian Prosopography 1500–1200 BC', *JNES* 5 (1946), 7–25. See 20 f.

[22] H. Ranke, *Die ägyptischen Personennamen* (Glückstadt, 1935, 1952, 1977).

these, *sr*, 'ist zu streichen'. Of the rest, *sr.ỉ* (317. 5) is not attested after the Old Kingdom, nor *sr.w* and *sr.y* (317. 4, 6) after the Middle Kingdom. None of these names are common. Mettinger does not, for some reason, suggest *sr* (316. 25), which is common in the New Kingdom, nor does he note in Ranke's *addenda* (ii. 316. 22, 23) the two names written *srỉ* from about the Twentieth Dynasty.[23] There are, then, some Egyptian names broadly similar to Seraiah, which were possibly in use at the time. Yet there is no reason whatsoever to suppose that any of these underlie the perfectly good Hebrew name Seraiah.

De Vaux, taking *šš'* as the original name, cites as possible originals Ranke, 330. 1–5. Of these, however, *šš* (330.1) is found only in the Old Kingdom, as a woman's name, while neither *šš.y* (330. 4, also a woman's name) nor *šš.w* (330.5) is attested after the Middle Kingdom. *šš* (330. 2), on the other hand, is not attested before a single occurrence in the Twenty-sixth Dynasty. The only one of all these names commonly attested is *ššỉ* (330. 3), but this is not found after the Old Kingdom either. An Egyptian origin for *šš'*, which does not appear to be a Hebrew name, remains a possibility, but the prototypes suggested by de Vaux are unconvincing.[24] Kitchen has suggested that names using the elements *s3ỉ* 'satisfaction', or *s3wỉ* 'his is' (cf. Ranke, i. 299. 4–10, 301. 24–302. 3), might form suitable prototypes, although his combination of the two, which comes closest to the Hebrew, is hypothetical.[25] He also notes the Hurrian names *šešwe* and *šešwiya*,[26] which, allowing the possibility of metathesis, seem closer than both his proposed Egyptian names and the other Hurrian forms suggested by Mazar.[27]

---

[23] See J. Černy, *Late Ramesside Letters* (Brussels, 1939), 57.11 (Pap. Geneva D.191, 1. 8) and A. H. Gardiner, *The Wilbour Papyrus* (Oxford, 1948), A77.52, A91.15, A97.28. (The group-writing of each name is slightly different.)

[24] See de Vaux, 'Titres et fonctionnaires égyptiens', 399.

[25] See pp. 112 f. in K. A. Kitchen, 'Egypt and Israel during the First Millennium BC', SVT 40 (1988), 107–23.

[26] See I. J. Gelb, P. M. Purves, and A. A. Macrae, *Nuzi Personal Names* (Chicago, 1943), 133.

[27] B. Mazar (Maisler) ingeniously suggests that the original name was *Ša/e-wa/ ešarri*, abbreviated and written *šwš'/šwā; śryh* is a Hebrew adaptation. See 'The Scribe of King David and the Problem of the High Officials in the Ancient Kingdom of Israel', *BJPES* 13 (1946–7), 105–14 (Heb.: Eng. summary on pp. iv–v); also his revised version, 'King David's Scribe and the High Officialdom of the United Monarchy of Israel', in *The Early Biblical Period* (Jerusalem, 1986), 126–38.

Turning to the sons, Mettinger's suggestion that the Hebrew name Ahijah reflects here an original Egytian ₃ḥ-ỉꜥḥ (Ranke, i. 2. 22) seems unnecessary. The Egyptian name, moreover, is attested only once, in the Nineteenth Dynasty, and the reading is doubtful. The questions surrounding the name of the other son, Elihoreph, are altogether more interesting. Mettinger and de Vaux here follow the theory of Marquart,[28] that Elihoreph is a distortion of a name originally containing a theophoric element *ḥp* = Apis,[29] which has been altered to the consonants of *ḥrp*, and given the vowels of *bōšet*. De Vaux cites in this connection the fifth-century Phoenician names *bnḥp* and *ytnḥp* from Elephantine, which both appear to contain this theophoric element. The first of these is uncertain,[30] but we may add the Aramaic *[ꜥ]bdḥp*, again from Elephantine, which has the same characteristic.[31] Attractive though this theory is, it is worth recalling that these parallels are about half a millennium later than the individual in question, and, moreover, that they are Semitic names borne by Semites in Egypt, and are not, therefore, strong evidence that such a name might be adopted by an Egyptian in Israel. In any case, the use of an Egyptian theophoric element in a name does not necessarily imply Egyptian ancestry, and it is noteworthy that in his epigraphic study of names from Israel, Tigay finds more names compounded with Horus than with Baal.[32] It is, moreover, quite possible that the '-horeph' element of the name is to be explained in some other way, especially since names with those consonants are found in Neh. 7. 24; 10. 20 (ET 19) and an inscription.[33] In general, the

---

[28] J. Marquart, *Fundamente israelitischer und jüdischer Geschichte* (Göttingen, 1986).

[29] See Jer. 46. 15 MT and 26. 15 LXX for Hebrew *ḥp* = Apis. Mazar, in 'The Scribe of King David' and 'King David's Scribe', takes -*ḥrp* to be the Hurrian deity Harpa; Tigay, however, notes that this deity is no longer found in personal names of the first millennium: see J. H. Tigay, *You Shall Have No Other Gods* (Atlanta, 1986), p. 77 n. 15.

[30] The names are from 5th-cent. Elephantine ostraca; see M. Lidzbarski, *Phönizische und aramäische Krugaufschriften aus Elephantine* (Berlin, 1912), nos. 2, 5, and 35b. Lidzbarski notes that *bnḥp* might be read *bnhr*, which occurs in 14a.

[31] This name is found in Frag. 7, 3, 2 in G. R. Driver, *Aramaic Documents of the Fifth Century* BC (Oxford, 1954), 41. See also W. Kornfeld, *Onomastica aramaica aus Ägypten* (Vienna, 1978), 65.

[32] See Tigay, *You Shall Have No Other Gods*, 13.

[33] Ibid. 77. See also E. Lipiński, 'Scribes d'Ugarit et de Jérusalem', in H. L. J. Vanstiphout et al. (eds.), *Scripta Signa Vocis* (Groningen, 1986), 143–54, who sees a N. Syrian origin for both Elihoreph and his father.

oddness of (possibly) two out of the three names in the family may suggest a non-Israelite ancestry, and Egypt is a strong candidate. However, this is a long way from saying that David's *sôpēr* was an Egyptian, brought in as the first holder of an office based on an Egyptian model.

We have reviewed at some length the rather complicated evidence adduced for the suggestion that the *sôpēr* was an office based on an Egyptian model, and have found it unconvincing on almost every point. Ultimately, the problem is simply that we know too little about the duties of this official to make any realistic comparison, and the arguments for direct evidence, the use of the Egyptian title in Israel, prove untenable. We may deal with the other offices more briefly, since the evidence is less convoluted.

(b) *The mazkîr*

Mettinger confesses that the information available for the duties of this official is very scanty, and he relies almost entirely on an etymological study, from which he deduces that the term has the sense 'he who mentions, proclaims', and so describes the official as the 'Royal Herald'. After a brief examination of the possibility that the office was modelled on the Mesopotamian *nāgiru*, he finally concludes that a more probable model was the Egyptian *wḥmw nsw*, the king's herald, whose title is possibly a semantic equivalent of the Hebrew. This conclusion was reached also by de Vaux and Begrich.

I do not intend to discuss this comparison in depth since, apart from the vague semantic link, there is no evidence at all for any similarity between the duties of these officials; more importantly, the very existence of the Egyptian office in the time of David and Solomon is questionable. As Redford has remarked:

the sobering fact is, and it has been taken into account upon occasion by those who maintain the identity of the two, that the heyday of the *wḥmw* in the royal administration was during the New Kingdom before 1100 BC. Thereafter references peter out until, in the late Twenty-first Dynasty and under the Libyans, the *wḥmw* is conspicuous by his absence. If David were looking for models, would he not be more liable to copy from contemporary Egyptian titles than to choose an obsolescent function over a century out of date?[34]

[34] Redford, 'The Taxation System of Solomon', p. 144 n. 7.

In view of this, it seems unlikely that the comparison can be sustained.

(c) The Official *'ašer 'al-habbāyit*

This official 'over the house' is absent from the Davidic lists, making his first appearance in 1 Kgs. 4. 6, but he appears frequently thereafter, and the term *'ašer 'al-habbāyit* is found used of individuals in epigraphic material.[35] Its use in the Joseph Narrative (especially in Gen. 41. 40) has given some impetus to the quest for an Egyptian original. Mettinger rightly rejects the arguments of de Vaux, that the Egyptian vizier was the model,[36] and prefers the royal chief steward, the *ỉmy-r pr wr*. His argument that the Hebrew title probably refers to management of the royal estates is reasonable, but this connection with the Egyptian official seems somewhat tenuous, resting as it does on two observations of questionable value.

The first of these is that the Israelite official in question is found often in association with the two officials examined above: since we have rejected the suggestion that these officials were certainly modelled on Egyptian prototypes, the implication that association with them suggests an Egyptian origin cannot be sustained. It is a pretty feeble argument anyway. The second concerns the title itself, which Mettinger regards as a 'semi-calque' on the Egyptian title, the meaning of which is 'great overseer of the house', the element *wr*, 'great', distinguishing the official from *ỉmy-r pr*, the Egyptian for 'steward'. Yet this element *wr* is absent from the supposed translation, making the Hebrew an equivalent of 'steward', rather than 'High Steward'. The precise literal meaning of *ỉmy-r* is uncertain, but it is used as a set expression for 'overseer': that *ỉmy* has some relative implication, makes it attractive to see in this the origin of the *'ašer* in the common expression *'ašer 'al-habbāyit*, but the relative is not a part of the Hebrew title, being used only when the title is in apposition or as an independent relative, while *ỉmy* is not actually a relative particle, but an adjective formed from the preposition *m*. Further, the form *'al* + noun is used for other titles: the official 'over the

---

[35] See N. Avigad, *Hebrew Bullae from the Time of Jeremiah* (Jerusalem, 1986), nos. 1–3 (21–3) and the references there.

[36] See de Vaux, 'Titres et fonctionnaires égyptiens', 401 ff., and Mettinger, *Solomonic State Officials*, 77.

city', for example, in 2 Kgs. 10. 5. It is highly improbable, then, that the Hebrew relative reflects the Egyptian *ỉmy* in the set phrase *ỉmy-r*. Mettinger himself, in an earlier chapter, acknowledges that 'the mere form and syntactic function of the title *'ašer 'al-habbāyit* cannot be taken as an indication that this title is a loan translation.'[37] The Hebrew title is '(one who is) over the house', the Egyptian title 'great overseer of the house': the similarity is not striking, and is confined to the use of 'house' in each. There is, then, no force in either of the arguments used to show an Egyptian origin for this official, and there is no particular reason to look to Egypt for the inspiration. A recent study of this office by S. C. Layton rejects imitation of Egypt in favour of a Canaanite prototype.[38]

(d) *The State Officials: General Observations*

If we have found little evidence to suggest any direct imitation of Egypt in the establishment of the Israelite administration, that is hardly a matter for surprise. Our information about the state officials is limited, and comparisons with any nation would be difficult. Mettinger's apparent confidence in his results would be misplaced, given the limitations of the evidence, even were all his arguments unassailable. One must turn eventually to the question of inherent likelihood: is Mettinger's theory in accordance with, or does it fly in the face of historical probability?

The whole discussion about the state officials is posited on the belief that the Davidic and Solomonic lists of officials reflect the historical facts. If so, two of the three offices which we have discussed already existed at the time of David. If a case can be made out for strong links between Israel and Egypt under Solomon, no such case can be made out for the reign of David, whose activities and contacts were, according to the biblical account, confined to Palestine and Transjordan. It is inherently far more probable that David's officials, if they were modelled on any foreign prototypes, were modelled on the officials to be found in the Canaanite or other city states within Palestine, with which David would have been familiar. We know little about the administration of these states, although inferences are possible

---

[37] Mettinger, *Solomonic State Officials*, 16 f.

[38] S. C. Layton, 'The Steward in Ancient Israel: A Study of Hebrew *('ăšer) 'al-habbāyit* in its Near Eastern Setting', *JBL* 109 (1990), 633–49. See also Kitchen, 'Egypt and Israel during the First Millennium BC', 115.

from elsewhere, and it is conceivable that Egyptian influence was mediated indirectly through them.[39] In this context it is interesting to note that the terms *sôper* and *mazkîr* both appear on Moabite seals, which might indicate that the terms are 'Palestinian' rather than specific to Israel.[40] There is no reason to suppose that David created senior administrative posts along Egyptian lines, or that Solomon substantially changed those posts.

Finally, this issue has to be put into context. If Jamieson-Drake is right, then Solomon's state was not heavily centralized and the apparatus of state in Jerusalem may have been fairly small. Indeed, it is hard to believe that, in the short period between Saul and Solomon, any large and entrenched administrative class could have evolved which was remotely comparable to that of Egypt. Furthermore, it is doubtful that the Egyptian administration, geared to a wholly different scale and a quite dissimilar economy, could usefully have served as a model for Israel. Whatever the prestige of Egypt, and it may not have been so very great at this time, it is far more likely that an Israelite king would have developed his administration with a view both to the structures of more similar states and to the existing power-structures in Israel itself. To claim imitation of Egypt in this area requires, then, some very convincing evidence. Mettinger presents no such evidence, resorting instead to doubtful etymologies and guesses about the function of officials. Let us bear this in mind when we turn to some other supposed imitations of Egypt which have had less impact on biblical scholarship.

2. *Solomon's Provisioning System*

In 1 Kgs. 4. 7 we are told that 'Solomon had twelve officers over all Israel, who provided food for the king and his household; each

---

[39] Canaanite influence on the administration of Israel has been perceived by a number of scholars, most notably H. Donner. U. Rüterswörden argues persuasively that the new Davidic state officials were derived from the system in pre-Israelite Jerusalem, in his *Die Beamten der israelitischen Königszeit* (Stuttgart, 1985). See his remarks on the individual officials on pp. 77–91, and 120 f. of his conclusion. Mazar, 'The Scribe of King David' and 'King David's Scribe', argues that both the office of *sôpēr* and its first holder were Canaanite.

[40] For the *sôpēr*, see p. 289 of N. Avigad, 'Ammonite and Moabite Seals', in J. A. Sanders (ed.), *Essays in Honor of Nelson Glueck: Near Eastern Archaeology in the Twentieth Century* (Garden City, NY, 1970), 284–95. The term may be used here, of course, in the more general sense of 'scribe'. For the *mazkîr*, see M. Abu Taleb, 'The Seal of plty bn m'š the Mazkir', *ZDPV* 101 (1985), 21–9.

man had to make provision for one month in the year.' The list
which follows, apparently naming the individuals and towns or
regions responsible, presents grave problems of interpretation, but
these need not detain us here.[41] Redford believes that the system
described reflects Egyptian influence upon Solomon's administration, and the most precise analogy, he suggests, is in a near-
contemporary stela of Shoshenq I, where the king describes his
restoration of the daily sacrifice at the temple of Arsaphes in
Herakleopolis.[42] This details the source of the levy in twelve
monthly sections, with a final section to cover the epagomenal
days. In each section are listed the officials and towns responsible
for supplying the temple during that month, and the amount which
is to be levied. Less precise analogies are to be found in other
Egyptian texts. In a twist to this argument, A. R. Green has
argued that in fact it was Solomon's system which influenced
Shosenq.[43]

The similarity between the system at Herakleopolis and that in
Israel is that they each involve the appointment of officials
responsible for provisioning during one month at a time.[44] However, the provisioning in each case is for very different purposes:
on the Herakleopolis stela the levy is for oxen, which are to be
sacrificed daily at the temple, while the Israelite list refers to
provisioning for the royal household.[45] Furthermore, although
many of the Egyptians are implicitly associated with particular
areas or estates by virtue of their offices, the Egyptian system,
unlike the Israelite, is not explicitly related to geographical areas.

The appointment of officials to collect provisions for the royal
household in particular areas is attested in Mesopotamia,[46] and

[41] For the main problems, see J. M. Miller and J. H. Hayes, *A History of
Ancient Israel and Judah* (London, 1986), 205–7.

[42] Redford, 'The Taxation System of Solomon'.

[43] A. R. Green, 'Israelite Influence at Shishak's Court?', *BASOR* 233 (1979),
59–62. Kitchen, 'Egypt and Israel during the First Millennium BC', 116, rightly
describes this as far-fetched.

[44] The number twelve is a product of the division into months: the OT text does
not appear to relate the system to the twelve tribes.

[45] Redford's speculation, 'The Taxation System of Solomon', 154 ff., that the
provisions listed in 1 Kgs. 5. 2 f. (ET 4. 22 f.) are actually the provisions for sacrifice
in the Jerusalem Temple, runs counter to the assertions of the text itself.

[46] For the Neo-Babylonian evidence, see R. P. Dougherty, 'Cuneiform Parallels
to Solomon's Provisioning System', *AASOR* 5 (1923–4), 23–65. Dougherty does
not succeed in demonstrating the responsibility of officials for provisioning in
certain months of the year only.

the responsibility of certain areas for certain months may have been known in Persia.[47] Such systems are sensible and obvious, spreading the burden of the royal household across the state. While the coincidence of time makes it particularly tempting to see a connection between the systems of Solomon and Shoshenq, it would, then, hardly be a strain on credulity to suppose that they arose independently. On the other hand, it would be distinctly curious if Solomon borrowed, as the basis for his national system of provisioning for the palace, a method of providing temple sacrifices in a small area of Egypt. It is far more probable that Solomon's system goes back to Canaanite practices, and Kitchen has adduced evidence from Ugarit for palace levies and monthly regulation.[48] In short, it is possible that Solomon's provisioning system was inspired by Egyptian methods, but it is not especially probable.

3. *Hieratic Numerals, Weights and Measures*

Finally, there are some miscellaneous issues relevant to the discussion but of a rather different nature. Foremost amongst these is the use of Egyptian hieratic numerals in Israel, which is widely attested. These numerals were less long-winded than those of the rival Phoenician system, and were doubtless adopted for this reason: it is not clear, however, that this is evidence for more widespread adoption of Egyptian practices under the Israelite monarchy. Indeed, on the face of it, it seems more likely that the numerals became established in Palestine during the earlier period of Egyptian domination, when they would have been used widely in trade and administration.[49] Mettinger objects that all the evidence for their use comes from the time of the monarchy,[50] but this is substantially just an argument from silence: we have little or no evidence for the normal Canaanite practices in Palestine.[51]

---

[47] See Herodotus, i. 192.

[48] See Kitchen, 'Egypt and Israel during the First Millennium BC', 116 f.

[49] See e.g. O. Goldwasser, 'Hieratic Inscriptions from Tel Sera' in Southern Canaan', *TA* 11 (1984), 77–93, and M. Gilula, 'An Inscription in Egyptian Hieratic from Lachish', *TA* 3 (1976), 107 f.

[50] Mettinger, *Solomonic State Officials*, 49.

[51] Cross suggests that the broken horizontal line at the end of the Qubūr el-Walaydah bowl inscription (*c.*1200 BC) may be a Phoenician-style '10', but this is speculative: F. M. Cross, 'Newly Found Inscriptions in Old Canaanite and Early

Apparent use of the numerals in Ammonite texts tells against a specifically Israelite borrowing.[52]

A related issue is that of the hieratic numerals on 'shekel weights', although these may have come into use only under the later monarchy. The weights themselves seem to correspond to multiples and fractions of 8 shekels (the most common denomination), but the numbers on them seem to express the equivalent number of Egyptian *ḳdt* units.[53] This suggests not adoption of, but assimilation to Egyptian measures, and is most probably to be explained in terms of trading convenience.

Finally, Aharoni has suggested that the enlargement of the dimensions in the Stratum X temple at Arad reflects a change in the length of the cubit under the early monarchy, from approximately 45 cm. to approximately 52.5 cm.[54] He associates this with a general restandardization of measurements, in which the Israelite cubit, previously equivalent to the 'common' cubit of Egypt, was made equivalent to the 'royal' cubit. We have little evidence for the length of the cubit, and none to suggest that the change at Arad marks a more general change. If the cubit lengths at Arad were based on Egyptian ones, as is possible, the change from short to long is unlikely to have been inspired by any change in Egypt, where such an alteration did not occur until much later, under the Twenty-sixth Dynasty.[55] In fact, then, the change tells against any general move to conformity with Egyptian usage, and also against equivalence to the common cubit being itself a recent innovation.

Phoenician Scripts', *BASOR* 238 (1980), 1–20, esp. 1–4. The only non-hieratic numeral from the Israelite period is on the 8th-cent. ostracon 2 from Tell Qasîle, see B. Maisler (Mazar), 'The Excavations at Tell Qasîle', *IEJ* 1 (1950/1), 194–218, esp. see 209 f. This may be Philistine, cf. J. Naveh, in 'Writing and Scripts in Seventh-Century BCE Philistia: The New Evidence from Tell Jammeh', *IEJ* 35 (1985), 8–21.

[52] See W. E. Aufrecht, *A Corpus of Ammonite Inscriptions* (Lewiston, NY, Queenston, Ont., and Lampeter, 1989), 355. The numerals appear to reflect an adaptation or hybrid from the hieratic system.

[53] Y. Aharoni, 'The Use of Hieratic Numerals in Hebrew Ostraca and the Shekel Weights', *BASOR* 184 (1966), 13–19, esp. 18.

[54] Y. Aharoni, 'Arad: Its Inscriptions and Temple', *BA* 31 (1968), 2–32. See 22–4.

[55] See E. Iversen, *Canon and Proportion in Egyptian Art*[2] (Warminster, 1975), 16–19.

4. *Egypt and the State administration: Conclusions*

I have not tried to pinpoint the actual origins of the state administrative system in Israel, but only to examine the claim that it was modelled on the Egyptian system. This claim has, it appears, little to commend it, and it follows that we cannot use any supposed imitation of the Egyptian administration as evidence for the nature of Israelite wisdom. More generally, it seems unwise to overemphasize the changes wrought in Israel by the Davidic monarchy. To be sure, the consolidation of the nation and conquests abroad would bring with them the need for some new political structures (though it is unlikely that these would have obtruded into such inherently conservative areas as the systems of weights and measures). Yet, as historians tend more and more to emphasize the cultural continuity between Canaan and Israel, the idea that Canaanite or other Palestinian administrative practices would have been ignored or rejected by Israel seems increasingly out of step. That Canaanite and pre-monarchic Israelite usage was the most probable source for the state administration should be an a priori assumption, and our limited knowledge about such usage does not somehow make Egypt a more likely source. The sort of discontinuity central to the hypothesis of a Solomonic Enlightenment cannot be accepted as plausible without far better evidence than has hitherto been produced.

8

Schools in Israel

Proverbs does not set its material in the context of formal education, but in the home or on the lips of royalty and wise men. It is, however, widely asserted that early wisdom was 'educational' or 'pedagogical' in origin and purpose, rather than simply improving or didactic in some broader sense. Such claims are hard to prove or disprove, although they should not be based, as often they are, on the false assumption that Egyptian instructions certainly had such a character. There is, however, a broader issue which involves more than simple assertions and counter-assertions: the nature of education in Israel. This is a question which has concerned scholars for many years, and Klostermann's classic treatment of it predates the recognition of a relationship between Proverbs and Egyptian instructions.[1]

The very existence of written documents indicates that some sort of education must have been available in Israel. This might have taken one or more of various forms, from parental teaching or apprenticeship through to an established system of schools, and might have included anything from basic literacy through to professional training and familiarization with classic literature. Pointing to the systems in other, larger nations, many scholars have been inclined to believe that formal schooling existed, at least for the administrative class, from a relatively early time; a few have attempted to describe that schooling in detail. I shall devote much of this last chapter to assessing the evidence for schools, before returning to a final discussion of more general issues.

1. *Old Testament Evidence for Schools in Israel*

The Old Testament is notoriously reticent on this subject, and there is no explicit reference to a 'school' in Hebrew before Sir.

[1] A. Klostermann, 'Schulwesen im alten Israel', in N. Bonwetsch *et al.*, *Theologische Studien, Theodor Zahn* (Leipzig, 1908), 193–232.

51. 23. Three passages used by Klostermann,[2] Isa. 28. 9–13; 50. 4–9; and Prov. 22. 17–21, have continued to be prominent in subsequent discussions, although the last of these is too closely related to *Amenemope* to be of definite relevance to the situation in Israel, and I shall not examine it here.[3] The first is very obscure:

9. To whom will he teach knowledge, and to whom will he explain the message?
   Those weaned off milk, those removed from breasts?
10. For *ṣaw lāṣāw ṣaw lāṣāw qaw lāqāw qaw lāqāw*
    zĕʿêr šām zĕʿêr šām
11. For through men of unintelligible speech and alien tongue will Yahweh speak to this people,
12. to whom he has said, 'This is rest; let the weary rest: and this is repose'; yet they would not listen.
13. And the word of Yahweh will be to them
    ṣaw lāṣāw ṣaw lāṣāw qaw lāqāw qaw lāqāw
    zĕʿêr šām zĕʿêr šām
    That they may go, and fall back, and be broken and trapped and taken.

The untranslated text is the crux: *zĕʿêr šām zĕʿêr šām* can be taken to mean 'a little here, a little there', but attempts to understand the rest as Hebrew are unconvincing. Klostermann takes *ṣaw* and *qaw* to be the names of letters (cf. '*waw*', '*taw*') being used to teach children how to write. By this reckoning, vv. 9–10 are a pastiche of a school lesson, in which the drunken prophets and priests of the preceding verses complain that Isaiah is talking to them as though to school children.

Despite its popularity, this interpretation encounters several difficulties. It may well be that children of that time were weaned later than in our society,[4] but it is still unlikely that those just weaned would be taught to read.[5] Equally, there is no evidence that these sounds ever were the names of letters. More importantly, this interpretation gives no weight to the following verse, which is

[2] Ibid. 211 ff.
[3] Cf. p. 603 of J. L. Crenshaw, 'Education in Ancient Israel', *JBL* 104 (1985), 601–15.
[4] 1 Sam. 1. 22 ff. implies only a period of at least three months' breast-feeding, but the later 2 Macc. 7. 27 mentions a period of three years.
[5] Contra Lang, Prov. 4. 3 has nothing to do with the formal schooling of small children; see p. 191 of B. Lang, 'Schule und Unterricht im alten Israel', in M. Gilbert (ed.), *La Sagesse de l'Ancien Testament* (Louvain, 1979), 186–201.

surely connected with vv. 9–10 by its reference to incomprehensible speech. A. Van Selms has taken this seriously by attempting
to understand the strange words as a prophecy in Akkadian,
contrasting with v. 12, but his translation, alas, makes little sense:
'Go out! Let him go out! Go out! Let him go out! Wait! Let him
wait! Wait! Let him wait! Servant, listen! Servant, listen!'[6] André
Lemaire wishes to have his cake and eat it, believing that the
repetition of the words in v. 13 is a piece of prophetic sleight of
hand, whereby the school lesson of v. 10 is revealed to be, in fact,
an announcement of the Assyrian invasion.[7] Even apart from the
problem of understanding the 'Assyrian', it is most improbable
that the same words would coincidentally be recognizable to
the listeners as both a Hebrew writing lesson and an Assyrian
exclamation.

Rather closer to the mark, I suspect, is the interpretation of the
words as 'baby talk'. Lindblom thus argues that:

> What the enemies meant was that the message of disaster proclaimed by
> Isaiah was pure nonsense. They were grown-up people and had under-
> standing enough to comprehend the ways of Yahweh. Isaiah's reply is
> ironical and biting: one day Yahweh will speak to this people by babbling
> lips and an alien tongue, when the Assyrian armies with their barbaric
> language come down upon the land of Israel.[8]

It seems clear, in view of v. 9, that the words are indeed intended
to sound like baby talk: however, it seems probable that they are
also intended to represent the babbling of drunkards. To take
vv. 9–10 as the words of Isaiah's opponents about him is not
justified by anything in the text except the sudden use of singular
verbs without an explicit subject. Rather than taking these as the
words of the opponents, it would, in fact, be more natural to take
them as a continuation of the description of the drunken priest and
prophet of v. 7, especially since the hiphil of *yārāh*, 'teach', is used
pre-eminently of priestly directions, and the 'message' may be the
prophetic revelation of coming destruction (cf. 28. 19; Jer. 49. 14;
Ezek. 21. 12 (ET 7); Obad. 1). Then the singular verbs are

---

[6] A. Van Selms, 'Isaiah 28: 9–13: An Attempt to Give a New Interpretation',
ZAW 85 (1973), 332–39.

[7] A. Lemaire, *Les Ecoles et la formation de la Bible dans l'ancien Israël*
(Freiburg and Göttingen, 1981), 39.

[8] J. Lindblom, *Prophecy in Ancient Israel* (Oxford, 1962), 201.

explained by their separate references: 'whom will (the priest) teach knowledge, and to whom will (the prophet) explain the message?' The drunken burblings of these supposed teachers of the divine will are comprehensible only as baby talk; so it is that God's kindly words to Israel come across to them as an incomprehensible babble, which they ignore, to their eventual ruin.

Whether or not this is the correct interpretation, it must be clear that the interpretation of the words as part of a primary-school lesson is very far from certain, and the evidential value of this verse is therefore very limited. The same is true of the second passage, Isa. 50. 4–9, although for somewhat different reasons. This is the third of the 'Servant Songs' in Deutero-Isaiah, and was almost certainly composed after the period of the monarchy: it does not, therefore, necessarily reflect the situation of an earlier age. Its value as evidence for schools rests upon a perception of educational vocabulary in vv. 4 f.:

> 4. The Lord God has given me the tongue of those who are taught,
> that I may know how to sustain the weary with a word.
> Morning by morning ‹he wakens›, he wakens my ear to hear as those who are taught.
> 5. The Lord God has opened my ear, and I was not rebellious, I turned not backward.

In Israel, as in Egypt, the ear is characteristically associated with the apprehension of knowledge (cf. Prov. 5. 13). In the OT, however, the expression 'open the ear', which occurs in v. 5, has a particular association with ideas of divine communication. So in Job 33. 16 and 36. 10, God opens the ears of men to warn them and persuade them to obedience. In Isa. 42. 20, the reference is probably to the literal ability to hear (cf. 35. 5), but in 48. 8 the implication is similar to that of the passages in Job: the fact that Israel's ear 'has not been opened from of old' is associated with her long-standing rebellion against God. It is probable that the same is true of 50. 5, where the expression is again associated with rebelliousness: the speaker's obedience follows from God's opening of his ear, and the expression does not mean that the speaker has received some sort of formal education from God, but that he is obedient to God.

What, then, of verse 4? God enables the prophet to speak and to listen like a *limmûd*, literally 'one taught', but there is no reference to school education here, unless we really think that the schools taught how 'to sustain the weary with a word'. The obscure Jer. 2. 24 or Jer. 13. 23 may suggest that *limmûd* means no more than 'trained' or 'accustomed', but its use in Isa. 8. 16 suggests that the reference here may be to prophetic discipleship (see also 54. 13). In that case there may also be a reference to the sustaining of the weary by Yahweh in 40. 29 ff.: the prophet has learnt to listen properly to Yahweh, like a disciple, and to pass on his word effectively. In any case, there is no clear reference to schooling in these verses, only to education in broader terms.

These examples, often cited in favour of there having been schools, illustrate the problems of all the OT evidence adduced: those passages which are not too vague or general require exegesis which is too tortuous or uncertain to be convincing. Only once is there any apparent reference to the payment of fees for tuition, in Prov. 17. 16, and that reference is more apparent than actual. The Hebrew word-order very clearly stresses not the fool but the fee (*měḥîr*): 'What use is a *fee* in the hand of a fool? To *buy* wisdom when he has no mind?'[9] Far from proving that the payment of fees was common, as argued by Oesterley and others,[10] the verse appears to express incredulity at the idea. We have, of course, no way of knowing whether the writer is being disingenuous, or drawing a distinction between wisdom and education, but the saying certainly provides no evidence for formal schooling.

Rather than run through all the evidence, I refer the reader to the lists of Lemaire and Crenshaw.[11] Crenshaw concludes that it provides no definitive answer,[12] while Lemaire, a keen advocate of schools, concedes uncomfortably that it is vague and far from explicit.[13] Clearly, we need to consider other evidence.

---

9 For this common use of *lămmāh-zeh* for 'what is the point of . . . ?', see e.g. Gen. 33. 15.

10 W. O. E. Oesterley, *Proverbs* (London, 1929), ad loc.

11 Lemaire, *Les Ecoles et la formation de la Bible*, 34–41; Crenshaw, 'Education in Ancient Israel', 602–4.

12 Crenshaw, 'Education in Ancient Israel', 604.

13 Lemaire, *Les Ecoles et la formation de la Bible*, 41.

2. *Epigraphic Evidence*

(a) *Abecedaries and School Exercises*

If the OT evidence for schools is inconclusive, the epigraphic evidence is, according to André Lemaire, overwhelmingly decisive.[14] He contends that a number of Palestinian inscriptions from eight different sites are to be interpreted as the work of students, and testify to the activity of a network of Canaanite and Israelite schools. This is an important claim, and deserves at least a brief examination in detail.

Lemaire never sets out his criteria explicitly, but we may set out some of our own: if it is to be demonstrated beyond reasonable doubt, and that is at least the level of proof which Lemaire claims to have attained, that there was a school at a given site, it is necessary to produce at least one text that is most plausibly interpreted as the work of a pupil at a school in that place. It is not sufficient merely to produce material which demonstrates the acquisition of literacy, since we know that there were literate people in Israel, and our concern is not with their literacy but with the context in which they learnt to read and write. It is necessary also, then, to show that there could have been a school at which the inscriptions were produced. In other words, evidence of someone learning to write is of no significance if it is discovered where there could not have been a school; in fact, such evidence would contradict Lemaire by suggesting that writing was taught outside schools. The physical and historical context of the inscription is, then, of as much significance as its content, and this will become clear in the first of the sites to be examined.

(i) *'Izbet Ṣarṭah* On an ostracon discovered in a silo close to the four-room house in Stratum II of 'Izbet Ṣarṭah, there are five lines of writing, comprising over eighty letters altogether. One of these lines, in which the characters are larger and more deeply cut than in the others, appears to be an abecedary in the (proto-) Canaanite

---

[14] Ibid., ch. 1 (pp. 7–33). See also Lemaire's 'Abécédaires et exercises d'écolier en épigraphie nord-ouest semitique, *JA* 266 (1978), 221–35, and 'Sagesse et écoles', *VT* 34 (1984), 270–81, esp. 277 ff.

script,[15] written from left to right.[16] The other four lines make no
obvious sense, and are generally taken to be writing exercises, in
which a student practised his letters, singly or in groups, sometimes writing them very badly; Demsky argues that the exercise is
in fact the work of a second writer.[17] Such an explanation is
plausible, but somewhat belied by the regularity of size and
spacing, indicative of a continuous text. Two scholars, indeed,
have chosen to take it as continuous: Garbini believes the script
to be a precursor of the Canaanite alphabet, used to write an
unknown, non-Semitic language,[18] while Dotan has attempted to
make sense of the lines as three short sentences.[19] Neither has won
general acceptance for his view.

   Given that the inscription demonstrates some sort of literacy,
and that where there is literacy there are likely to be writing
exercises, whether taught in schools or elsewhere, it is not really
the content of the sherd which concerns us at present, but the
likelihood of a connection with some local school. Some three
kilometres from 'Izbet Sarṭah is the site of Aphek, and cuneiform
texts have been found in the Late Bronze Age palace there,
testifying to scribal activity in the period preceding its destruction.
Lemaire supposes that our text is the work of an Israelite pupil
attending a Canaanite school at Aphek. Now, the 'Izbet Sarṭah
ostracon is probably to be associated with the Israelite settlement

---

[15] See M. Kochavi, 'An Ostracon of the Period of the Judges from 'Izbet
Sarṭah', *TA* 4 (1977), 1–13; A. Demsky, 'A Proto-Canaanite Abecedary Dating
from the Period of the Judges and its Implications for the History of the Alphabet',
TA 4 (1977), 14–27; F. M. Cross, 'Newly Found Inscriptions in Old Canaanite and
Early Phoenician Scripts', *BASOR* 238 (1980), 1–20; A. Demsky, 'The 'Izbet
Sarṭah Ostracon Ten years Later', in I. Finkelstein (ed.), *'Izbet Sarṭah: An Early
Iron Age Site Near Rosh Ha'ayin, Israel* (Oxford, 1986), 186–97. References to
other articles may be found in the last of these, with photographs of the ostracon
on p. 190, and on p. 64 of M. Kochavi *et al.*, *Aphek-Antipatris 1974–1977: The
Inscriptions* (Tel Aviv, 1978).

[16] But cf. J. Naveh, 'Some Considerations on the Otracon from 'Izbet Sarṭah',
IEJ 28 (1978), 31–5. The direction of writing does not seem to have yet been fixed;
cf. the earlier Canaanite inscription from Lachish, which is apparently to be read
boustrophedon, in F. M. Cross, 'An Old Canaanite Inscription Recently Found at
Lachish', *TA* 11 (1984), 71–6.

[17] Demsky 'A Proto-Canaanite Abecedary', 18 ff.

[18] G. Garbini, 'Sull' alphabetario di 'Izbet Sarṭah', *OA* 17 (1978), 287–95. See
also his *I fenici: storia e religione* (Naples, 1980), 23 ff.

[19] A. Dotan, 'New Light on the 'Izbet Sarṭah Ostracon', *TA* 8 (1981), 160–72.

in Stratum II of 'Izbet Ṣarṭah,[20] which has been dated to the end of the eleventh century BC,[21] somewhat later than the destruction by fire of the LB palace at Aphek in the second half of the thirteenth century. We may well question Lemaire's assertion that the scribal tradition there 'a vraisemblablement continué au xii–xième siècle',[22] since the Canaanites apparently did not continue to live there. Instead, Aphek seems to have been settled first by some unknown, non-Canaanite people (Stratum XI), and then, perhaps as early as the mid-twelfth century, by the Philistines (Stratum X). Israelite occupation did not begin until the early tenth century, around the same time that the Israelite settlement of 'Izbet Ṣarṭah finished.[23] Even the earliest settlement at 'Izbet Ṣarṭah (Stratum III), with which there is no reason to connect the text, would have overlapped only slightly, if at all, with Canaanite Aphek.[24] The writer of the 'Izbet Ṣarṭah ostracon could not, then, have attended either a Canaanite or an Israelite school in Aphek: if anything, the ostracon is evidence of the acquisition of literacy outside any school, unless we are to believe that even a small agricultural settlement the size of 'Izbet Ṣarṭah had its own school.[25]

(ii) *Gezer* The tenth-century inscription from Gezer, which apparently lists the agricultural activities associated with months, is well known, and has been viewed as a school exercise by a number of scholars.[26] The tablet is made of limestone, irregularly shaped and measuring 67–111 by 72 by 14–19 mm. The lower part is broken, but shows the top of what must have been a square or rectangular hole; on the reverse there is a deep indentation just above this. These holes may have been used for mounting the

[20] On the association of silo 605, in which the ostracon was found, with Stratum II, see Finkelstein, "Izbet Ṣarṭah', 18–20. For the identification of the site as Israelite: ibid. 201–4.

[21] Ibid. 201. M. Kochavi, 'An Ostracon of the Period of Judges', dated it slightly earlier, and Lemaire describes it as *c*. 12th–11th cent. BC. Finkelstein's date is to be preferred, but the earlier dates do not detract from my argument.

[22] Lemaire, *Les Ecoles et la formation de la Bible*, 10.

[23] For the history of Aphek, see M. Kochavi, 'The History and Archaeology of Aphek-Antipatris: A Biblical city in the Sharon Plain', *BA* 44 (1981), 75–86.

[24] See Finkelstein, "Izbet Ṣarṭah', 202 ff.

[25] The Stratum II population has been estimated at *c*. 100 people, living in twenty dwellings. Ibid. 114.

[26] References in Lemaire, *Les Ecoles et la formation de la Bible*, p. 87 nn. 16–18.

tablet in some way. The obverse has seven lines of script, written from right to left and parallel to the shorter side of the tablet, with a small, broken line of characters written vertically, apparently the name of the writer. The reverse seems to show traces of letters belonging to some previous text now erased; similar traces on the obverse have led scholars to describe the tablet as a 'palimpsest'.[27]

Lemaire compares this limestone tablet with three others, implying that they form a particular type of tablet used for school exercises. The first is a Phoenician tablet of unknown provenance, dated to the early eighth century. It seems originally to have been inscribed with an alphabet, written clumsily in boustrophedon, parallel to what would have been the longest side, were the tablet not broken. It now measures 42 by 30 by 17 mm., but Lemaire suggests elsewhere that the original width may have been about 80 mm.[28] The second is an Aramaic inscription from Tell Halaf, an abecedary which has recently been perceived amongst a mass of scratches on the stone. The fragment, however, although made of limestone, is clearly broken from a disc.[29] The third is a limestone tablet from Byblos, measuring 135 by 120 by 17 mm., with five lines of clumsy Phoenician script, apparently comprising a list of personal names; it too appears to be a 'palimpsest'.[30] Of these three, only the last is at all close in shape to the Gezer tablet, and there is no reason to believe that this one is a school exercise. Much closer in appearance are the incantation tablets from Arslan Tash (although their authenticity has recently been questioned), which are even less likely to be exercises.[31] They also resemble,

[27] Photographs in R. A. S. Macalister, *The Excavation of Gezer 1902–1905 and 1907–1909*, iii (London, 1912), pl. cxxvii, cf. ii. 24–8, and in D. Diringer, *Le iscrizioni antico-ebraiche palestinesi* (Florence, 1934), pls. I–II, cf. pp. 1–20.

[28] Published in A. Lemaire, 'Fragment d'un alphabet ouest-sémitique du viiie siècle av. J-C.', *Semitica*, 28 (1978), pp. 7–10 and pl. I.

[29] See R. Degen, 'Ein aramäisches Alphabet vom Tell Halaf', *NESE* 3 (1978), 1–9.

[30] Published in M. Dunand, *Fouilles de Byblos*, i. *1926–1932* (Paris, 1939), p. 95, no. 1452, and pl. 34 in vol. i. 'Atlas'.

[31] Published in R. du Mesnil du Buisson, 'Une tablette magique de la région du Moyen Euphrate', in *Mélanges syriens offerts à Monsieur René Dussaud*, i. (Paris, 1939), 421–34, and A. Caquot and R. du Mesnil du Buisson, 'La Seconde Tablette ou "petite amulette" d'Arslan-Tash', *Syria*, 48 (1971), 391–406. Their authenticity is questioned in J. Teixidor, 'Les Tablettes d'Arslan Tash au Musée d'Alep', *Aula Orientalis*, 1 (1983), 105–8, and P. Amiet, ibid. 109. A stone tablet from Zenjirli has a similar form and size: see F. von Luschan and W. Andrae, *Ausgrabungen in Sendschirli V* (Berlin, 1943), pp. 24 f., tb. 9–b, c.

much more closely than does the Gezer tablet, the type of wooden school exercise-boards found in Egypt.[32]

I doubt that any of this is significant. Lemaire's tablets do not constitute an obvious 'type', nor are they especially distinctive. More importantly, it seems most implausible that limestone would have been used in this way in schools. Pierced limestone tablets with a smooth surface would not be easy to make, which may account for the re-use of the Gezer tablet; they would be unwieldy in the hands of children, and readily chipped. Once used, the text could only be erased with difficulty, and would even then leave the sort of marks perceptible on the Gezer tablet. Is it really credible that such tablets would be thought preferable to tablets made of clay or wood?

The form of the tablet, then, is of little use as a guide to the interpretation of the contents, which have long been a source of scholarly debate. For Lemaire, the tablet is essentially a list of month names, 'un type d'exercice scolaire déjà connu en Égypte'.[33] On this view, the Egyptian examples, which are simple repetitive lists, numbering the months of each season, are possibly comparable.[34] The Gezer inscription, however, does not give simply the names of months, so far as we know them, nor is it a simple month-to-a-line calendar: although a total of twelve months can be reached, the inscription ceases then to be a simple list of each month, one at a time. The view that the inscription is a school exercise must remain only one of a number of possible explanations, and it is not an especially probable one. My own suspicion is that the purpose is in some sense magical or votive, as Wirgin argues.[35] Be that as it may, the content of the tablet no more requires the existence of a local school than does the form.

(iii) *Lachish* Lemaire cites three inscriptions from Lachish. The first was found scratched faintly on the rise of a limestone step,

---

[32] See G. Posener, 'Quatre tablettes scolaires de Basse Epoque (Aménémopé et Hardjédef)', *RdE* 18 (1966), 45–65. Egyptian writing-boards frequently had an appendix pierced by a hole for hanging them up.

[33] Lemaire, *Les Ecoles et la formation de la Bible*, 11.

[34] See U. Kaplony-Heckel, 'Schüler und Schulwesen in der ägyptischen Spätzeit', *SAK* 1 (1974), 227–46, esp. 234 f. and the translation of Bod. Eg. Inscr. 300 on p. 246.

[35] W. Wirgin, 'The Calendar Tablet from Gezer', *Eretz-Israel*, 6 (1960), 9*–12*.

under the upper stairway of Palace C,[36] and probably dates from
the ninth or eighth century. The first five letters of the alphabet
are written in order, along with some other, unintelligible signs
and some drawings, which include one of a lion roaring. Lemaire's
drawing follows that of the excavators,[37] which omits the large
space between the lion and the inscription on the 4-m.-wide step,
and gives an impression of a greater association between the two
than is necessarily the case.[38] The position from which the
inscription was written must have been rather awkward: 'Sitting
on a lower step with his back to the palace wall, the writer must
have stretched out his arm to scratch the letters diagonally across
the corner of the rise.'[39] This sounds more like the scrawling of
graffiti than the copying of a school exercise, which is how Lemaire
interprets it,[40] and in view of their position, his attempt to portray
both this and the drawings as formal exercises seems a little
absurd.[41]

The second inscription is on an ostracon found in the foundation
fill of Palace A and dated by Lemaire to the ninth century.[42] It is
partially erased, but Lemaire discerns an abecedary with some
letters misplaced, showing it to be the work of a beginner.[43] This
reading of the very faint characters is far from certain, which in
itself casts doubt on the evidential value of the ostracon.[44] If the
text is indeed an abecedary, then its writer has got it spectacularly
wrong, with three of the eleven letters misplaced, and too little
space left for many of the missing letters.

---

[36] See O. Tufnell *et al.*, *Lachish III* (London, 1953), pp. 67, 85, 118, 357 f., and
pl. 18: 2–4, 48B.   [37] Ibid., p. 118 fig. 10.

[38] See Diringer, in Tufnell, *Lachish III*, 357.   [39] Ibid.

[40] Cf. p. 256 of C. H. Inge, 'Excavations at Tell ed-Duweir', *PEQ* 70 (1938),
240–56.

[41] Cf. pp. 88 f. of M. Haran, 'Literacy and Schools in Ancient Israel', SVT 40
(1988), 81–95.

[42] No certain date can be ascertained from the archaeological context: see p. 31
of D. Ussishkin, 'Excavations at Tel Lachish 1973–1977: Preliminary Report', *TA*
5 (1978), 1–97. The ostracon was published by Lemaire in 'A Schoolboy's Exercise
on an Ostracon at Lachish', *TA* 3 (1976), pp. 109 f. and pl. 5. 2. Y. Aharoni has
appended to this a critical 'editor's note' (p. 110).

[43] Lemaire's opinion is broadly supported by E. Puech, who reconstructs the
inscription slightly differently, however, in p. 119 n. 4 of his 'Abécédaire et liste
alphabétique de noms hébreux du début du IIe s. AD', *RB* 87 (1980), 118–26.

[44] Aharoni, in his editor's note to Lemaire, 'A Schoolboy's Exercise', very
plausibly reads the characters at the end of the first line as hieratic numerals, which
suggests that this is not an abecedary. Lemaire's drawing is extremely optimistic.

The third inscription was incised on a jar before firing, and consists of a large symbol, a little like an arrow pointing upwards, followed by the letters '*b g d* (or *r*).[45] Lemaire assumes that this is the work of 'un jeune potier s'entraînant sur des vases non cuits'.[46] The first four letters of the alphabet crop up together elsewhere, in particular on a seal inscribed *l'bgd*, where they may be a name, 'Abigad'.[47] It is possible, then, that we are dealing with a name here, and that might be suggested by the context of the inscription. In any case, the jar, which was apparently fired and used, does not seem to have been merely a practice piece, and the letters are incised firmly and clearly. There is no special reason to suppose that it is the work of an apprentice, and no perceptible link with any sort of school, let alone the military academy about which Lemaire goes on to speak.

From these inscriptions, Lemaire concludes not only that Lachish had a school, possibly centred upon the palace fortress, but that it was a school for training army subalterns. With this he associates the complaint in Lachish ostracon 3, lines 8–13, where the writer protests at an accusation of illiteracy, perhaps a sarcastic comment on his failure to obey some order. According to Lemaire, he claims that he is able to repeat verbatim anything he has read. Such an ability, we are told, is the result of a school exercise, where pupils repeat what they have learnt off by heart from a document, another exercise 'qu'on connaissait déjà en Égypte'.[48] This repeats a claim made by Lemaire in an earlier work,[49] where

[45] See Ussishkin, 'Excavations at Tel Lachish', pp. 81 ff., fig. 25 and pl. 26.
[46] Lemaire, *Les Ecoles et la formation de la Bible*, 12.
[47] Published, appropriately, by N. Avigad in 'The Seal of Abigad', *IEJ* 18 (1968), pp. 52 f. and pl. 4c. The seal is probably 8th or 7th cent., and may be non-Israelite. Avigad cites an occurrence of the name in a much later Aramaic inscription, and it is perhaps also to be found on a Syrian seal of the 8th cent. published by P. Bordreuil and A. Lemaire in 'Nouveaux sceaux hébreux, araméens et ammonites', *Semitica*, 26 (1976), pp. 45–63, no. 25, where it is taken to be not a name, but a short abecedary. That the first of these reads *l'bgd* may indeed suggest the existence of the name, which is not attested in the OT, though Gad is known as an element in Hebrew and Phoenician names; see e.g. no. 64 on p. 220 of Diringer, *Le iscrizioni antico-ebraiche palestinesi*. However, Lemaire, 'Abecedaires et exercises' 226 f., cites a number of other seals in which the four letters, once preceded by *l*, are clearly part of an abecedary. For the view that they are apprentice pieces, see A. R. Millard, "BGD . . . -Magic Spell or Educational Exercise?', *Eretz-Israel*, 18 (1985), 39*–42*.
[48] Lemaire, *Les Ecoles et la Formation de la Bible*, 14 f.
[49] See A. Lemaire, *Inscriptions hébraïques*, i. *Les ostraca* (Paris, 1977), 100–9. E. Puech rejects Lemaire's interpretation in p. 199 n. 43 of his 'Les Ecoles dans l'Israël préexilique: données épigraphiques', *SVT* 40 (1988), 189–203.

he justifies his translation, reached by dividing a line rather differently from most scholars, and subsequently interpreting the letters as an unattested form of an unusual verb. Possibly such a treatment of this difficult text is justified, even if it has been rather literally interpreted; although there is no reference to school exercises in the *Ptahhotep* passage used to back the claim of an Egyptian model, where the reader is admonished to transmit faithfully the messages of his superiors, such exercises probably did exist in Egypt. However, like the ostraca cited, this evidence is far too weak to sustain Lemaire's detailed conclusions about a school in Lachish.

(iv) *Khirbet el-Qôm*   Three pairs of letters are scratched on the south wall of Tomb 1 at Khirbet el-Qôm. The first two are apparently '' and '*b*; the third is obscure, but may read *n l*.[50] Although the same juxtapositions of letters as in the first two pairs are found amidst the letters of the 'Izbet Ṣarṭah inscription, and although the second pair may be the beginning of an abecedary, Lemaire himself concedes that it would be hazardous to view this inscription as the work of a school pupil. Such reservations seem to be confirmed by the position of the inscription: the middle of an unlit, underground tomb, which has to be approached down a short shaft and through a narrow entrance (approx. 55 cm. sq.), is hardly likely to have served as a school.

(v) *Arad*   Lemaire lists a number of inscriptions from Arad which he believes to be school exercises, while admitting that such an interpretation remains very hypothetical for all but one of them. This exception is an inscription on a bowl, sherds of which were found in Stratum IX of the citadel (early eighth century). The name of the city is found engraved eight times on these sherds, written six times from right to left, but with the letters facing left to right in 'mirror writing', and twice from right to left; the writing is consistent only in its clumsiness.[51] Aharoni has suggested that the inscription was the work of an illiterate or an

---

[50] See pp. 157 f. of W. G. Dever, 'Iron Age Epigraphic Material from the Area of Khirbet el-Kôm', *HUCA* 40/41 (1969–70), 139–204.

[51] Description and photographs in Y. Aharoni and R. Amiran, 'Excavations at Tel Arad: Preliminary Report on the First Season, 1962', *IEJ* 24 (1964), 131–47, and in Y. Aharoni, *Arad Inscriptions* (English version: Jerusalem, 1981), 112 f.

apprentice, if it was not a game, while Yadin has proposed that it was the work of a Greek mercenary attempting to write Hebrew.[52] Whatever the purpose of the work, it seems improbable that it was done by somebody learning to write: the author had enough knowledge to form the letters correctly, and it is unlikely that he would not then be able to remember the direction of writing.[53] With one exception, which is incomplete and barely perceptible, all the writings of the name lie roughly on concentric circles around the plate. This suggests that the inscription is a crude and perhaps whimsical attempt to decorate the dish.

The second inscription cited is the intriguing ostracon 88, which appears to contain the pronouncement of a king. Although attributing it to differing circumstances, both Aharoni and Yadin have taken this to be an actual message.[54] Millard, on the other hand, has suggested tentatively that it may be a copy of a royal inscription, perhaps made by an apprentice scribe.[55] Lemaire is probably right to concede that the quality of the handwriting tells against it being an apprentice piece.

Ostracon 33, in which *ḥṭm*, 'wheat', recurs several times, followed by numbers and symbols of quantity, is almost certainly an inventory of some sort, and not a school exercise.[56] Ostracon 34 is probably also an inventory: it is difficult to read, but apparently contains a list of hieratic signs for goods and measurements, together with numerals.[57] It is possible that it was composed by an Egyptian scribe, as Aharoni suggests, but it is equally likely that the signs were employed by Israelites for their brevity and convenience. Ostracon 46 is probably another inventory. Ostraca 81 and 83 show some difficult and isolated symbols, the meaning of which is obscure; again, there is no reason to take them as school exercises.

---

[52] Y. Yadin, 'Four Epigraphical queries', *IEJ* 24 (1974), 30–6, esp. 30–2.

[53] Puech, 'Abécédaire et liste alphabetique', 194 f., argues that the plate must be regarded as a game, or in some way deliberate.

[54] Aharoni, *Arad Inscriptions*, 103 f.; Y. Yadin, 'The Historical Significance of Inscription 88 from Arad: A Suggestion', *IEJ* 26 (1976), 9–14. Aharoni attributes the message to Jehoahaz, Yadin to Aššur-uballiṭ. See also p. 290 n. 3 of D. Pardee, 'Letters from Tel Arad', *UF* 10 (1978), 289–336.

[55] See p. 26 of A. R. Millard, 'Epigraphic Notes, Aramaic and Hebrew', *PEQ* 110 (1978), 23–6.   [56] See Aharoni, *Arad Inscriptions*, 61.

[57] Ibid. 62–4 and S. Yeivin, 'A Hieratic Ostracon from Tel Arad', *IEJ* 16 (1966), 153–9.

down by Aharoni,[58] and is in fact an exercise in the drawing of the Egyptian hieroglyphs for 'year' (twice) and 'night'. There certainly is some resemblance to these signs (nos. M4 and N3 in Gardiner's sign-list),[59] but the combination makes no sense in Egyptian, and the symmetry of the piece supports Aharoni's view that it is a monogram or drawing. Ostracon 86 is unlikely to contain an exercise in writing letters, since there is no certainty that the strange signs upon it are, in fact, letters.[60] There is no reason to suppose that the isolated number on ostracon 87 is an exercise, not least because it is written regularly and confidently.[61] Finally, ostraca 50–7 each contain a single personal name, and Lemaire interprets these as exercises by school pupils learning to write their own names. Again, the high standard of writing tells against this, and Aharoni's idea that the names were used in a lottery or ballot, perhaps for priestly duties, is to be preferred.[62]

In general, then, Lemaire's evidence from Arad is unimpressive, as he concedes himself, and we cannot accept that any of it comes close to being credible evidence for the existence of a school in the town.

(vi) *Aroer* Lemaire cites two ostraca from Aroer in the Negev. On one there is apparently a single personal name, and he compares this to Arad ostraca 50–7. On the other is written *qr[* . . . , and he suggests that it may be a fragment of an abecedary.[63] However, there is no particular reason to suppose that the letters are not the beginning of a word, perhaps a name.[64]

(vii) *Qadesh-Barnea* Lemaire examines five ostraca from Qadesh-Barnea. The first is a triangular fragment, probably from the seventh century, at the bottom of which may be seen the tops of

---

[58] Aharoni, *Arad Inscriptions*, 102.

[59] A. Gardiner, *Egyptian Grammar*[3] (Oxford, 1957), 438–543.

[60] Aharoni, *Arad Inscriptions*, 102.   [61] Ibid.   [62] Ibid. 87.

[63] Lemaire, *Les Ecoles et la formation de la Bible*, 20; see also pp. 19 f. of his article 'Notes d'épigraphie nord-ouest sémitique', *Semitica*, 30 (1980), 17–32. For photographs and details of the locus, see A. Biran and R. Cohen, 'Aroer, 1977', *IEJ* 27 (1977), 250–1 and pl. 38.

[64] Maybe a place-name beginning *qryt* or a personal name like *qrh*. The combination *q r* is twice incised on the shoulders of pithoi at Kuntillet ʿAjrud, and Meshel suggests that they may stand for *qrbn*, 'sacrifice': see Z. Meshel, *Kuntillet ʿAjrud* (Jerusalem, 1978), p. 11 of the Eng. sect.

the letters z, ḥ, and ṭ. Lemaire reasonably supposes that it is part of an abecedary,[65] but it is clearly not the work of someone just learning to write: as he acknowledges elsewhere, the letters are 'écrites d'une main assurée.[66] On the second, Lemaire finds the words *mlʾ* and *wtʿsr*, each repeated once, and he supposes this to be a writing exercise. However, the ostracon is all but illegible, and the transcription speculative: the interpretation, as he concedes, must remain uncertain.

The remaining three ostraca all contain lists of hieratic numerals, the first and third having units of measure written beside the numerals.[67] The reading of the second is difficult, and the inscription may be a series of numbers all beginning with the same numerical signs, or a repetition several times of the same number. The third, which repeats whole sequences of numbers, is most plausibly interpreted, with Lemaire, as an exercise in the writing of numbers, and the same may be true of the others also, although in all the numbers are written confidently and apparently correctly. All are probably to be dated to the seventh century, and testify to the learning of the hieratic numeral system in Qadesh-Barnea at this time.

(viii) *Kuntillet ʿAjrud* Kuntillet ʿAjrud is set on the top of a steep hill in the desert, close to a junction of ancient trading roads and above some shallow wells. Traces have been found of only two structures, built close together on the plateau. One, the east building, was clearly of substantial size, but is very poorly preserved, and its function cannot be determined. The other, 'main' building, measuring about 25 by 15 m., is larger still and better preserved. It is centred on a courtyard, to the south and west of which lie large storerooms; the entrance to this courtyard is from the east, and bisects a long, narrow room lined with benches, the 'bench-

---

[65] See also R. Cohen on p. 72 of 'The Iron Age Fortresses in the Central Negev', *BASOR* 236 (1979), 61–79, and p. 98 of 'Excavations at Kadesh-Barnea 1976–1978', *BA* 44 (1981), 93–107. Photographs of the ostracon are to be found in both these articles.

[66] See p. 341 of A. Lemaire and P. Vernus, 'Les Ostraca paléo-hébreux de Qadesh-Barnéa', *Orientalia*, 49 (1980), 341–5.

[67] The third and largest of the ostraca had not yet been properly published when Lemaire wrote his 1981 book; see now A. Lemaire and P. Vernus, 'L'Ostracon paléo-hébreu No. 6 de Tell Qudeirat (Qadesh-Barnéa)', in M. Görg (ed.), *Fontes atque Pontes* (Wiesbaden, 1983), 302–26.

room'. At each end of this room are small rooms or compartments connected to it by windows above the benches: it was from these and from the bench-room itself that most of the inscriptions were recovered. The site is probably to be dated to the ninth and eighth centuries.[68]

The inscriptions which Lemaire cites as school exercises are of various types. First of all he discerns three abecedaries on the shoulder of the second large pithos recovered. The uppermost of these runs from *ṭ* to *t*,[69] the second, parallel to it and underneath, from ʿ to *t*, and the third, below that, from *k* to *t*. The first and third abecedaries are written in a highly cursive style, the second being smaller and squarer. Lemaire's interpretation is that the first and third are the work of an experienced writer, teaching a pupil who is responsible for the second. Such an interpretation is improbable, however, if Lemaire's own reading is correct: the first and third abecedaries adopt the order *pe ʿayin*, but the second has *ʿayin pe*. These orders are alternatives, both known from elsewhere, but it is unlikely that a pupil following a teacher's example would adopt a different, alternative order. It is equally unlikely that such a pupil would also write his letters in a fashion which is quite correct but radically different in style: nothing in the second abecedary suggests that its writer is attempting to imitate either the first or the third, and there are some grounds for supposing that it was written before them.[70]

On the same pithos, the word *šʿrm* is supposedly written twice, between the second and third abecedaries, although the first

---

[68] See Z. Meshel, *Kuntillet ʿAjrud*.

[69] Lemaire curiously omits the last two letters from his drawing (*Les Ecoles et la Formation de la Bible*, 27).

[70] As regards the order of the letters, there is a round mark above and to the right of the *ṣade* in Meshel's photograph, but the *ʿayin* is clearly visible to the right of the *pe*, where Lemaire places it in his drawing. Puech has noted this discrepancy, and in his own drawing takes the mark to be the *ʿayin*. However, he denies that the alphabets are a school exercise, since: *1.* the second abecedary is, on paleographic grounds, to be dated earlier than the first and third; *2.* the first and third alphabets are written over the margin line of another text, and therefore after it, while the second is well to the right of it; *3.* that the writer of the first abecedary had to write on the handle of the pot shows that his space was more restricted than that of the writer of the second. So the second abecedary predates the first and third, and cannot be a copy. See p. 363 and fig. 3 of E. Puech's response to the papers by Lemaire and Levine, in J. Amitai (ed.), *Biblical Archaeology Today* (Jerusalem, 1985), 354–65. See also Puech, 'Les Ecoles dans l'Israël préexilique', 191 f.

occurrence is barely legible, and seems to be preceded by a *he*. Lemaire takes this to be an exercise in the repeated writing of a word. If so, and his reading is questionable, it is a very brief exercise indeed.[71] Two short sentences from the first and second pithoi, both beginning with '*mr*, and ending with blessings, are taken to be letter formulae, and compared with formulae from elsewhere. The resemblance is not striking: the first sentence is too fragmentary for a proper grammatical analysis, but in the second the '*mr* is clearly the 3 m.s. perf. qal of the verb, while in the letter formulae it is an imperative.[72] Next, Lemaire takes the drawings on the pithoi to be the result of drawing classes: the good ones on the first pithos are the work of the teacher, and the somewhat cruder attempts on the second the work of pupils.[73] Finally, he suggests that the various inscriptions in Phoenician which were found at the site, of which a number are benedictions, were intended as aids in the teaching of Phoenician.

From this evidence Lemaire concludes that there was a school at Kuntillet ʿAjrud: the bench-room served as a classroom, and the pithoi as blackboards. However, this room is only about 2 m. wide, with less than a metre between the benches, and about 7 m. long, with the main entrance to the building running through the middle. It would not make a comfortable or practical classroom. More importantly, where are the pupils supposed to have come from? Kuntillet ʿAjrud was two buildings on the top of a steep hill in the desert, many miles from any known settlement. Even if Lemaire's interpretation of the inscriptions were plausible, the position and nature of the site would rule out the possibility that there was a school there. Far more likely is the view of most scholars that the bench-room served some religious purpose, with which the inscriptions are to be associated, while the position of the site as a whole, and its abundant storage facilities, may suggest

---

[71] Puech reads not a repeated word, but the two words *šmrn* and *šʿrm*: 'Response to Lemaire and Levine' and 'Les Ecoles dans l'Israël préexilique'.

[72] See D. Pardee, *Handbook of Ancient Hebrew Letters* (Chico, Calif., 1982), 120 f.; the '*mr* . . . *l* formula is attested only twice in N. W. Semitic letters of the first millennium.

[73] On the wall-paintings and drawings, see P. Beck, 'The Drawings from Horvat Teiman (Kuntillet ʿAjrud)', *TA* 9 (1982), 3–68. This emphasizes the Phoenician–Syrian background of the iconography and suggests that the wall-paintings, at least, were the work of itinerant artisans.

that it served as an ancient equivalent of the motorway service station.[74]

(ix) *Abecedaries: General Considerations.* We have encountered a number of abecedaries, partial abecedaries, and groups of letters which may be partial abecedaries. If not commonplace, such inscriptions are certainly not very rare: many have been found outside Israel and from a later period within Israel. Yet even among the few we have discussed, some, most especially those in the tomb at Khirbet el-Qôm and in the bench-room at Kuntillet ʿAjrud, cannot plausibly mark the site of a school. As Haran has pointed out, this is true also of some later abecedaries, including that in the cave at Naḥal Michmash, which was home to a single family and approachable only by rope ladder.[75] It seems clear that no link necessarily exists between abecedaries and schools. Are abecedaries, in fact, writing exercises at all? There is no simple answer to such a question: Haran suggests that some should be viewed as practice work by apprentice craftsmen, which has a ring of plausibility, but he rightly acknowledges that this is unlikely to be the full explanation. The letters on the step at Lachish seem to be a simple graffito, and it may be that this doodling of letters was quite common. I have speculated that the repetition of the name of the city on the bowl from Arad was an attempt to decorate it, and this seems quite clearly to have been the case with an abecedary inscribed around a dish from Deir ʿAlla.[76] Given the possibly religious context of the abecedaries at Kuntillet ʿAjrud, on the other hand, there is surely some weight in the suggestion that writing, and abecedaries in particular, were seen to be endowed with some magical or mystical significance, as was the case in classical times.[77] In this context, it is worth noting the

[74] Analysis of the material used in the pottery shows that it was not made locally, but probably brought in along the nearby trade routes: the site cannot be connected with any local settlement. See J. Gunneweg, I. Perlman, and Z. Meshel, 'The Origin of the Pottery of Kuntillet ʿAjrud', *IEJ* 35 (1985), 270–83. Meshel's identification of the site as a religious shrine has also been rejected, in favour of the view that it was a way-station, by J. M. Hadley in 'Yahweh's Asherah in the Light of Recent Discovery', Ph.D. thesis (Cambridge, 1989), 143–58.

[75] M. Haran, 'Literacy and Schools in Ancient Israel'.

[76] See Lemaire, 'Abécédaires et exercises', 225 f.; also J. Hoftijzer and G. Van der Kooij, *Aramaic Texts from Deir ʿAlla* (Leiden, 1976), p. 267 and pl. 22.

[77] Cf. pp. 354 f. of J. Teixidor, 'Bulletin d'épigraphie sémitique 1978–1979', *Syria*, 56 (1979), 353–405.

particular association of biblical and Babylonian acrostics with hymns, prayers, and, perhaps, the cult.[78] There is probably no single interpretation to be put on all the abecedaries which have been recovered, and the automatic association of abecedaries with the learning of writing, let alone with schools, is to be regarded with profound suspicion.

(b) *Schools and Writing*

Learning to write was not a simple process in Egypt or Mesopotamia, where the sheer number of phonetic signs employed, the use of non-phonetic determinatives, and archaizing orthography all contrived to make considerable experience in the reading of texts a virtual prerequisite. There is, however, a fundamental difference between the alphabetic system used in Israel and the writing-systems of these nations: it was designed to be easy to learn, and they were not. Albright's well-worn dictum is still worth quoting:

Since the forms of the letters are very simple, the 22-letter alphabet could be learned in a day or two by a bright student and in a week or two by the dullest; hence it could spread with great rapidity. I do not doubt for a moment that there were many urchins in various parts of Palestine who could read and write as early as the time of the Judges . . . [79]

Albright's assumption that the ease of writing must in itself have led to widespread literacy has very properly been challenged,[80] but his main point is surely indisputable: the Phoenician alphabet adopted and then adapted in Israel is neither complicated nor arcane. The system of writing was not an obstacle to the acquisition of literacy in Israel, and it is not necessary to suppose that lengthy schooling and a course in reading literature was necessary for a good grasp of the essentials. The argument has been advanced, however, that such schooling *must* be hypothesized, as the only explanation for a perceived uniformity of script and orthography in Hebrew inscriptions.[81]

---

[78] See W. M. Soll, 'Babylonian and Biblical Acrostics', *Biblica*, 69 (1988), 305–83.

[79] W. F. Albright in C. H. Kraeling and R. M. Adams (eds.), *City Invincible* (Chicago, 1960), 123.

[80] See S. Warner, 'The Alphabet: An Innovation and its Diffusion', *VT* 30 (1980), 81–90.

[81] See Lang, 'Schule und Unterricht im alten Israel', 190–2, Puech, 'Les Ecoles dans l'Israël préexilique', 201, and Aharoni, *Arad Inscriptions*, 130.

There would be some force in this argument if orthography and script in the early Israelite inscriptions showed any marked tendency toward conservatism or any other form of artificiality, but they do not. In fact, as regards orthography, there is regional variation in the representation of vowels, expressing differences in pronunciation, while the use of *matres lectionis* is far from consistent, and shows considerable development over time. Even as late as the sixth century, orthographic variation is found within the official correspondence from Arad and Lachish.[82] Such adaptation and development is hardly evidence of a static tradition of orthography, and the general uniformity of orthography is explained simply by the nature of the script: it is really quite hard to come up with alternative spellings of a word when the alphabet offers little or no choice of characters to represent a given sound; it was only with the widespread use of the more ambiguous vowel letters, in a later period, that great variation was able to occur. As regards the script, it is simply a fallacy to suppose that it was uniform: it went through periods of very rapid development, and different styles certainly existed side by side.[83] There is nothing in the fact of writing, in the orthography, or in the development of the script which demands the existence of schools or of lengthy schooling.

We cannot go into the question of literacy here, beyond saying that there seems to be some consensus emerging among scholars that writing in Israel before the Exile was not simply confined to a small class of professional scribes. Many of the inscriptions discovered, especially those incised on pots before firing and carved on seals, are clearly the work of artisans rather than scribes, while there is biblical and epigraphic evidence to suggest

[82] The classic review of the subject, now rather dated, is F. M. Cross and D. N. Freedman, *Early Hebrew Orthography* (New Haven, Conn., 1952). See esp. pp. 45–60 there, and also D. N. Freedman, 'The Orthography of the Arad Ostraca', *IEJ* 19 (1969), 52–56, although some of the views expressed in the latter must also be corrected in the light of new material: see Aharoni, *Arad Inscriptions*, 142. J. Naveh, *Early History of the Alphabet* (Leiden, 1982), 76 ff. gives a useful summary, but the most thorough recent work is Z. Zevit, *Matres Lectionis in Ancient Hebrew Epigraphs* (Cambridge, Mass., 1980).

[83] See F. M. Cross, 'Epigraphic Notes on Hebrew Documents of the Eighth to Sixth Centuries BC.; ii. The Murabba'at Papyrus and the Letter Found near Yabneh Yam', *BASOR* 165 (1962), 34–42, and *idem*, iii. 'The Inscribed Jar Handles from Gibeon', *BASOR* 168 (1962), 18–23. Also J. Naveh, A. Palaeographic Note on the Distribution of the Hebrew Script', *HTR* 61 (1968), 68–74.

that many Israelites who were neither scribes nor artisans possessed some degree of literacy.[84] Arguments from silence, against the existence of anything, draw their strength from the reasonableness of the expectation that there should be evidence of that thing if it existed. If literacy was acquired only or mainly through schooling, a lot of literate people would imply the existence of a lot of schools, and the expectation that there should be some clear biblical or archaeological evidence for such schools becomes correspondingly more reasonable. Since such evidence is almost negligible, consisting only of evidence for instruction in numerals and measures at Qadesh-Barnea in the closing decades of the southern kingdom, it is difficult to maintain that the use of writing in Israel was dependent upon the existence of schools.

(c) *Schools: Conclusions*

The biblical and epigraphic evidence adduced for schools in Israel seems very weak indeed, and can certainly not support any hypothesis of a large, integrated, school system. If the existence of schools cannot be proved, though, it cannot be disproved either: all we can say for certain is that it should not be presumed. For the rest of this chapter, I wish to look more specifically at the education of administrators in Israel, and the relevance of this to the wisdom literature.

3. *Schools, Scribes, and the Wisdom Literature*

The difference in the type of script, and the evidence for some degree of literacy far outside the scribal profession, mean that we should be very wary of assuming that Egyptian or Mesopotamian education can be used as a guide to the nature of education in Israel. Even Ugarit, which possessed an alphabetic script, is a poor potential analogy, since Akkadian seems to have played a role there which is unattested in Israel. Furthermore, the different histories and different administrative needs of each nation are likely to have necessitated different systems and different types of education.[85] For these reasons, the sporadic debate about relative

[84] See A. R. Millard, 'An Assessment of the Evidence for Writing in ancient Israel', in Amitai (ed.), *Biblical Archaeology Today*, 301–12, and the responses by A. Demsky and J. Naveh on 349–54; also Haran, 'Literacy and Schools'.
[85] Cf. D. W. Jamieson-Drake, *Scribes and Schools in Monarchic Judah* (Sheffield, 1991), 152–4.

stages of advancement in the various nations is misguided:[86]
administration and education are a function of structures, needs,
and history within a society, and there is no uniform path of
development. Equally, there is no evidence of some universal
scribal culture towards which the administrators of each nation
might aspire. Relevant to this, of course, is the evidence studied
in the last chapter. If, as we have seen, concrete evidence is
lacking for the suggestion that Israel imitated the administrative
system of Egypt, it is hardly something which we should suppose
on theoretical or analogical grounds. The needs of the Israelite
administration, and the skills required, therefore, of administrators, must be assessed in terms of the archaeological and
biblical evidence for Israelite society, economy, and organization,
not on the basis of the quite different systems which evolved
elsewhere. That is not a study which I can undertake here, but
there are some assumptions about officials in Israel which do need
to be questioned.

Chief among these is the belief that officials must have been
involved in the production of literature. This is not a pursuit or
skill which follows necessarily from administrative skill: literacy
may be a *sine qua non* for the composition of literature, but one
can be literate and yet not feel the urge to write books. The Old
Testament itself demonstrates quite clearly that literature in Israel
was not a scribal monopoly, and there is no pre-exilic literature,
indeed, which can unequivocally be attributed to the activity of
officials.[87] That does not, of course, rule out the possibility that
individual scribes, along with anyone else sufficiently literate,
might have composed literature.

Furthermore, I see no good reason to presuppose that literature
was employed in the education of scribes. Since there were, to our
knowledge, no 'classical' or literary languages to be learnt, and no
requirement for extensive reading in order to master the script, an
education similar to that of an Egyptian or Babylonian scribe
would have been both unnecessary and extravagant in Israel. The

---

[86] See Crenshaw, 'Education in Ancient Israel', 609 f.

[87] M. Weinfeld's argument for the scribal origin of Deuteronomy rests upon the
assumption that wisdom is scribal, and also upon a misinterpretation of Jer 8. 8:
see M. Weinfeld, *Deuteronomy and the Deuteronomic School* (Oxford, 1972), esp.
158–78, 244–97, and cf. J. Malfroy, 'Sagesse et loi dans le Deuteronome: Etudes',
VT 15 (1965) 49–65. The post-exilic situation, and 'scribes', are to be understood
rather differently.

degree of literacy required and the specialist knowledge to be learned are quite compatible with the idea of training through apprenticeship or within hereditary families of scribes. Although it is again an argument from silence, it is worth recalling that Israel has yielded no counterparts to the numerous Egyptian ostraca which reflect the copying of literature in schools there. Particular things might, of course, be taught formally to those who needed them: hence, perhaps, the instruction in hieratic numerals at Qadesh-Barnea.

One area of specialized learning which might well have been taught formally, using literature, is that of foreign languages. It seems possible, moreover, that this was one route through which foreign wisdom literature might have entered Israel and been translated. This must, however, be put in context. In the first place, the number of scribes actually involved in foreign relations, and requiring foreign languages, is likely to have been fairly small, and probably, from about the eighth century, Aramaic would have sufficed for most purposes.[88] It is difficult to think of any practical reason for Israelite scribes to have learnt Middle Egyptian (which was archaic many hundreds of years before Solomon) or Sumerian: the languages in which much of the foreign literature was written are most unlikely to have played any role in international affairs.

Furthermore, only in the case of *Amenemope* do we have good reason to suppose that an actual text, or some version of it, was known in Israel. Most of the close parallels to other works are scattered and isolated. In part this may be due to the influence of texts or traditions unknown to us, but I think it is also probable that some proportion of the transmission was oral and piecemeal. The number of people who spoke Hebrew or some closely related language but were able to understand spoken Egyptian is likely to have been much higher than the number able to read Egyptian,[89] and sayings may have been spread through trade or via the many Semites resident in Egypt at various times. Finally, the Exile and the settlement of Jews in Mesopotamia and Egypt may have played an important role, though this importance varies according to the date one assigns to the wisdom literature. Scribal training

[88] Cf. 2 Kgs. 18. 26 for knowledge and use of Aramaic by Israelite officials at this time.

[89] It is interesting to note that the teaching of Egyptian to a Semite is one of the examples given in the epilogue to *Any* for the educability of man.

in foreign languages may, then, have had some part in the transmission of foreign wisdom literature, but it is not the only way of understanding that transmission, nor should skill in languages be assumed to have been a part of the training for all scribes.

On other areas of administrative expertise, the relationship to the wisdom literature is very general: there is nothing in Proverbs which would have been of interest or use solely to a scribe. However, the assumption that wisdom is 'scribal' has led to some curiously narrow interpretations of wisdom interests. The emphasis on the value of speech and persuasiveness, for example, need hardly be interpreted in terms of rhetorical skill,[90] nor counsel viewed solely as political advice: where these are related to the court or to government, this is simply an aspect of them, and sometimes, clearly, just illustrative.[91]

4. *Schools: Conclusions*

Its use in schools has long been viewed as a central influence on the development of the wisdom literature, and has been seen by some scholars as the medium through which wisdom literature exerted an influence on other areas of the biblical tradition. Were it reasonably clear that schools actually existed, then we might at least entertain the possibility that wisdom literature was used in them, or even composed for use in them. However, there is neither any strong evidence for schools nor any convincing reason to suppose that they would have existed. Our ignorance of educational methods in Israel remains profound, and claims for the use of wisdom literature in schools are entirely speculative.

[90] This idea may have been influenced by misconceptions about the idea of 'perfect speech' in the Egyptian instructions. This does not indicate rhetorical ability but the embodiment of perfection and truth in speech: the first maxim of *Ptahhotep* points out that it is rare and hidden, but may be found among maids at the grindstone. On this, see e.g. R. B. Parkinson, *Voices from Ancient Egypt* (London, 1991), 66.

[91] Thus Prov. 24. 5 f. uses the value of wisdom in war to illustrate the general principle that brains are better than brawn.

Conclusions

In the preceding chapters I have reviewed the main issues and evidence involved in the theory that wisdom literature arose as an administrative and pedagogical literature. Other evidence has, of course, been adduced from time to time. In some cases I have omitted discussion of this because I believe it to constitute not evidence for the theory so much as an assumption based upon it; admittedly, it is sometimes difficult to disentangle the two, particularly in form-critical discussions. A few common claims have also been passed over because lengthy discussion seems inappropriate where a little common sense will do. An example of this is the assertion that wisdom's 'internationalism' shows it to be scribal. This may distinguish the wisdom literature from many historical and prophetic texts, but the conventional non-nationalism of wisdom literature is hardly 'scribal' in itself: Egypt's scribal culture was supremely nationalistic and disdainful of other nations. More important issues are raised, I think, by the other ways in which wisdom literature seems 'different', and there is much work to be done on these distinctive characteristics, and on the question of whether they are attributable more to origin than to convention within the genre. Such problems are outside the scope of this study, and need not be linked to a scribal theory of wisdom's origins. That theory relies principally on some or all of the evidence reviewed above, and it stands or falls with such evidence.

Literature similar to that preserved in Proverbs is amongst the earliest literature recovered from Egypt and Mesopotamia. In those regions it appears to have been 'high literature', composed by members of the literate, scribal élite and reflecting their outlook, but not designed solely or specifically to meet their professional and educational needs. Its wide interests and applicability allowed it to spread beyond national boundaries in a way quite unparalleled by any other known ancient literature of the region, but the mechanisms which enabled this are not clearly

known. When we consider a work like *Ahikar*—probably Syrian
in origin, but set in Assyria, read by Jews on an island in the Nile,
and adapted into numerous different versions—all bets must be
off.

However they reached Israel, such works do seem to have
influenced the Israelite wisdom literature very strongly. There is
little or no reason to suppose that this reflects any broader
imitation of a foreign scribal class or administration, let alone an
Egyptian one in particular. After all, cross-influences between the
foreign texts are often perceptible without any indication of
corresponding political influences. There is evidence for both
Egyptian and Mesopotamian influence on Israelite wisdom, as well
as close parallels with *Ahikar*, so such influence is unlikely to have
come from a single direction, and may, of course, have happened
over a long period.

Most of the material in Proverbs conforms to structural and
thematic conventions known from other countries. In some cases,
sayings, themes, or types of unit have clearly been borrowed with
little substantial change. There is also, however, some indication
of creative adaptation and of alignment to Hebrew poetic conventions. The sentence literature, as elsewhere, shows signs of careful
arrangement, but with a view more to a smooth flow and formal
consistency than to the treatment of particular themes. The
sayings and instructions themselves embrace many topics and
situations, often displaying great pithiness or wit. Some show
an interest in the king and his court, but vary considerably in
their opinion. The few which are unabashedly loyal show many
close correspondences to foreign sayings, and little sign of any
specifically Israelite input.

Religious ideas are important in the foreign texts from earliest
times, and are a major theme in Egyptian instructions from the
New Kingdom onwards. They seem to have been important in
Israel also, and there is no reason to suppose that this is a late
innovation within Israelite wisdom. Often entwined with sayings
about the king, religious observations in the sentence literature
may reflect the common wisdom preoccupations with justice and
with the forces which have power over the individual. It is likely,
although not demonstrable, that religious sayings and motifs
borrowed from elsewhere were understood within the context of
mainstream Israelite beliefs.

When we come to consider the authorship of the texts, it is obviously tempting to associate the wisdom literature with the 'wise men' mentioned elsewhere in the OT. On closer examination, however, these references do not appear to be to any single group or class. The story of Joseph is of no more help: it bears little resemblance to the wisdom literature, and its protagonist cannot be considered an embodiment of wisdom ideals. In short, our best chance of establishing authorship is through a consideration of the assumptions made in the literature itself, bearing in mind the complication of conventions inherited from abroad. That is too lengthy a study to undertake here.

Finally, there is the question of purpose. In broad terms, the wisdom literature is certainly educational, although the sentence literature, in particular, blends in a strong element of humour and cynicism. It is, however, preceptive and exhortatory, not informative. Thus, for all the sayings about the importance of speech, there is no instruction on *how* to speak well; nor, for that matter, is there even any description of what constitutes 'righteousness'. Proverbs moralizes, and encourages its readers to pursue certain ideals or patterns of behaviour, but assumes that they will know about them already. This is never clearer than in chs. 1–9, but it is true of the book as a whole. Nobody seeking rhetorical skill, a precise knowledge of etiquette, or almost any practical ability, would turn to the wisdom literature, which is at best sporadically helpful in such matters. It should be said that the same is true of most comparable non-Israelite literature.

In view of this, the Israelite literature might make elevating reading for adults or children, but would be of little use in training them either for a profession or for a way of life. There is, moreover, no evidence to suggest that it was ever more functionally orientated. When the arrangement of the material is also taken into account, with topic so frequently subsidiary to sound, it seems highly unlikely that it could ever have been intended primarily to teach at an elementary level. Instructions were used in Egyptian schools because they were classic works, written in a high literary style in the classical languages, and were morally elevating; if there were any Israelite schools, and if they did use the wisdom literature, both suppositions for which we have no evidence, then this would be a reasonable explanation for educational use in Israel too.

Without specifying the date or the authors, who may indeed have included scribes or anyone else able to write, it is clearly possible to present a strong case for the wisdom literature being 'high literature' in Israel too. By such a reckoning, its authors or redactors composed or sought out sayings, from near and far, for their pithiness or pointedness; they then adapted and arranged them to pleasing effect. This is, substantially, the technique attributed to Qoheleth in Qoh. 12. 9 ff. As for Qoheleth, the audience may have been 'the people', or at least those to whom books were accessible, and the purpose similarly to combine pleasure with a moral prod.

It is much harder to make out a case for wisdom literature in Israel having been composed specifically for the professional and educational purposes of the state administrators. First of all, this theory demands that the material we possess now has changed very substantially from the earliest, more practical, wisdom literature. McKane, perhaps, sees this rather more clearly than von Rad. The proportion of material specifically relevant to administrative matters is all but negligible in Proverbs, and its position insignificant. If the earliest material was much the same as that which we have now, then the redactors' status as administrators seems quite incidental, and hardly worth mentioning. There is, however, no evidence to suggest that any substantial change or reinterpretation has occurred, while the closest foreign parallels would hardly lead us to look for such a change.

In order to justify the assumption of change, then, other evidence has to be adduced. McKane's preference, as we have seen, is to rest his case on suppositions about 'wise men' elsewhere in the OT. This does not seem a very strong basis. Other scholars concentrate on Solomon and his administration. This has the merit of some biblical support in the account of Solomon's reign and in the association of his name with wisdom literature. On the other hand, these may reflect much later interpretations of the original Solomon tradition, and more weight is normally put upon evidence for his imitation of Egyptian practices. From what we know of Solomon's administration, however, it was largely derived from that of his father, and if Solomon looked north and south, David's view seems to have been confined to Palestine and Transjordan. Those few official posts for which Egyptian models are suggested seem mostly to predate Solomon, and anyway, we know too little about them for any proper judgement about their origins.

In other words, then, the theory is forced to posit changes in the literature which are improbable, and for which there is no evidence. It is forced to assume that Israel ignored the general nature of wisdom literature abroad, in order to imitate only its role in the Egyptian school system, but is unable to present any evidence for the existence of such a system in Israel or any reason why Israel should wish to copy the structures of such a different society. It is forced to emphasize a tiny proportion of Proverbs for no good exegetical reason, and to make historical assumptions for which the evidence is, at the very best, extremely slender. In short, it is a theory for which little or no direct evidence can be found, and which requires many improbable assumptions. At the very least, it is not a theory which should be taken for granted as an 'assured result'.

Appendix: The Non-Israelite Sources

This list is intended to provide a brief introduction to the available ancient Near Eastern texts which are directly relevant to the study of Proverbs. The selection is not based entirely, however, on close similarity to the biblical material: for Egypt I have tried to include all those texts which properly belong to the genre 'instruction', not just those which resemble material in Proverbs; for Mesopotamia, where some of the distinctions are less clearcut, I have attempted to include all texts which belong to the tradition of sayings-collection. A few of the works do not fall clearly into these categories, but their relevance should be obvious. Egyptian texts which are certainly later than Proverbs have been included in order to indicate the development of the traditions there, but I have not dealt with the Greek collections, the *Syriac Sentences of Menander*, the later versions of *Ahikar*, or any of the numerous other works which are important for later Israelite wisdom literature, but less so for Proverbs. For discussion of such later works, the reader is referred to M. Küchler, *Frühjüdische Weisheitstraditionen* (Freiburg and Göttingen, 1979).

In my treatment of the individual works, I have been constrained by the information available and by the limits of my own competence in the languages. For unpublished texts and Mesopotamian material available only in facsimile or transcription, I have been entirely dependent on the secondary literature. For practical reasons, I have only summarized in detail the contents of texts which are short or limited in their scope, and have avoided lengthy discussion of issues which are of little relevance to the biblical material. Egyptian sources have been arranged by period and then, where relevant, by language or script. For Mesopotamia, where dating is often more difficult, the sources are arranged by language.

I have provided general bibliographies for Egypt and Mesopotamia, and a select bibliography for each text. Where appropriate this is in two parts: the first includes editions, descriptions, and similar works, while the second covers more general articles relevant to specific points in my description. Neither is intended to be exhaustive. Much of the Akkadian material has been collected previously in W. G. Lambert, *Babylonian Wisdom Literature* (Oxford, 1960): for such works I have given only a reference to *BWL* and a supplementary bibliography.

A. EGYPT

Collected translations:

M. Lichtheim, *Ancient Egyptian Literature* (Berkeley, Calif., Los Angeles, and London; 1973, 1976, 1980) has many of the texts, plus bibliographical and other information. H. Brunner, *Altägyptische Weisheit* (Darmstadt, 1988) has fuller coverage, bibliographies, and a lengthy introduction. J. Lévêque, *Sagesses de l'Egypte ancienne* (Paris, 1983), is useful.

Bibliographies and surveys:

E. Hornung and O. Keel (eds.), *Studien zu altägyptischen Lebenslehren* (Freiburg and Göttingen, 1979), 363–91; M. V. Fox, 'Two Decades of Research in Egyptian Wisdom Literature', *ZÄS* 107 (1980), 120–35, esp. 131–5. R. J. Williams, 'The Sages of Ancient Egypt in the Light of Recent Scholarship', *JAOS* 101/1 (1981), 1–19, complements the bibliography in J. Leclant, 'Documents nouveaux et points de vue récents sur les sagesses de l'Egypte ancienne', in *Les Sagesses du Proche-Orient ancien: Colloque de Strasbourg 17–19 mai 1963* (Paris, 1963), 5–26, esp. 18 ff. For the Middle Kingdom literature, R. Parkinson, 'Tales, Teachings and Discourses from the Middle Kingdom', in S. Quirke (ed.), *Middle Kingdom Studies* (New Malden, 1991), supplements G. Posener, 'Les Richesses inconnues de la littérature égyptienne', *RdE* 6 (1951), 27–48, *RdE* 9 (1952), 117–20. See also M. Bellion, *Egypte ancienne: Catalogue des manuscrits hiéro-glyphiques et hiératiques et des dessins, sur papyrus, cuir ou tissu publiés ou signalés* (Paris, 1987), 328–41. For a general treatment and bibliography of the major instructions, see the relevant articles on pp. 963–92 of vol. 3 in the *Lexikon der Ägyptologie* (Wiesbaden, 1980). G. Burkard, *Textkritische Untersuchungen zu ägyptischen Weisheitslehren des alten und mittleren Reichs* (Wiesbaden, 1977), examines textual issues in several of the earlier instructions.

1. Before the New Kingdom

(i) *The Instruction of Hardjedef* (= *Djedefhor*)   The attribution to a famous Fourth Dynasty Prince is probably pseudonymous, and a date after the Old Kingdom seems likely. The extant text advocates the establishment of a household and careful preparations for the treatment of one's body after death.

1. E. Brunner-Traut, 'Die Weisheitslehre des Djedef-Hor', *ZÄS* 76 (1940), 3–9; G. Posener, 'Le Début de l'enseignement de Hardjedef (Recherches littéraires iv)', *RdE* 9 (1952), 109–17, and 'Quatre tablettes scolaires de Basse Epoque (Aménémopé et Hardjedef)', *RdE* 18 (1966), 45–65, esp. 62 ff.; W. Helck, *Die Lehre des*

Djedefhor und die Lehre eines Vaters an seinen Sohn (Wiesbaden, 1984).
2. W. Helck, 'Zur Frage der Enstehung der ägyptischen Literatur', *WZKM* 63/64 (1972), 6–26, esp. 16–19; H. Brunner, 'Zitate aus Lebenslehren', in E. Hornung and O. Keel (eds.), *Studien zu altägyptischen Lebenslehren* (Freiburg and Göttingen, 1979), 105–71, esp. 117 f., 122.

(ii) *The Instruction of Kagemni*   The beginning is lost; our copy precedes *Ptahhotep* on Papyrus Prisse. Attributed to a vizier under the Third Dynasty, it too is most probably later and pseudonymous. The instruction commends silence and respectfulness, the avoidance of gluttony, and discreet behaviour at the table of the glutton or drunkard. It concludes with the advice to let one's reputation spread without resort to self-advertisement or bragging, lest one arouse opposition and divine punishment. A narrative epilogue describes the grateful acceptance of the vizier's instruction by his children, and the accession to office of Kagemni, who is among them.

G. Jéquier, *Le Papyrus Prisse et ses variantes* (Paris, 1911), pl. I, cf. p. 9; A. Scharff, 'Die Lehre für Kagemni', *ZÄS* 77 (1942), 13–21; A. H. Gardiner, 'The Instruction Addressed to Kagemni and his Brethren', *JEA* 32 (1946), 71–4.

(iii) *The Instruction of Ptahhotep*   Several copies are extant, but the only complete one, Papyrus Prisse, differs from the others in important respects, and we must reckon with early divergent textual traditions. The work was probably composed in the Twelfth Dynasty, despite the attribution to a Fifth Dynasty vizier: the language is Middle Egyptian and other evidence points to a Middle Kingdom date. In a long prologue, the vizier describes the onset of his old age, and receives royal permission to instruct his son. Thirty-seven maxims follow, typically giving advice on the proper behaviour in particular situations. This behaviour is marked by self-restraint and discretion, and intended to win prosperity and respect. Different maxims address men in different positions; special admiration is reserved for the self-made man. The maxims extend into family life and other non-professional areas. An epilogue extols the value of teaching and of hearing, of fine speech and of self-control; the value of instructions lies in their truth and benefit to posterity.

1. E. A. Wallis Budge, *Facsimiles of Egyptian Hieratic Papyri in the British Museum* (London, 1910), pls. 34–8; G. Jéquier, *Le Papyrus Prisse et ses variantes* (Paris, 1911); E. Devaud, *Les Maximes de Ptahhotep* (Freiburg, 1916); Z. Žàba, *Les Maximes de Ptahhotep*

(Prague, 1956); G. Posener, *Catalogue des ostraca hiératiques littéraires de Deir El Médineh*, i. (Cairo, 1972), 34, pl. 58.
2. E. Blumenthal, 'Ptahhotep und der "Stab des Alters"', in J. Osing and G. Dreyer (eds.), *Form und Mass, Beiträge zur Literatur, Sprache und Kunst des alten Ägypten. Festschrift für Gerhard Fecht* (Wiesbaden, 1987), 84–97; P. Seibert, *Die Charakteristik*, i. (Wiesbaden, 1967), 70.

(iv) *The Instruction of Merikare* The royal authorship is probably a fiction, and so may be the First Intermediate Period date. The beginning is fragmentary, and the more legible text starts with a long section in which the king is admonished by his father to act with wisdom and justice, and to avoid oppression. Specific advice is given on the proper performance of royal duties. In the next section, the king draws lessons from his own past actions, with reference to specific names and events. Finally, the instruction examines the office of kingship itself, before ending with a hymn in praise of the god's actions for mankind, and an admonition to follow the instruction, as it lays down the principles for kingship.

W. Golénischeff, *Les Papyrus hiératiques 1115, 1116A et 1116B de l'Ermitage Impérial à S‑Pétersbourg* (St Petersburg, 1913); A. Volten, *Zwei altägyptische politische Schriften* (Copenhagen, 1945), 3–105; W. Helck, *Die Lehre für König Merikare* (Wiesbaden, 1977).

(v) *The Instruction of King Amenemhet* An unusually large number of extant texts reflects the later popularity of this work. Though it claims to be the instruction of a Twelfth Dynasty king for his son, the pseudonymity of the work is certain, since the assassination attempt which it describes appears to have been successful. Later acknowledgement of this may be reflected in the ascription of the work to Khety in Pap. Chester Beatty IV. Hardly a didactic text at all, the only advice given is to trust nobody: a pessimism justified by a description of the cowardly assassination. After a list of his own achievements, the king's thoughts turn to his son and successor Sesostris (Senwosret), and he affirms the right of the latter to the crown. This reinforces the impression that the work is party-political in intent, as has been suggested by a number of scholars.

F. Ll. Griffith, 'The Milligan Papyrus (Teaching of Amenemhat)', *ZÄS* 34 (1896), 35–51; A. Volten, *Zwei altägyptische politische Schriften* (Copenhagen, 1945, 106–28; W. Helck, *Der Text der 'Lehre Amenemhets I, für seinen Sohn'* (Wiesbaden, 1969). On recent textual discoveries: E. Blumenthal, 'Die Lehre des Königs Amenemhet (Teil i)', *ZÄS* 111 (1984), 85–107, esp. 85 n. 3; H. Goedicke, *Studies in 'The Instructions of King Amenemhet I for his Son'*, (San Antonio, 1988). Also J. L. Foster, 'The Conclusion to *The Testament of Ammenemes, King of Egypt'*, *JEA* 67 (1981), 36–47.

(vi) *The Instruction of Khety* (= *Dua(f)-Khety* and *The Satire of the Trades*)   Also widely copied, this work is supposedly the instruction given by Khety to his son as he took the boy South to be enrolled at school. Most of it is devoted to a systematic, and probably light-hearted, denigration of professions lowlier than that of the scribe, who can look forward to a fine career and comfortable working conditions. This has a biblical counterpart in Sir. 38. 24–39. 11. Khety does, however, include a section of 'instruction' proper, formally quite distinct from the other material, which deals with behaviour and speech when at table, visiting important men, or in other situations conventional for the élite.

E. A. Wallis Budge, *Facsimiles of Hieratic Papyri in the British Museum. Second Series* (London, 1923), pls. 65–73, p. 19; H. Brunner, *Die Lehre des Cheti, Sohnes des Duauf* (Gluckstadt and Hamburg, 1944; W. Helck, *Die Lehre des Dw3-Htjj* (Wiesbaden, 1970). See also R. J. Williams, 'The Sages of Ancient Egypt in the Light of Recent Scholarship', *JAOS* 101/1 (1981), 1–19, esp. 2.

(vii) *The Loyalist Instruction*   A version of the first part of this instruction is attributed on his stela at Abydos to the senior official Sehetepibre, who lived in the late Twelfth Dynasty. The name of the original protagonist is now lost, but the titles in NK versions of the preamble are appropriate to a vizier. The instruction falls into two parts, explicitly separate (cf. 9. 1–4). The first demands loyalty to and veneration of the king, who can discern thoughts and who will punish his opponents, but nourish and protect his supporters. The second concerns the importance of a good workforce for the landowner: he should treat his workers well and not overburden them with dues, lest they up and leave, ruining him. It is these workers who are the real creators of wealth. Towards the end, this is expressed in more conventional terms: the generous and silent man will win respect. The workers will, it is claimed, prove useful even after one's death, and this provides a link with the closing advice, that one should gain the assistance of a dead noble by tending to his body. A party-political purpose has been suggested for this work.

G. Posener, *L'Enseignement loyaliste* (Geneva, 1976). Sehetepibre only: H. O. Lange and H. Schäfer, *Grab- und Denksteine des mittleren Reichs in Museum von Kairo No. 20001–20780* (Berlin, 1908), 145–50; K. Sethe, *Ägyptische Lesestücke* (Leipzig, 1924), 68–70, and *Erläuterungen zu den ägyptischen Lesestücken* (Leipzig, 1927), 99–104.

(viii) *The Instruction by a Man for his Son*   Not yet reconstructed in full from the many fragmentary copies, this instruction shares certain features with the last, and may also have served a political purpose. Its deliberate anonymity makes explicit, perhaps, the universal aspect of its wisdom. The preamble is followed by four short and general sayings (i. 3–6), which seem to serve as an introduction, and then a short section on speech. A lengthy discourse next praises the king: he makes the ignorant wise, the hated loved, the lowly great and the last first; the poor man becomes rich, and the landless a householder; he causes one who is adrift to become moored, teaches the dumb to speak, and opens the ears of the deaf. Obviously, his favour is to be sought. The remainder of the work, too fragmentary to be read in places, includes exhortations to impartiality, silence, and discretion; one should not involve oneself in disputes, nor argue with members of one's family.

W. Helck, *Die Lehre des Djedefhor und die Lehre eines Vaters an seinen Sohn* (Wiesbaden, 1984). Major additional texts: G. Posener, 'Pour la reconstitution de l'Enseignement d'un homme à son fils', *RdE* 36 (1985), 115–19, and 'L'Enseignement d'un homme à son fils: Cinq nouveaux ostraca', in J. Osing and G. Dreyer (eds.), *Form und Mass* (Wiesbaden, 1987), 361–67; J. L. Foster, 'Texts of the Egyptian Composition "The Instruction of a Man for his Son" in the Oriental Institute Museum', *JNES* 45 (1986), 197–211.

(ix) *Amherst Papyrus III* All that remains of this Twelfth Dynasty papyrus are five tiny fragments. *sb3.i tw*, 'I shall(?) instruct you', appears on fragment J, and suggests that the work may have been an instruction, but there is little else left to read.

P. E. Newberry, *The Amherst Papyri* (London, 1899), pl. I, frags. H–L.

(x) *Pap. Ramesseum II* Two sizeable strips of papyrus from the Ramesseum collection, dated by Gardiner to the Thirteenth Dynasty, appear to contain a work consisting of short maxims, set out one to a line until, near the end, the scribe resorted to writing them continuously, separated only by red punctuation. Even where it is not fragmentary, the text is frequently incomprehensible, but the sayings appear to vary considerably in both form and theme. Especially in the first four sayings, which all seem to concern servants, there seems to have been some attempt to juxtapose sayings on similar topics. More obviously, catchwords are used to link sayings. Also worthy of note are the mixture of statements with admonitions, and the cast list: the wise man, the fool, the silent man, and the ignoramus all appear. An apparent lament over the state of wisdom in verso ii, 4 is reminiscent of more pessimistic Egyptian wisdom literature.

A. H. Gardiner, *The Ramesseum Papyri: Plates* (Oxford, 1955), 8 f., pls. III–VI; J. W. B. Barns, *Five Ramesseum Papyri* (Oxford, 1956), 11–14, pls. 7–9.

(xi) *Oxford Wisdom Text (Ashmol. 1964.489 a,b)*   This text is found on
the pieces of plaster which are all that remain of a plastered wooden
writing-board, probably from Thebes. The copy seems to date from the
Hyksos period. If one takes the 'god' of the text to be the king, the theme
seems to be similar to that of the 'king' sections in *The Loyalist Instruction*
and *The Instruction by a Man for his Son*: the benefits accruing to those
who are loyal to the king.

J. W. B. Barns, 'A New Wisdom Text from a Writing-Board in
Oxford', *JEA* 56 (1968), 71–6, pls. XA, X.

2. *The New Kingdom*

(xii) *The Instruction of Any*   Its preamble describes this as the 'educational' or 'testimonial' instruction composed for his son by a scribe in the
funerary temple of Queen Nefertari. The instruction may reflect the
milieu of the 'middle class' of scribes to which such a man would belong,
but there is no explicit address to any particular group, and it advises the
reader to guard his position 'be it lowly or high' (8, 10). Probably
composed in the Eighteenth Dynasty, *Any* covers a range of themes
from daily life, including religious observance, the treatment of family,
sobriety, adultery, and the avoidance of quarrels. The instruction itself is
followed by an epilogue in which the son fails to accept his father's
instruction with the expected gratitude, but protests that he cannot take
to heart so many maxims. In the ensuing debate the father insists that a
capacity for learning and virtue need not be innate, but may be taught.

A. Mariette, *Les Papyrus égyptiens du Musée de Boulaq* (Paris, 1871),
pls. 15–28; E. Suys, *La Sagesse d'Ani* (Rome, 1935); extracts only: A.
Volten, *Studien zum Weisheitsbuch des Anii* (Copenhagen, 1937).
Additional texts: J. Černy, *Papyrus hiératiques de Deir el Médineh*, i.
(Cairo, 1978), pp. 2–4, pls. 1–8a; G. Posener, *Catalogue des ostraca
hiératiques littéraires de Deir el Médineh*, iii (Cairo, 1977, 1978, 1980),
nos. 1639, 1658–60.

(xiii) *The Instruction of Amenemope*   This work, composed no later than
the Twenty-First Dynasty and probably in the Ramesside period, is
apparently attributed to a middle-ranking government official, responsible for the administration of land, agricultural produce, and revenues in
a region of Egypt. A prologue is followed by thirty chapters, the first and
last commending the work to the reader. The chapters vary in form, and
do not always mark a change of subject. As a whole, the work commends
a self-restraint and trust in god which verges on passivity. The future is
unforeseeable, resting wholly in the hands of god, who will protect and

punish as he sees fit. Trusting in him, one must not react to provocation, seek human protection, or try to advance oneself without divine aid: god does not help those who help themselves. One must be discreet and generous to the less fortunate, and though respect should be shown to elders and betters, one should not kowtow to the rich. The instruction stresses honesty above all, and prohibits cheating others through fraud or perjury. Such attempts to gain advantage to the detriment of others incur condemnation, confuse the plans of god, and lead inexorably to disgrace and punishment. The advice in *Amenemope*, then, is set in a world where the supernatural intrudes constantly, and somewhat unpredictably, into human life, and it is motivated by an intense personal piety, characteristic of the New Kingdom.

E. A. Wallis Budge, *Facsimiles of Hieratic Papyri in the British Museum. Second Series* (London, 1923), pp. 9–18, 41–51, pls. 1–14; H. O. Lange, *Das Weisheitsbuch des Amenemope* (Copenhagen, 1925); I. Grumach, *Untersuchungen zur Lebenslehre des Amenope* (Munich and Berlin, 1972).

(xiv) *The Instruction of Amennakhte*   Only the prologue is extant from this instruction by the scribe Amennakhte for his apprentice, but we do possess several copies. One of these affirms that the author was a scribe of the House of Life, apparently an academic and educational centre attached to a temple. Posener's desire to connect this prologue with the material on Pap. Chester Beatty IV is conjectural, but the work may indeed have been a 'miscellany', rather than an instruction proper.

G. Posener, 'L'Exorde de l'instruction éducative d'Amennakhte (Recherches littéraires, v)', *RdE* 10 (1955), 61–72. Additional texts: J. von Beckerath, 'Ostracon München ÄS 396', *SAK* 10 (1983), 63–9; G. Posener, *Catalogue des ostraca hiératiques littéraires de Deir el Médineh*, iii (Cairo, 1977, 1978, 1980), no. 1596 (corresponds to O. BM 41541, ll. 7–10).

(xv) *The Instruction According to Ancient Writings*   Petrie Ostracon 11 contains a distinctive series of prohibitions with *ỉmỉ:k*, 'do not', followed by motive clauses. Though verso 3 f. and 6 f. seem to be pairs of sayings, most are independent, and the overall arrangement is loose. The advice is not addressed to specific situations, but is general in its applicability. It has long been acknowledged that a relationship exists between this ostracon and several others on which similar sayings appear; it is now clear that some, in fact, overlap with it, showing that O. Petrie 11 does not stand alone, and allowing the reconstruction of a substantial, if somewhat fragmentary, portion from the original collection of which it is a copy. Given the distinctive nature of the sayings, it is reasonable to suppose that some other fragments in which they appear are from the same work, even when there is no overlap, although it is possible that they reflect similar but distinct works. One such, the verso of O. BM 5631, contains a preamble, declaring that the text is the *sb3yt mtrt*, the 'educational/testimonial instruction', which is 'according to ancient writings'. The only other line consists of a prohibition with *ỉmỉ:k*, and although this lacks a corresponding motive clause, it is not unreasonable to suppose that we possess here the title of the work found on the other ostraca. Despite the title, there is no evidence beyond the usual literary archaisms for a date earlier than the New Kingdom.

> O. Petrie 11: J. Černy and A. H. Gardiner, *Hieratic Ostraca*, i. (Oxford, 1957), pl. I; A. H. Gardiner, 'A New Moralizing Text', *WZKM* 54 (1957), 43–5. Overlapping texts: rt. 1–7 correspond to ll. i. 9–15 of O. IFAO 1632, and rt. 4–7 to O. IFAO 1633: on these, see G. Posener, *Catalogue des ostraca hiératiques littéraires de Deir el Médineh*, iii (Cairo, 1977, 1978, 1980), pl. 62. Finally, O. Turin 57089 corresponds to O. IFAO 1632 i. 5–9, and its fifth line, therefore, to rt. 1 of O. Petrie 11: on this text, see G. Posener, 'Ostraca inédits du Musée de Turin (Recherches littéraires iii)', *RdE* 8 (1951), 171–89, pl. 14A (under its inventory no., 6391); J. Lopez, *Catalogo del Museo Egizio di Torino*, serie II, vol. iii (Milan, 1978–80), pl. 38. Other texts: G. Posener, *Catalogue des ostraca hiératiques littéraires de Deir el Médineh*, i (Cairo, 1938), pl. 49 (O. IFAO 1090); Černy and Gardiner, *Hieratic Ostraca*, pls. VII 2, LXXXVIII (O. Petrie 45, O. BM 5631).

(xvi) *Pap. Chester Beatty IV verso*   This is a 'miscellany', including passages of didactic instruction along with other material. A eulogy of literature and ancient sages is preceded by a section of instruction in seven parts. The beginning of the first is lost: what remains seems to prohibit encroachment on the boundaries of another, and to advise on the transfer of property to one's children. The following four parts deal with speech and paying one's way, the value of perseverance over sloth, acting properly to win respect, attaching oneself to a magistrate in order to win favour, and avoiding the proximity of women. The last two admonish the successful man against pretending not to know acquaintances, and urge him to protect the defenceless. At 4. 6, five more sections of instruction begin. The first consists of miscellaneous sayings: do not sit in the presence of one greater, respect that you may be respected, love that you may be loved, do not speak too much, and avoid ostentation. The next four concern dealings with one's god. A separate section urges the reader not to claim that a man's character and destiny are already determined by god, and that instruction is thus futile. This theme appears also in the epilogue to *Any*. Finally, the text ends with a blessing and the beginning of a eulogy of the scribe Akhthoy (= Khety), in which he is described as the author of the instruction attributed to Amenemhet I. Posener associates this text with the *Instruction of Amennakhte*.

A. H. Gardiner, *Hieratic Papyri in the British Museum. Third Series, Chester Beatty Gift* (London, 1935), i, pp. 37–44, ii, pls. 18–22.

(xvii) *Ostracon IFAO 1250* This ostracon from Deir el-Medinah preserves fragments of seven lines from an unknown text, apparently an instruction, since at least some of the sayings are admonitions.

G. Posener, *Catalogue des ostraca hiératiques littéraires de Deir el Médineh*, ii (Cairo, 1951, 1952, 1972), pl. 62.

(xviii) *Ostracon Berlin P. 14371* A short fragment containing three or four sayings, with some affinities to the vocabulary of *Any*. The first two seem to concern speech.

F. Hintze, 'Ein Bruchstück einer unbekannten Weisheitslehre', *ZÄS* 79 (1954), 33–6.

(xix) *Ostracon Oriental Institute 12074 (= Instruction of Men(e)na; Letter to a Wayward Son)* A literary letter written by a draughtsman to his son, this text lacks any prologue describing it as an instruction, but seems related to the genre. There are good grounds for supposing that the father, the son, and the general situation described are all historical, but the text is poetic in character. Menna laments the decision of his son to go to sea, and chides him for disregarding his advice and maxims, declaring 'If a son obeys (his) father, instruction (*sb3yt*) is great for eternity, it is said: but look, you heeded no warning which I spoke to you formerly.' The ostracon is from the Ramesside period.

J. Černy and A. H. Gardiner, *Hieratic Ostraca*, i. (Oxford, 1957), p. 22, pls. 78, 78A; W. Guglielmi, 'Eine "Lehre" für einen reiselustigen Sohn (Ostrakon Oriental Institute 12074)', *Die Welt des Orients*, 14 (1983), 147–66; J. L. Foster, 'Oriental Institute Ostracon 12074: "Menna's Lament" or "Letter to a Wayward Son"', *SSEA Journal*, 14 (1984), 88–99.

3. *The Late Period*

(a) *Hieratic*

(xx) *Pap. Brooklyn 47.218.135* This text is still unpublished, but descriptions are available. The extant text consists of five pages, reconstructed from numerous small fragments of a papyrus from about the fourth century BC. The actual composition may have been somewhat earlier, and there is evidence to support a date in the Twenty-Sixth Dynasty (seventh/sixth centuries). This is a period for which we possess few literary remains, and no other instructions. From the descriptions, it seems that formally the text represents something closer to the classical than the Demotic type of instruction, with themes treated in integrated sections. Many of the themes and sayings are also reminiscent of earlier works. Posener and Garnot recognize two major concerns: the importance of leadership and the value of agricultural workers (cf. *The Loyalist Instruction*). The concentration on the good labourer's life in a substantial section may be a response to the more common praise of the scribal profession in other literature. The sayings which are cited suggest an unusually high dependence on figurative language and similes.

> G. Posener and J. Sainte Fare Garnot, 'Sur une sagesse égyptienne de Basse Epoque (Papyrus Brooklyn no. 47.218.135)', in *Les Sagesses du Proche-Orient ancien* (Paris, 1963), 153–7; M. Lichtheim, *Late Egyptian Wisdom Literature in the International Context* (Freiburg and Göttingen, 1983), 11 f.

(b) *Demotic*

(xxi) *The Instruction of 'Onchsheshonqy* This text is some twenty-eight columns long, although fragmentary in places, and begins with the story of 'Onchsheshonqy's imprisonment after he fails to report an abortive coup against Pharaoh. The instruction which follows is supposed to have been written daily by him for his son on the sherds of jars. This possibly reflects a certain self-consciousness about the form and arrangement of the sayings, which are mostly monostichs, occasionally combined to form longer sayings, and frequently organized into chains by the use of verbal, formal, or thematic links. The fragmentary col. 26 may have a paradoxical structure, comparable to that of Pap. Insinger (below). The range of topics is considerable, and it is unfortunate that a small proportion of sayings on country matters has led to the work being described as 'agricultural wisdom'. Between the story and sayings is a sort of lament, about the consequences for a land of Pre's anger; the interests of this section are in justice and good government. The date of the instruction is disputed. Early commentators put it as early as the Saite period, but a Ptolemaic date is more likely.

> 1. S. R. K. Glanville, *Catalogue of Demotic Papyri in the British Museum*, ii. *The Instructions of 'Onchsheshonqy (British Museum Papyrus 10508)* (London, 1955). B. H. Stricker, 'De wijsheid van Anchsjesjonq', *OMRO* 39 (1958), 56–79; H. J. Thissen, *Die Lehre*

des Anchscheschonqi (P. BM 10508) (Bonn, 1984); M. Lichtheim, *Late Egyptian Wisdom Literature in the International Context* (Freiburg and Göttingen, 1983); H. S. Smith, 'The Story of 'Onchsheshonqy', *Serapis*, 6 (1980), 133–56.

2. B. Gemser, 'The Instructions of 'Onchsheshonqy and Biblical Wisdom Literature', SVT 7 (1960), 102–28.

(xxii) *Papyrus Insinger (= The Demotic Wisdom Book)* This work usually goes under the name of the principal text, Papyrus Insinger, but other copies are known, and show significant variants in content and order. Some biblical scholars call it 'Phibis' or, more properly, 'Phebhor', but this is probably the name of the copyist, not the author or protagonist. The work is divided into twenty-five numbered 'instructions', each containing a series of sayings on a particular theme; the number of sayings is given at the end of each. The sayings are generally independent of each other grammatically and syntactically, but there is a consistent attempt to impose a thematic structure on the material within each chapter, and even to achieve some development in the thought. Towards the end of each chapter the writer introduces sayings which wholly undermine what has gone before, and thus creates a paradox, which exists because the way things turn out is wholly in the hands of god, and cannot be predicted according to normal ideas of reward and punishment. The patient self-control and faith in god which are advocated hark back to the ideas of *Amenemope*, but there are possibly some links also with Hellenistic moral philosophy. With a view to Proverbs, the most striking feature is the consistent classification of people into types, especially the 'wise man' and the 'fool'.

Rijksmuseum, Leiden, *Suten-Xeft, le livre royal* (Leiden, 1905); F. Lexa, *Papyrus Insinger* (Paris, 1926); A. Volten, *Kopenhagener Texte zum demotischen Weisheitsbuch* (Copenhagen, 1940) and *Das demotische Weisheitsbuch* (Copenhagen, 1941). On reconstruction of the first column from recent discoveries, see Zauzich in M. Lichtheim, *Late Egyptian Wisdom Literature in the International Context* (Freiburg and Göttingen, 1983), 107–9.

(xxiii) *P. inv. Sorbonne 1260* Broken into three small and badly stained pieces, this is probably to be dated to about the third century BC. Only a few words are legible on fragments b and c. On fragment a, ll. 1–4 are very close to 'Onchsheshonqy 6. 13–15, but the order is different, and *sty*, 'fire', in line 5 rules out any exact equivalence. A fragmentary saying in line 11 is identical to the beginning of 'Onchsheshonqy 9. 23. Line 7 is of interest for a direct address to 'my son', and an appeal to hear the instruction. In view of the close similarities to 'Onchsheshonqy, Pezin wonders whether this text might not be from a personal collection of sayings drawn from various other instructions, or even a witness to a different recension of ʿ*Onchsheshonqy*.

M. Pezin, 'Fragment de sagesse démotique (P. inv. Sorbonne 1260)', *Enchoria*, 11 (1982), 59–61, pls. 7 f.

(xxiv) *Pap. Louvre 2377 verso* The papyrus upon which this text is written has been used as a palimpsest: drafts of Greek memoranda to the right of the column of Demotic are in the same hand as that on Pap. Louvre 2380 (below), and can be dated to the period 163–159 BC, giving a *terminus ad quem* for the copy. The extant text is part of a longer piece. The sayings are a mixture of statements and admonitions, including three vetitives with *m-ỉr* (lines 6, 7, 11), and are written in an extremely concise style. The themes are varied, and include some familiar from other material, but there are no especially close correspondences. Loose thematic linking is visible in lines 2–3 (willingness to listen to others), 6–7 (avoiding oppression of others), 8–9 (overcoming nervousness by prayer: a pair of very similar sayings), and 12–13 (crime). Rather more obvious is the arrangement of sayings by form in 3–4 (cf. 1), 6–7, and 8–10.

1. R. J. Williams, 'Some Fragmentary Demotic Wisdom Texts', in *Studies in Honor of George R. Hughes* (Chicago, 1976), 263–71, esp. 264–66, fig. 50.
2. M. Lichtheim, *Late Egyptian Wisdom Literature in the International Context* (Freiburg and Göttingen, 1983), 100–2.

(xxv) *Pap. Louvre 2380 verso* This text is closely associated with Pap. Louvre 2377 verso, but is much more fragmentary: none of the sayings in the twenty-one lines which survive is complete. Some of the legible words and phrases indicate the affinities of the text with other wisdom material: e.g., 'love of wo[rk . . .' (i. 3); 'instruct him (*mtr:f*)' (i. 4); '. . . foolish of his heart for his master, he will serve his wife(?)' (i. 5); 'The mind of a wise [man] . . .' (ii. 3); 'The wicked is swift(?)' (ii. 4); '. . . teaching of a foolish mind' (ii. 6). R. Jasnow has restored line i. 6 to read 'As for the one who does not] carry the wheat belonging to those of his house, he shall carry the [ch]aff of (other) households', a parallel to ʿ*Onchsheshonqy* 24. 18.

1. R. J. Williams, 'Some Fragmentary Demotic Wisdom Texts', in *Studies in Honor of George R. Hughes* (Chicago, 1976), 263–71, esp. 268–70, fig. 51.
2. R. Jasnow, 'An Unrecognised Parallel in Two Demotic Wisdom Texts', *Enchoria*, 11 (1982), 111.

(xxvi) *Pap. Dem. Louvre 2414: The Instruction of P3-wr-dl for his Son* Other material on the papyrus suggests a date in the mid-second century BC for our copy of this text. The script is generally neat, and the three columns tidily set out, but solecisms in the orthography and grammar, as well as the very loose organization of the material, have led to suggestions that it is a poorly copied extract or an early and incomplete draft. The work is described in the first line as 'The instruction of *P3-wr-dl*, ‹which› he gave to his beloved son': *p3-wr-dl* might be a title (Volten), but is more probably a name (Hughes, Lichtheim). The text has some parallels with, and a general resemblance to ʿ*Onchsheshonqy*, while various themes, such as the admonishments to avoid evil and foolish company, adultery, and slander, are reminiscent of the sentence literature in Proverbs. There is considerable variation in the length of the monostichs, which are sometimes juxtaposed to form longer sayings, while the organization of the material seems rather haphazard. The use of catch-words to form verbal links is, however, apparent in places, while there is a broad arrangement by form also, with the first column made up principally of statements, and the other two of vetitives. There is very little thematic arrangement.

1. A. Volten, 'Die moralischen Lehren des demotischen Pap. Louvre 2414', in *Studi in memoria di Ippolito Rosellini nel primo centenario della morte*, ii. (Pisa, 1955), 269–80, pls. xxxiv–xxxv; G. R. Hughes, 'The Blunders of an Inept Scribe (Demotic Papyrus Louvre 2414)', in G. E. Kadish and G. E. Freeman (eds.), *Studies in Philology in Honour of Ronald James Williams* (Toronto, 1982), 51–67.

2. M. Lichtheim, *Late Egyptian Wisdom Literature in the International Context* (Freiburg and Göttingen, 1983), 93–100.

(xxvii) *Pap. Michaelides I* Only two sayings can still be read in their entirety on this fragment from the first/second century BC: 'Do not be far from the way of god for the human word' (1. 10), and 'He who hastens (?) to find much does not find (even) a little' (1. 12). Unusually, the sayings are not written on separate lines, but separated only by spaces. The general sense of some other sayings is clear: one in line 8 urges association with the wise man, while line 13 cautions against becoming indebted to the overseer of one's pasture(?) land, and line 15 against covetousness. Isolated words mention cursing and speech, while a number of the sayings were clearly vetitives. Bresciani compares the beginning of a sentence in line 10, 'Do a deed . . .' with ʿ*Onchsheshonqy* 19. 10, 'Do a good deed and cast it in the flood; when it dries you will find it'; cf. Qoh. 11. 1.

1. E. Bresciani, *Testi demotici nella Collezione Michaelidis* (Rome, 1963), pp. 1–4.

2. M. Lichtheim, *Late Egyptian Wisdom Literature in the International Context* (Freiburg and Göttingen, 1983), 102 f.

(xxviii) *P. Dem. Cairo 30672* This Ptolemaic text is extremely fragmentary: barely enough remains to confirm that it was indeed a wisdom text.

W. Spiegelberg, *Die demotischen Denkmäler 30601–31270, 50001–50022*, ii. *Die demotischen Papyrus* (Strasbourg, 1908), text vol. pp. 102 f.

(xxix) *P. Dem. Cairo 30682* H. S. Smith has noted that the four lines of text on this fragment are very close to ʿOnchsheshonqy 7. 16–20, 9. 10, and 9. 14. The copy may be slightly later than that of ʿOnchsheshonqy, and the text either a version of that work or part of a closely related work.

W. Spiegelberg, *Die demotischen Denkmaler 30601–31270, 50001–50022*, ii. *Die demotischen Papyrus* (Strasbourg, 1908), text vol. p. 107; H. S. Smith, 'A Cairo Text of Part of the "Instructions of ʿOnchsheshonqy"', *JEA* 44 (1958), 121 f.

(xxx) *O.BM 50627 The Instruction of a 'Scribe of the House of Life'(?)* Only seven lines are preserved on this ostracon of the first century BC to first century AD, but they are very striking. I reproduce Williams's translation:

1. Here is a copy of a teaching that a 'scribe of the House of Life' (?) gave them
2. For a little child who is very, very young.
3. Do not sleep with a wife who is not yours,
4. that no fault may be found with you because of it.
5. Here is another one: Those who are . . . are not women in the street (to)
6. create your bad odour in(?) [. . .]
7. Here is another one: Do not listen [. . .]

The sayings seem, unusually, to be distichs. Lichtheim has drawn attention to the extraordinary way in which the sayings are prefaced with *k.t ʿn t3y*, 'here is another one', and suggested that the gleaning of sayings here is 'playful'. Perhaps there is also a certain humour evident in the nature of the sayings addressed to the 'little child who is very, very young': this tiny tot is admonished to avoid adultery and disreputable women! It is tempting to suppose that what we have here is a sort of pastiche.

1. R. J. Williams, 'Some Fragmentary Demotic Wisdom Texts', in *Studies in Honor of George R. Hughes* (Chicago, 1976), 263–71, esp. 270 f., fig. 52.

2. M. Lichtheim, *Late Egyptian Wisdom Literature in the International Context* (Freiburg and Göttingen, 1983), 103 f.

(xxxi) *P. Berlin 15658*   An unpublished fragment. Zauzich describes it as containing wisdom sayings, and compares the script to that of two fragments of the first century AD which mention the name 'Ahikar'. He is unable, however, to identify it with any known version of the *Sayings of Ahikar*.

K. T. Zauzich, 'Neue literarische Texte in demotischer Schrift', *Enchoria*, 8/2 (1978), 33–8, esp. p. 34.

(xxxii) *Pap. Tebtunis Tait 15*   Some fifteen fragmentary lines survive on this papyrus fragment of the second/third centuries AD, which is torn on all sides and probably part of a longer text. Although it does seem that this is a wisdom piece, Tait's reconstruction shows little indication of traditional themes and vocabulary, and it is hard to make sense of any of the surviving bits of sayings.

W. J. Tait, *Papyri from Tebtunis in Egyptian and Greek (P. Tebt. Tait)* (London, 1977), 53–6.

4. Other Egyptian 'Instructions'

A number of other texts claim or are claimed to be 'instructions'. Foremost amongst these are the omnivorous 'miscellanies'. *Khety* is perhaps a prototype of these works, and Pap. Chester Beatty is certainly one, but both of those texts include distinct passages which are clearly didactic, employing forms and style characteristic of the instruction genre. The same is not true of the works attributed to Kageb, Pentwere, and Nebmaranakhte, better known, perhaps, as papyri Anastasi IV, Sallier I, and Lansing. The last of these may, incidentally, have absorbed a similar work, attributed to one Pyay on O. Cairo 25771 recto. Each of these texts is described as a *sb3yt š<(w)t*, an 'instruction in letter-writing', and this should, perhaps, be regarded as distinct from the classical instruction genre. The miscellanies gather together a variety of literary and non-literary material, and their apparent purpose is the provision of material for educational exercises in writing and composition. It seems likely that the initial lines scrawled on the Ramesseum ostraca 3 and 4 belonged to similar works; they are attributed respectively to a scribe whose name is lost, and to the treasury-scribe Setekhmose. The instruction of Hori (O. Gardiner 2) is called a *sb3yt mtrt*, like, for example, *Any*, but its advice to the recipient, that he should follow in his father's footsteps and become a scribe, identifies it with the 'Be a scribe' literature, beloved of the miscellanies, but represented only by *Khety* among the classical texts.

Anastasi IV, Sallier I, Lansing: A. H. Gardiner, *Late-Egyptian Miscellanies* (Brussels, 1937), 34–56, 79–88, 99–116; R. A. Caminos, *Late Egyptian Miscellanies* (London, 1954), 125–221, 303–29, 373–428.
Pyay: J. Černy, *Catalogue général des antiquités égyptiennes du Musée du Caire Nos. 25501–25832*, i (Cairo, 1935), 96.
Ramesseum ostraca: W. Spiegelberg, *Hieratic Ostraka and Papyri Found by J. E. Quibell in the Ramesseum, 1895–6* (London, 1898), pl. I nos. 3 f.
Hori: J. Černy and A. H. Gardiner, *Hieratic Ostraca*, i. (Oxford, 1957), pl. VI, no. 1; H.-W. Fischer-Elfert, *Literarische Ostraka der Ramessidenzeit in Übersetzung* (Wiesbaden, 1986), 1–4.

An old and close relationship exists between the instructions and Egyptian tomb inscriptions, some of which include, indeed, the term 'instruct(ion)'. As we have seen, the inscription of Sehetepibre goes so far as to appropriate a section of *The Loyalist Instruction* for its own use. A few scholars, see the 'instruction' on certain other inscriptions as genuinely didactic; it is hardly to be denied that some relationship exists between many of the declarations made in what Miriam Lichtheim calls the 'moral self-presentation' of the dead, and the advice given in the instructions. There is a considerable resemblance between both the language and the outlook in each: broadly speaking, what the instructions advise that one should do, the dead man claims to have done, and there is often extensive reference to the high reputation that he enjoyed thereby. Short didactic sections are sometimes found also. On the literary level, it is highly unlikely that the instructions can be said to have influenced the form of the tomb inscriptions, and though the opposite is possible, we must more probably reckon with a complicated interrelationship between the two, stretching back to pre-literary times.

See, e.g., H. G. Fischer, 'A Didactic Text of the Late Middle Kingdom', *JEA* 68 (1982), 45–50, on the tomb of Inpy. This text is very fragmentary, and is hardly 'didactic' in any meaningful sense. W. Schenkel, in 'Eine neue Weisheitslehre?', *JEA* 50 (1964), 6–12, has challenged Goedicke's claim that the stela of Menuhotep contains a 'didactic' section, described as an 'instruction': see H. Goedicke, 'A Neglected Wisdom Text', *JEA* 48 (1962), 25–35. The best known of these tomb 'instructions' is that of the priest Amenemhet (not to be confused with the king of that name): his 'instruction' is, however, almost wholly autobiographical; see A. H. Gardiner, 'The Tomb of Amenemhet, High-Priest of Amon', *ZÄS* 47 (1910), 87–99, esp. 92–7. More generally, see M. Lichtheim, *Ancient Egyptian Autobiographies Chiefly of the Middle Kingdom* (Freiburg and Göttingen, 1988), p. 7; J. Assmann, 'Schrift, Tod und Identität: Das Grab als Vorschule der Literatur im alten Ägypten', in A. Assmann *et al.* (eds.), *Schrift und Gedächtnis* (Munich, 1983), 64–93.

B. MESOPOTAMIA

Translations, bibliographies, and surveys:
W. G. Lambert, *Babylonian Wisdom Literature* (Oxford, 1960), covers most of the bilingual and Akkadian texts; a few are translated also in *ANET*³. For general surveys and bibliographies, see especially E. I. Gordon, 'A New Look at the Wisdom of Sumer and Akkad', *Bi. Or* 17 (1960), 122–52, and the article 'Literatur', in the *Reallexikon der Assyriologie und vorderasiatischen Archäologie* (Berlin, 1987), vii. 35–75.

1. Unilingual Sumerian

(xxxiii) *The Instructions of Šuruppak*   Several versions of this work are known, of which the archaic text from Abu Salabikh (mid-third mill.) and the OB 'classical version' (early second mill.) are most complete. The classical version, which was translated into Akkadian (see below), seems to be an expansion of the earlier one. Much less is preserved of another archaic version from Adab. The prologue to the work describes it as the instructions given by Šuruppak to his son, the legendary Ziusudra, an association with the far-distant past which is emphasized in the classical version. The prologue concludes with a paternal exhortation to heed the instructions. Restatements of the prologue occur later in the work, dividing it into parts, or, in the classical version, three separate 'instructions'. In all versions, the first of these parts is a series of bipartite prohibitions, in a few of which the motive clause is expanded to form a longer saying. Elsewhere, the short sayings which make up the work are more diverse, but adjacent sayings or whole series are often linked by associative methods.

B. Alster, *The Instructions of Šuruppak: A Sumerian Proverb Collection* (Copenhagen, 1974), and *Studies in Sumerian Proverbs* (Copenhagen, 1975); C. Wilcke, 'Philologische Bemerkungen zum *Rat des Šuruppag* und Versuch einer neuen Übersetzung', *ZA* 68 (1978), 196–232; B. Alster, 'Additional Fragments of the Instructions of Šuruppak', *Aula Orientalis*, 5 (1987), 199–206; M. Civil, 'Notes on the "Instructions of Šuruppak"', *JNES* 43 (1984), 281–98, and 'More Additional Fragments of the Instructions of Šuruppak', *Aula Orientalis*, 5 (1987), 207–10.

(xxxiv) *A Sumerian Preceptive Work*   The date of this work is uncertain, but it is unusual among the Sumerian texts in presenting advice through integrated units of varied length, rather than individual short sayings. The content is very interesting and may be summarized:

rev. 5. 1:   Obey your mother as you obey your god.
     2–3:   Don't go to the mighty, but provide for yourself with your own work.

4–7: Respect for your elder brother and sister.

8–10: Do not let your advice be influenced by enmity, and put the man of strife in his place.

11–13: Do not trust in prayers; the god will do what he has decided for you on the appointed day, when you should celebrate with a party.

14–16: Men swoop like an eagle on party after party; do not be too proud to hold one.

17–20: Do not show irritation where there is strife, but learn to calm the angry and to ignore insults.

rev. 6. 1a: Vows are dangerous.

1: Do not let your judging be prejudiced by hatred.

2–6: Know how to be generous: it pays dividends.

2–12: If approached by a poor foreigner, feed him and give him a bed: if he becomes rich in the future he will remember.

12b–12c: Do not harm, but rather befriend strangers and new arrivals.

13: The vengeance(?) of someone hurt by you.

14–22: The advantages of keeping local children on your side when things have gone wrong.

J. J. A. Van Dijk, *La Sagesse suméro-accadienne* (Leiden, 1953), 102 ff. (note that his text 'C' (TRS 93) is in fact from *Šuruppak*); M. Civil, 'Supplement to the Introduction to *ISET* I', *Orientalia*, NS 41 (1972), 83–90.

(xxxv) *The Farmer's Instruction* This long text gives direct and practical advice on farming. However, it seems improbable that many farmers would have been able to read it, and it should be regarded as evidence for an early literary interest in agriculture. The work is portrayed as the instruction once given by a farmer to his son. The farmer is not named in the prologue, but appears to be identified with Ninurta in the epilogue.

A. Salonen, *Agricultura Mesopotamica nach sumerisch-akkadisch Quellen* (Helsinki, 1968), 202–12.

(xxxvi) *Collections of Sayings* With most of the collections still unedited and many tablets unpublished, the information available is often limited. For a general description of each, see E. I. Gordon, 'A New Look at the Wisdom of Sumer and Akkad', *Bi. Or* 17 (1960), 122–52, esp. 126–30, 151. Textual information is summarized by B. Alster on pp. 98–102 of his 'Sumerian Proverb Collection Seven', *RA* 72 (1978), 97–112. Of the twenty-four collections which Gordon originally identified, several have now turned out to be different parts of the same collection: coll. 20 is the continuation of coll. 8, and coll. 19 of coll. 11; further such relationships may be uncovered by future textual discoveries.

Collection One: *C.*200 sayings on a great variety of themes, mostly arranged in groups of sayings which share the same initial sign, but with some thematic links also. E. I. Gordon, *Sumerian Proverbs: Glimpses of Everyday Life in Ancient Mesopotamia* (Philadelphia, 1959), 23–150, 448–73, 491–517, 547–50.

Collection Two: 166 sayings, mostly in initial-sign groups, but nos. 119–38 are antithetical sayings grouped by form. The collection begins with a section about destruction, which bears little relationship to what follows: part of this also precedes coll. 7. Coll. 6 may be a continuation of coll. 2. Ibid., pp. 151–284, 473–87, 518–45, 550.

Collection Three: 201 sayings, many of them well preserved. Gordon finds no overall principle of arrangement.

Collection Four: 62 sayings, no apparent principle of arrangement. E. I. Gordon, 'Sumerian Proverbs: "Collection Four"', *JAOS* 77 (1957), 67–79.

Collection Five: 125 animal sayings and fables arranged in groups where each saying begins with the same animal's name. E. I. Gordon, 'Sumerian Animal Proverbs and Fables: "Collection Five"', *JCS* 12 (1958), 1–21, 43–75.

Collection Six: Possibly a continuation of coll. 2. The sayings are grouped by initial sign or internal key-word.

Collection Seven: 114 sayings, many of which are found also in colls. 1–3 and 6. One of the Neo-Assyrian bilingual collections (K4327 etc.) is apparently based on this collection. B. Alster, 'Sumerian Proverb Collection Seven', *RA* 72 (1978), 97–112.

Collection Eight + Twenty: Animal sayings and fables, grouped as in coll. 5.

Collection Nine: The first 8 sayings also begin coll. 10. In the present context, they form a series with the next 5 sayings, each linked by a key-word, but this arrangement is subsequently abandoned.

Collection Ten: On the first 8 sayings, see on coll. 9 above. Sayings 9–12 are found with variants in the *Dialogue between a King, an Old Man and a Maiden* (ll. 28–31), and also in colls. 11 + 19 and 17. B. Alster, *Studies in Sumerian Proverbs* (Copenhagen, 1975), 90 ff.

Collection Eleven + Nineteen: *C.*300 sayings with no apparent ordering: many appear to have been excerpted from other collections.

Collection Twelve: Arranged in groups by initial word (*lugal*, 'king', in the first group).

Collection Thirteen: Arranged in groups by initial word.

Collection Fourteen: *C.*43 sayings, arranged in groups by initial word. Gordon believes one group to have been arranged by its final word, but Alster sees this section as a separate work.

Collection Fifteen: *C.*50 sayings, some found also in colls. 3, 14, and 15, and in the bilingual collections. No apparent ordering.

Collection Sixteen: *C.*30 sayings, some also in colls. 3, 14, and 15 and in the Neo-Bab. bilingual BM 38283. No apparent ordering.

Collection Seventeen: Gordon suggests a relationship with colls. 10 or (11 +)19, with which this shares a group of 4 sayings; 5 others are found also in colls. 2 or 3. No apparent ordering.

Collection Eighteen: 15 sayings; the last appears to underlie the introduction to the *Assyrian Dream Book*.

Collection Twenty-one: well attested. Includes a section of sayings and fables grouped by initial word or internal key-word, and also a lengthy 'parable', 'The Fowler and his Wife' (cf. coll. 24).

Collection Twenty-two: 3 sayings only: barely legible, but all beginning with the same (obscure) name of a bird.

Collection Twenty-three: no apparent ordering, and only slight links with other collections.

Collection Twenty-four: 11 sayings, including 'The Fowler and his Wife' (cf. coll. 21), and one saying also in coll. 23.

2. *Bilingual Sumerian/Akkadian*

(xxxvii) *Collections of Sayings*   Most of these texts are edited in *BWL*, to which the reader is referred for more detailed discussion and bibliography; see also Gordon's survey in *Bi. Or* 17. Almost all were probably composed originally in Sumerian, but Gordon notes that in two of the texts the Sumerian may be late, and perhaps even secondary.

N-3395: a poorly preserved fragment from Nippur, either OB or a Cassite copy. Apparently animal sayings. *BWL* 272 f.

UM 29-15-330: confusingly, Lambert and Gordon disagree as to which side is the obverse of this small fragment. (Lambert's) obv. 3–4 seem to be saying 42 of Sum. coll. 1, and the traces in obv. 1 may reflect saying 41. The other side of the tablet is obscure, but does not reflect the Sum. coll. 1. *BWL* 273 f.

BE (unnumbered): an exercise tablet from Babylon, on which 2 sayings are preserved: the first is found in Sum. coll. 3. 149 and elsewhere, including BM 38283 (below). The second is found in Sum. coll. 3. 179 and 7. 77: a man exclaims as disasters happen to his boat, but reaches shore safely. *BWL* 274.

'The Assyrian Collection': the Sumerian of this well-attested text may be late. Much is obscure, and overall there seems to be little connection between the sayings, although some associative links are visible. A series in ii. 23–32 concerns the god (cf. 42–5), while ii. 33–7 concern friendship, 38–41 profit, and iv. 9–26 the king; iii. 13–18 seem to confront a situation of disaster. *BWL* 225 ff. Sumerian of VAT 10251 translated in J. J. A. Van Dijk, *La Sagesse suméro-accadienne*, i (Leiden, 1953), 9–11.

VAT 10810: most of the Sumerian is lost, and little of the Akkadian unbroken. Two sayings are translated by Lambert: one concerns ignorance, the other the relations between a bride and her mother-in-law. *BWL* 260 ff.

RS 25.130; 23.34 (+) 494+ 363; 25.434: three closely related texts from Ras Shamra, which have much of their material in common but differ substantially in matters of orthography and presentation. Nougayrol suggests that they were written by school pupils attempting an exercise in composition, and in that case they should, strictly speaking, perhaps, be described as 'Syrian' texts. The subject-matter of each is the terrible state of the world: men know neither themselves nor their actions, and the meaning of their lives lies with the gods who have ordained events. See J. Nougayrol *et al.* (eds.), *Ugaritica V* (Paris, 1968), 291–300.

K4160 + 13184: 2 sayings are legible, both about the king: in the power of his word and in his righteousness he is comparable to Anu and Šamaš. *BWL* 233 f.

K4207: the sense and interrelationship of the few sayings preserved is unclear. *BWL* 234 f.

K4327 + 4605 + 4749 and K15227, 80-7-19.130: apparently a bilingual version of Sum. coll. 7. *BWL* 235 ff., 257 ff.

K4347 + 16161: a long text, in which the Sumerian may be late, though Gordon notes that iv. 30 is very close to Sum. coll. 1. 157. The subject-matter is varied and the arrangement loose, though formal and thematic links are apparent in places. *BWL* 239–50.

K5688: the only saying preserved is a bilingual version of Sum. coll. 4. 61, where a chattering mouth is compared to an anus breaking wind. *BWL* 251.

K7654: 3 sayings are preserved. 2–5 = Sum. coll. 1. 89, about the wreckage of a ferry. *BWL* 251.

K7674 + 11166 + 13568: Lambert translates only ll. 19–24 of this badly broken text: 'Long life begets for you a sense of satisfaction; concealing a thing—sleepless worry; wealth—respect.' *BWL* 252 f.

K8216: most of the Sumerian is lost, but 4 sayings can be read in the Akkadian. Although Lambert suggests that 10–11 may be a riddle, it seems more likely that all the sayings are ironic comments on the claims of a braggart. *BWL* 253 f.

K8315: 2 sayings are preserved. The first = Sum. coll. 2. 46, an obscure comparison of something with lapis lazuli; the second = Sum. coll. 3. 189: the reaction of a proletarian to an aristocrat on fire. *BWL* 254 f.

K8338: 3 sayings are preserved. 11–14 is similar to Sum. coll. 1. 153, but different in meaning; on other links, see Lambert's comments. *BWL* 255.

K9050 + 13457: The 2 partially legible sayings are obscure. *BWL* 256.

K11608: the Akkadian is lost; 2 sayings are preserved in the Sumerian: 7–10, 11–13 = Sum. coll. 4, 11, 12. *BWL* 256.

K16171: the Akkadian is lost, and too little of the Sumerian left to establish the meaning. *BWL* 258.

Sm 61: several sayings are preserved: 2–4 has a number of parallels, while the pair 9–11, 12–15 occurs also in Sum. coll. 3. 17, 18. The sayings in 5 and 6 differ only in their second half: 'Giving pertains to a king, doing good to a cupbearer / showing favour to a steward' (Lambert); the first occurs alone in Sum. coll. 3. 85. In 19, the scribal art is praised as the 'mother of orators and father of scholars'. *BWL* 258 f.

BM 98743 = Th 1905-4-9.249: 1 saying: the unprecedented event of a young girl breaking wind in her husband's embrace. Lambert compares an Akkadian saying, and there is probably some connection with Sum. coll. 1. 12. *BWL* 260.

BM 38283=80-11-12.165: All of the sayings preserved have parallels or equivalents in the unilingual Sumerian literature: obv. 1–5 = Sum. coll. 2. 69; 6–11 = Sum. coll. 1. 3–5; 12–16 = Sum. coll. 14. 1 (Lambert's refs. to Sum. coll. 6 are apparently a misprint: the cited texts belong to coll. 14). Rev. 1–3 and 4–8 are of a type found in Sum. colls. 14, 15, and 16, while 9–10 has equivalents in Sum. colls. 15 and 16; 11–14 occurs in Sum. coll. 3. 149 and elsewhere. Finally, 15–17 occurs in Sum. coll. 15. *BWL* 262 ff.

BM 38486 = 80-11-12.370: Lambert translates 2 sayings, obv. 8–9 on the impotence of mighty men in the face of flood and fire, and rev. 7–8 on the unknowability of divine will. *BWL* 264 ff.

BM 38539 = 80-11-12.480: lines 4–7 lament thriftlessness in the family, incorporating 2 sayings found in Sum. colls. 1 and 14: Sum. coll. 1. 151 has a line lacking in 4–5 here and the Sum. coll. 14 version. Lines 12–13 comment ironically that when you find something you always lose it immediately, but when you mean to throw something away, it hangs around for ever. *BWL* 266 f.

BM 38596 = 80-11-12.480: the tone of the extant sayings is unusual. i. 2–9 complains of Enlil's treatment of a woman who has carried out the ordinances of the gods and multiplied the rules of kingship (?); 12–15, where the Akkadian differs somewhat from the Sumerian, lists three actions which are not properly humane: 13–15 = rev. 2–3 of SU 1952, 15 + 91 + 186 + 350 etc., see below. iii. 5–7 wonders who will oppose single-minded warriors, and 8–12 seems to commend grovelling to those who are present, and slandering those who are not. On the relationship of this seemingly somewhat cynical text to other Akkadian material, see Lambert's notes. *BWL* 267 ff.

BM 56607 = 82-7-14.989: the 3 sayings in A. 7–13 may be linked by some vague association of ideas—beer, river, malt—but those in B. 8–18 are clearly linked by theme: when prosperous, be generous to your family (8–15), for 'flesh is flesh, blood is blood. Alien is alien, foreigner is indeed foreigner' (Lambert). *BWL* 270 f.

(xxxviii) *Hymn to Ninurta (VAT 10610)* Lambert describes this as a 'preceptive hymn'. While the reverse addresses the god entering his shrine, the obverse condemns the man guilty of certain actions, all common bugbears in wisdom literature: adultery, slander, malicious gossip and charges, oppression of the poor, and surrender of the weak to the powerful. Such ethical material is found in some other Sumerian hymns (see also the Akkadian hymn below). It is not really preceptive, since the listener here is not addressed, nor is it expressed in a 'wisdom literature' form. I have included it as an excellent illustration of the extent to which 'wisdom' themes and opinions may be found outside wisdom literature and even in the cult. Though found in Assur, the tablet probably originated in Babylonia during the Cassite period.

BWL 118ff.

3. *Unilingual Akkadian*

(xxxix) *The Instructions of Šuruppak* The Akkadian text VAT 10151 seems to be a direct translation of the classical Sumerian work. A more recently discovered text from Sippar is apparently larger and better preserved.

> *BWL* 92 ff. Report of Sippar text: p. 199 of B. Alster, 'Additional Fragments of the Instructions of Šuruppak', *Aula Orientalis*, 5 (1987), 199–206.

(xl) *Counsels of Šube'awilum* Fragmentary unilingual copies of this lengthy work have been found at Ras Shamra (RS 22. 439) and Emar (Nos. 778–80); a bilingual fragment from Boghazköy (KUB 4. 3) has an incomplete Hittite translation. In the prologue to the Ras Shamra text, Nougayrol reads the names Šube'awilum and Zurranku for the father who is giving the instruction and his son, but Arnaud does not take these to be proper names in his edition of the Emar text. The latter has made it possible to reconstruct much more of the text than previously, and it now seems that the instruction is in two parts: the father's instruction, and the son's reply. This is, of course, reminiscent of *Any*. The first part gives conventional advice on behaviour, mostly in the form of prohibitions, while the son's reply appears to be a much more pessimistic wisdom, stressing the vanity of toiling for wordly wealth and the inevitability of death. The mixture of pessimistic and didactic wisdom in a text is not uncommon, but the apparent confrontation of the two here is notable. Like *Šuruppak*, the work begins some sayings 'My son . . .' (i. 9, ii. 6; cf. Prov. 1–9, P. inv. Sorbonne 1260, a. 7, above, and *Counsels of Wisdom*, below), and sets the whole within a framework of paternal instruction. However, the sayings are typically much longer than those of *Šuruppak*. iii. 5–9, indeed, appears to be a much expanded version of the saying found in *Šuruppak* 17, and iii. 10–14 of Šuruppak 217 and 213 (cf. also 220).

Ras Shamra: J. Nougayrol *et al.* (eds.), *Ugaritica V* (Paris, 1968), 273–93. Boghazköy: ibid. 779–84. Emar: D. Arnaud, *Recherches au pays d'Astata. Emar vi. 4* (Paris, 1987), 377–83.

(xli) *Counsels of Wisdom* Lambert suggests that this work was composed in the Cassite Period. The beginning is probably lost, but in view of 'my son' in line 81, it seems likely that it is supposed to be viewed as paternal instruction. Lambert suggests that K 13770 or 80-7-19.283 may be from the beginning. The advice is as follows:

8–21:	(broken)
21–30:	Do not associate with tale-bearers, but guard your speech.
31–40:	Avoid disputes.
41–48:	Disarm your adversary with kindness.
50–55:	(broken)
56–65:	Do not insult the unfortunate, but be charitable.
66–71:	Do not honour a slave girl.
72–80:	Do not marry a prostitute.
81–94:	If put in a position of trust by the prince, do not defraud him.
96–126:	(broken)
127–134:	Do not slander or speak carelessly.
135–147:	Worship and sacrifice to your god.
148–166:	Do not break trust with a friend.

Typically, the sections are composed of commands or vetitives followed by motive clauses, though no strict pattern is followed.

BWL 96; cf. 106 f.

(xlii) *Counsels of a Pessimist (K1453)* The date of this text is uncertain. The first eight lines of the obverse are fragmentary, but seem to refer to the transitoriness of human achievement, clearly the theme of lines 9 f. and the basis for Lambert's title. Lines 11–13 contain injunctions to religious observance: pray to your god, make offerings to the god who created you, and bow down to the city goddess that she may grant you offspring. Line 14 suggests that one should remember one's agricultural responsibilities, and 15 f. concern one's eldest son and daughter, though their meaning is obscure. Finally, an extended saying about the effect of misery on one's sleep begins in line 17, and continues to the end of the text on the reverse: it seems to advocate banishing discontent and being happy. The text thus contains three long sayings in 1(?)–10, 11–13, and 17–22. It is not clear whether some thematic connection should be perceived between 14, 15 f., and the previous section; on the whole it seems likely that the link is verbal: 13–15 all begin with the preposition *ana*, and 14 shares with 15 the same third sign also.

BWL 107 ff.

(xliii) *K 13770* A fragment from the beginning of a text, and apparently part of a prologue; cf. on *Counsels of Wisdom*, above. A learned man seems to be exhorting his son to hear his teaching.

BWL 106 f.

(xliv) *80-7-19.283* Another fragment from the beginning of a text, exhorting the reader to take hold of truth. Cf. on *Counsels of Wisdom*, above.

BWL 107.

(xlv) *Advice to a Prince (DT 1 = The Babylonian Fürstenspiegel)* I include this because it is relevant to the king sayings in Proverbs, and is of interest in the light of Egypt's 'royal' instructions. The genre and nature of the text are, however, quite unclear. Phrased in an apparent imitation of omen texts (the first line seems to be a virtual quotation from the series *šumma ālu*), it consists of conditions in the form: 'If a king (does something bad) then . . .'. The first few conditions are very general, but the text becomes very precise and refers to the treatment of major cities. Various attempts have been made to place either the events or the composition of this literary text in a particular historical context.

1. *BWL* 110 ff.
2. I. M. Diakonoff, 'A Babylonian Political Pamphlet from about 700 BC', in H. G. Güterbock and Th. Jacobsen (eds.), *Studies in Honor of Benno Landsberger on his Seventy-Fifth Birthday* (Chicago, 1965), 343–49; E. Reiner, 'The Babylonian Fürstenspiegel in Practice', in M. A. Dandamayev *et al.* (eds.), *Societies and Languages of the Ancient Near East: Studies in Honour of I. M. Diakonoff* (Warminster, 1982), 320–26, with an appendix by M. Civil.

(xlvi) *Collections of Sayings*
SU 1952, 15+91+186+350, SU 1952, 23: Fragmentary. In the opening section of *c*.30 lines, the sayings are all of the form 'to do *x* is an abomination to Nammu'; after this, the text consists of ethical admonitions. Rev. 2–3 of the first fragment is about human nature, and is found also on BM 38596 (i. 13–15, Akk.) and the school tablet Leiden 853; rev. 4–5 = *Dialogue of Pessimism*, pp. 32 f., itself broken and obscure. *BWL* 117.

K9908: a small fragment, which Lambert suggests may be part of an ethical text. *BWL* 117.

CBS 14235: several sayings are more or less complete in ll. 5–15 of this text from Nippur, which is either OB or a Cassite copy. Line 5 mentions the actions of someone in the king's presence, perhaps linked with the anointing in 6 f. Lines 8–11 assert that a man must toil for a living, and cannot expect to be given one; 12 concerns vain acts, while 13–15 asks: 'He who has not king and queen, who is his lord? He(?) is either an animal or one who lies . . .' (Lambert). *BWL* 276 f.

BO 3157: there are several legible sayings on this fragment of a prism found at Boghazköy. Lines 4–6 appear to consist of bipartite sayings: the first part states something good, the second something bad which qualifies it, rather like a good news/bad news joke. Lines 7–8 are quite different: the speaker expresses his total lack of concern at the actions of another. *BWL* 278.

(xlvii) *Hymn to Šamaš* For a discussion of date, sources, and other issues, see *BWL*. The work as a whole is not comparable to Proverbs, but substantial parts are: between lines 85 and 129 we find condemnation of false oaths, coveting one's neighbour's wife, calculated villainy, corrupt judgement, false trade (especially, the use of false weights), and hypocrisy. Praise is reserved for those who champion justice and the weak, trade honestly, and act straightforwardly. The fate of all is entrusted to Šamaš, who makes plain everything that is obscure.

BWL 121 ff.

4. Bilingual: Akkadian with Hittite or Hurrian

(xlviii) *Counsels of Šube'awilum* A partially bilingual (Akk./Hitt.) fragment of the Akkadian work.

J. Nougayrol *et al.* (eds.), *Ugaritica V* Paris, 1968), 779–84 (Laroche).

(xlix) *RS 15. 10* This Akkadian/Hurrian text from Ras Shamra includes extended sayings about the swearing of false oaths (1–4) and prayer by the guilty (10–13).

BWL 116.

(l) *BO4209 + 4710* Little is preserved of the Hittite version on this text from Boghazköy. Lambert translates two sayings from the Akkadian, one concerning prematurely ripe fruit (7 f.) and the other irrigation (9 f.); if, however, the obscure saying in 11 f. is indeed about male prostitution, the 'collection' as a whole is not exclusively agricultural.

BWL 279.

C. SYRIA

(li) *Aramaic Sayings of Ahikar* The fifth century Aramaic text of *Ahikar* found at Elephantine is the earliest known version of a work found, with substantial variations, in many other languages. A collection of sayings is set within a story, as in *'Onchsheshonqy*, and this tells how the scribe Ahikar, senior adviser to the Assyrian kings Sennacherib and then Esarhaddon, adopts and educates his nephew Nadin, who betrays him. Ahikar, with the help of the officer sent to kill him, fakes his own execution and goes into hiding. At this point the Aramaic version begins, without warning, the lengthy collection of sayings: the end of this and of the story is lost. In the other versions, Ahikar is restored and performs miraculous acts for the king; Nadin is imprisoned and tortured, expiring horribly after a long series of reproaches by Ahikar. Recent linguistic studies suggest that the narrative and sayings in the Elephantine version were not composed at the same time, and place the composition of the sayings in Syria, no later than the seventh century BC. This view is supported by Lindenberger's study of the deities mentioned. There is no evidence to suggest the existence of any earlier version from Mesopotamia. As it stands, the collection is incomplete, but still contains well over a hundred sayings. Some of these are fables or other relatively long units, but most are short and pithy; there is considerable variety in both form and theme, but paronomasia within the sayings and associative, especially verbal, links between them are obvious and very common.

1. E. Sachau, *Aramäische Papyrus und Ostraca aus einer jüdischen Militärkolonie zu Elephantine* (Leipzig, 1911), vol. i, tables 44–50, vol. ii, pp. 147–82; A. Cowley, *Aramaic Papyri of the Fifth Century BC* (Oxford, 1923), 204–48; J. M. Lindenberger, *The Aramaic Proverbs of Ahiqar* (Baltimore and London, 1983), sayings only; I. Kottsieper, *Die Sprache der Ahiqarsprüche* (Berlin, 1990). F. C. Conybeare, J. Rendel Harris, and A. S. Lewis, *The Story of Ahikar*[2] (Cambridge, 1913), gives translations of many of the major versions.

2. J. C. Greenfield, 'The Background and Parallel to a Proverb of Ahiqar', in A. Caquot and M. Philonenko (eds.), *Hommages à André Dupont-Sommer* (Paris, 1971), 49–59; J. M. Lindenberger, 'The Gods of Ahiqar', *UF* 14 (1982), 105–17.

Bibliography of Works Cited

This bibliography does not include works cited only in the Appendix.

AHARONI, Y., 'The Use of Hieratic Numerals in Hebrew Ostraca and the Shekel Weights', *BASOR* 184 (1966), 13–19.

—— 'Arad: Its Inscriptions and Temple', *BA* 31 (1968), 2–32.

—— *Arad Inscriptions* (Hebrew version: Jerusalem, 1975; English version: Jerusalem, 1981).

—— and AMIRAN, R., 'Excavations at Tel Arad: Preliminary Report on the First Season, 1962', *IEJ* 24 (1964), 131–47.

ALBRIGHT, W. F., 'Cuneiform Material for Egyptian Prosopography 1500–1200 BC', *JNES* 5 (1946), 7–25.

ALETTI, J. N., 'Séduction et parole en Proverbes I–IX', *VT* 27 (1977), 129–44.

ALSTER, B., *Studies in Sumerian Proverbs* (Mesopotamia, 3; Copenhagen, 1975).

ALT, A., 'Die Weisheit Salomos', *Th. LZ* 76 (1951), cols. 139–44. ET in J. L. Crenshaw (ed.), *Studies in Ancient Israelite Wisdom* (New York, 1976), 102–12.

AMIET, P., 'Observations sur les 'tablettes magiques' d'Arslan Tash', *Aula Orientalis*, 1 (1983), 109.

ASSMANN, J., 'Schrift, Tod und Identität: Das Grab als Vorschule der Literatur im alten Ägypten', in A. Assmann *et al.* (eds.), *Schrift und Gedächtnis, Beiträge zur Archäologie der literarischen Kommunikation* (Munich, 1983), 64–93.

AUFRECHT, W. E., *A Corpus of Ammonite Inscriptions* (Ancient Near Eastern Texts and Studies, 4; Lewiston, NY, Queenston, Ont., and Lampeter, 1989).

AVIGAD, N., 'The Seal of Abigad', *IEJ* 18 (1968), 52 f., pl. 4c.

—— 'Ammonite and Moabite Seals', in J. A Sanders (ed.), *Essays in Honor of Nelson Glueck: Near Eastern Archaeology in the Twentieth Century* (Garden City, NY, 1970).

—— *Hebrew Bullae from the Time of Jeremiah* (Jerusalem, 1986).

BAINES, J., 'Literacy and Ancient Egyptian Society', *Man*, NS 18 (1983), 572–99.

BAUMGARTNER, A., *Etude critique sur l'état du texte du livre des Proverbes d'après les principales traductions anciennes* (Leipzig, 1890).

BAUMGARTNER, W., 'The Wisdom Literature', in H. H. Rowley (ed.), *The Old Testament and Modern Study* (Oxford, 1951), 210–37.

BECK, P., 'The Drawings from Ḥorvat Teiman (Kuntillet ʿAjrud)', *TA* 9 (1982), 3–68.

BEGRICH, J., 'Sōfēr und Mazkīr: Ein Beitrag zur inneren Geschichte des davidisch-salomonischen Großreiches und des Königreiches Juda', *ZAW* 58 (1940), 1–29.

BIRAN, A., and COHEN, R., 'Aroer, 1977', *IEJ* 27 (1977), 250–1, pl. 38.

BLUMENTHAL, E., 'Ptahhotep und der "Stab des Alters"', in J. Osing and G. Dreyer (eds.), *Form und Mass, Beiträge zur Literatur, Sprache und Kunst des alten Ägypten: Festschrift für Gerhard Fecht* (Wiesbaden, 1987), 84–97.

BOER, P. A. H. de, 'The Counsellor', SVT 3 (1960), 42–71.

BORDREUIL, P., and LEMAIRE, A., 'Nouveaux sceaux hébreux, araméens et ammonites', *Semitica*, 26 (1976), 45–63.

BOSTRÖM, G., *Paranomasi i den Äldre Hebreiska Maschallitteraturen* (LUÅ NF Avd. 1 Bd. 23.8; Lund and Leipzig, 1928).

BOYD, W. J. P., 'Notes on the Secondary Meanings of 'ḤR', *JTS* NS 12 (1961), 54–6.

BRENNER, A., *The Israelite Woman* (Sheffield, 1985).

BROWN, F., DRIVER, S. R., and BRIGGS, C. A., *A Hebrew and English Lexicon of the Old Testament* (Oxford, 1907).

BRUNNER, H., *Altägyptische Erziehung* (Wiesbaden, 1957).

—— 'Gerechtigkeit als Fundament des Thrones', *VT* 8 (1958), 426–28.

—— 'Zitate aus Lebenslehren', in E. Hornung and O. Keel (eds.), *Studien zu altägyptischen Lebenslehren* (OBO 28; Freiburg (Sw.) and Göttingen, 1979), 105–71.

BRYCE, G. E., 'Another Wisdom-"Book" in Proverbs', *JBL* 91 (1972), 145–57.

—— *A Legacy of Wisdom: The Egyptian Contribution to the Wisdom of Israel* (Lewisburg, Pa., and London, 1979).

BUDGE, E. A. W., *Facsimiles of Egyptian Hieratic Papyri in the British Museum: Second Series* (London, 1923).

BUISSON, R. DU MESNIL DU, 'Une tablette magique de la région du moyen Euphrate', in *Mélanges syriens offerts à Monsieur René Dussaud*, vol. i. (Paris, 1939), 421–34.

BURNEY, C. F., *Notes on the Hebrew Text of the Books of Kings* (Oxford, 1903).

CAMP, C. V., 'The Wise Women of 2 Samuel: A Role Model for Women in Early Israel', *CBQ* 43 (1981), 14–29.

—— *Wisdom and the Feminine in the Book of Proverbs* (Sheffield, 1985).

CAQUOT, A., and BUISSON, R. DU MESNIL DU, 'La Seconde Tablette ou "petite amulette" d'Arslan-Tash', *Syria*, 48 (1971), 391–406.

ČERNY, J., *Late Ramesside Letters* (Brussels, 1939).

CHEYNE, T. K., *Job and Solomon or The Wisdom of the Old Testament* (London, 1887).

CHILDS, B. S., 'A Study of the Formula "Until This Day"', *JBL* 82 (1963), 279–92.

—— 'The Birth of Moses', *JBL* 84 (1965), 109–22.

COATS, G. W., 'The Joseph Story and Ancient Wisdom: A Reappraisal', *CBQ* 35 (1973), 285–97.

—— *From Canaan to Egypt: Structural and Theological Context for the Joseph Story* (CBQMS 4; Washington, DC, 1976).

CODY, A., 'Le Titre égyptien et le nom propre du scribe de David', *RB* 72 (1965), 381–93.

COHEN, R., 'The Iron Age Fortresses in the Central Negev', *BASOR* 236 (1979), 61–79.

—— Excavations at Kadesh-Barnea 1976–1978', *BA* 44 (1981), 93–107.

CRENSHAW, J. L., 'Method in Determining Wisdom Influence upon "Historical" Literature', *JBL* 88 (1969), 129–42.

—— 'Education in Ancient Israel', *JBL* 104 (1985), 601–15.

CROSS, F. M., *The Ancient Library of Qumran* (London, 1958).

—— 'Epigraphic Notes on Hebrew Documents of the Eighth to Sixth Centuries BC; ii. The Murabbaʿat Papyrus and the Letter Found near Yabneh Yam', *BASOR* 165 (1962), 34–42; *idem*, iii. The Inscribed Jar Handles from Gibeon', *BASOR* 168 (1962), 18–23.

—— 'Newly Found Inscriptions in Old Canaanite and Early Phoenician Scripts', *BASOR* 238 (1980), 1–20.

—— An Old Canaanite Inscription Recently Found at Lachish', *TA* 11 (1984), 71–6.

—— and FREEDMAN, D. N., *Early Israelite Orthography* (American Oriental Series, 36; New Haven, Conn., 1952).

DEGEN, R., 'Ein aramäisches Alphabet vom Tell Halaf', *NESE* 3 (1978), 1–9.

DELITZSCH, FRANZ, *Biblischer Commentar über die poetischen Bücher des Alten Testaments*, iii. *Das Salamonische Spruchbuch* (Leipzig, 1873). ET *Biblical Commentary on the Proverbs of Solomon* (Edinburgh, 1874–5).

DEMSKY, A., 'A Proto-Canaanite Abecedary Dating from the Period of the Judges and its Implications for the History of the Alphabet', *TA* 4 (1977), 14–27.

—— 'The ʿIzbet Ṣarṭah Ostracon Ten Years Later', in I. Finkelstein (ed.), *ʿIzbet Ṣarṭah: An Early Iron Age Site Near Rosh Haʿayin, Israel* (BAR International Series, 299; Oxford, 1986), 186–97.

DEVER, W. G., 'Iron Age Epigraphic Material from the Area of Khirbet el-Kôm', *HUCA* 40/41 (1969/70), 139–204.

DIRINGER, D., *Le iscrizioni antico-ebraiche palestinesi* (Florence, 1934).

DONNER, H., and RÖLLIG, W., *Kanaanäische und aramäische Inschriften* (Wiesbaden, 1962–4).

Dotan, A., 'New Light on the 'Izbet Ṣarṭah Ostracon', *TA* 8 (1981), 160–72.

Dougherty, R. P., 'Cuneiform Parallels to Solomon's Provisioning System', *AASOR* 5 (1923/4), 23–65.

Driver, G. R., *Aramaic Documents of the Fifth Century* BC (Oxford, 1954).

Driver, S. R., *Introduction to the Literature of the Old Testament*⁹ (Edinburgh, 1913).

—— *Notes on the Hebrew Text and the Topography of the Books of Samuel²* (Oxford, 1913).

Dunand, M., *Fouilles de Byblos, i. 1926–1932* (Paris, 1939).

Eissfeldt, O., *Einleitung in das Alte Testament³* (Tübingen, 1964). ET: *Introduction to the Old Testament* (Oxford, 1965).

Emerton, J. A., 'Notes on Some Passages in the Book of Proverbs', *JTS* NS 20 (1969), 201–20.

Erman, A., 'Eine ägyptische Quelle der "Sprüche Salomos"', *SPAW* 15 (1924), 86–93, tab. VI f.

Ewald, H., *Jahrbücher der biblischen Wissenschaft, i* (Göttingen, 1848).

—— *Die Dichter des alten Bundes²* ii. *Die salomonische Schriften* (Göttingen, 1867).

Fichtner, J., 'Jesaja unter den Weisen', *Th. LZ* 74 (1949), cols. 75–80; ET in J. L. Crenshaw (ed.), *Studies in Ancient Israelite Wisdom* (New York, 1976), 429–38.

Finkelstein, I. (ed.), *'Izbet Ṣarṭah: An Early Iron Age Site Near Rosh Haʿayin, Israel* (BAR International Series, 299; Oxford, 1986).

Fontaine, C., *Traditional Sayings in the Old Testament: A Contextual Study* (Sheffield, 1982).

Fox, M. V., 'Two Decades of Research in Egyptian Wisdom Literature', *XÄS* 107 (1980), 120–35.

—— 'Egyptian Onomastica and Biblical Wisdom', *VT* 36 (1986), 302–10.

Frankfort, H., *Ancient Egyptian Religion: An Interpretation* (New York, 1948).

Freedman, D. N., 'The Orthography of the Arad Ostraca', *IEJ* 19 (1969), 52–6.

Fritsch, C. T., 'God Was With Him', *Interpretation*, 9 (1955), 21–34.

Frye, R. N., *The Heritage of Persia²* (London, 1976).

Garbini, G., 'Sull' alphabetario di 'Izbet Ṣarṭah', *OA* 17 (1978), 287–95.

—— *I fenici: storia e religione* (Naples, 1980).

Gardiner, A. H., *Ancient Egyptian Onomastica* (London, 1947).

—— *The Wilbour Papyrus* (Oxford, 1948).

Gardiner, A. H., *Egyptian Grammar³* (Oxford, 1957).

Gelb, I. J., Purves, P. M., and Macrae, A. A., *Nuzi Personal Names* (Chicago, 1943).

Gemser, B., *Sprüche Salomos¹* (Tübingen, 1937).

GILULA, M., 'An Inscription in Egyptian Hieratic from Lachish', *TA* 3 (1976), 107 f.

GOLDWASSER, O., 'Hieratic Inscriptions from Tel Sera' in Southern Canaan', *TA* 11 (1984), 77–93.

GOLKA, F. W., 'Die Königs- und Hofsprüche und der Ursprung der israelitischen Weisheit', *VT* 36 (1986), 13–36.

—— 'Die Flecken des Leoparden: Biblische und afrikanische Weisheit im Sprichwort' in R. Albertz *et al.* (eds.), *Schöpfung und Befreiung: Für Claus Westermann zum 80. Geburtstag* (Stuttgart, 1989), 149–63.

GRAPOW, H., and WESTENDORF, W., *Handbuch der Orientalistik* I. i. 2 (Leiden, 1970).

GREEN, A. R., 'Israelite Influence at Shishak's Court?', *BASOR* 233 (1979), 59–62.

GREENFIELD, J. C., 'The Background and Parallel to a Proverb of Ahiqar', in A. Caquot and M. Philolenko (eds.), *Hommages à André Dupont-Sommer* (Paris, 1971), 49–59.

GRESSMANN, H., 'Die neugefundene Lehre des Amen-em-ope und die vorexilische Spruchdichtung Israels', *ZAW* 42 (1924), 272–96.

GUNNEWEG, J., PERLMAN, I., and MESHEL, Z., 'The Origin of the Pottery of Kuntillet 'Ajrud', *IEJ* 35 (1985), 270–83.

HADLEY, J. M., 'Yahweh's Asherah in the Light of Recent Discovery', PhD. dissertation (Cambridge, 1989).

HARAN, M., 'Literacy and Schools in Ancient Israel', SVT 40 (1988), 81–95.

HEATON, E. W., *Solomon's New Men: The Emergence of Ancient Israel as a National State* (London, 1974).

HELCK, W., *Zur Verwaltung des mittleren und neuen Reichs* (Leiden, 1958, index: 1975).

—— 'Zur Frage der Enstehung der ägyptischen Literatur', *WZKM* 63/64 (1972), 6–26.

HERDNER, A., *Corpus des tablettes en cunéiformes alphabétiques découvertes à Ras Shamra-Ugarit de 1929 à 1939* (Paris, 1963).

HERMISSON, H.-J., *Studien zur israelitischen Spruchweisheit* (WMANT 28; Neukirchen, 1968).

HOFTIJZER, J., 'David and the Tekoite Woman', *VT* 20 (1970), 419–44.

—— and VAN DER KOOIJ, G., *Aramaic Texts from Deir 'Alla* (Leiden, 1976).

HOGLUND, K., 'The Fool and the Wise in Dialogue', in K. Hoglund *et al.* (eds.), *The Listening Heart: Essays in Wisdom and the Psalms in Honor of Roland E. Murphy, O. Carm.* (JSOTS 58; Sheffield, 1987), 161–80.

HOLZINGER, H., *Genesis* (Kurzer Hand-Kommentar zum A. T. i; Freiburg, 1898).

HUMBERT, P., *Recherches sur les sources égyptiennes de la littérature sapientale d'Israël* (Neuchâtel, 1929).

HUMPHREYS, W. L., 'The Motif of the Wise Courtier in the Old Testament', dissertation (New York, 1970).

—— 'A Life-Style for Diaspora: A Study in the Tales of Esther and Daniel', *JBL* 92 (1973), 211–23.

—— 'The Motif of the Wise Courtier in the Book of Proverbs', in J. Gammie (ed.), *Israelite Wisdom: Theological and Literary Studies in Honor of Samuel Terrien* (New York, 1978), 177–90.

—— *Joseph and his Family: A Literary Study* (Columbia, SC, 1988).

INGE, C. H., 'Excavations at Tell ed-Duweir', *PEQ* 70 (1938), 240–56.

IRVIN, D., 'The Joseph and Moses Stories as Narrative in the Light of Ancient Near Eastern Narrative', in J. H. Hayes and J. M. Miller (eds.), *Israelite and Judean History* (London, 1977), 180–203.

JAMIESON-DRAKE, D. W., *Scribes and Schools in Monarchic Judah: A Socio-Archaeological Approach* (Sheffield, 1991).

JASTROW, Marcus, *A Dictionary of the Targumim, the Talmud Babli and Yerushalmi, and the Midrashic Literature* (London and New York, 1903).

KAISER, O., *Der Prophet Jesaja: Kap. 13–39* (Göttingen, 1973). ET: *Isaiah 13–39*[2] (London, 1980).

KAPLONY, P., 'Die Definition der schönen Literatur im alten Ägypten', in J. Assmann *et al.* (eds.), *Fragen an die altägyptische Literatur: Studien zum Gedenken an Eberhard Otto* (Wiesbaden, 1977), 289–314.

KAPLONY-HECKEL, U., 'Schuler und Schulwesen in der ägyptischen Spätzeit', *SAK* 1 (1974), 227–46.

KAYATZ, C., *Studien zu Proverbien 1–9: Eine form- und motivgeschichtliche Untersuchung unter Einbeziehung ägyptischen Vergleichsmaterials* (WMANT 22; Neukirchen, 1966).

KENT, C. F., *The Wise Men of Ancient Israel and their Proverbs*[2] (New York, 1899).

KITCHEN, K. A., 'Proverbs and Wisdom Books of the Ancient Near East: The Factual History of a Literary Form', *Tyndale Bulletin*, 28 (1977), 69–114.

—— 'The Basic Literary Forms and Formulations of Ancient Instructional Writings in Egypt and Western Asia', in E. Hornung and O. Keel (eds.), *Studien zu altägyptischen Lebenslehren* (OBO 28; Freiburg (Sw.) and Göttingen, 1979), 235–82.

—— 'Egypt and Israel during the First Millennium BC', *SVT* 40 (1988), 107–23.

KLOSTERMANN, A., 'Schulwesen im alten Israel', in N. Bonwetsch *et al.*, *Theologische Studien, Theodor Zahn* (Leipzig, 1908), 193–232.

KOCHAVI, M., 'An Ostracon of the Period of the Judges from 'Izbet Ṣarṭah', *TA* 4 (1977), 1–13.

—— 'The History and Archaeology of Aphek-Antipatris: A Biblical City in the Sharon Plain', *BA* 44 (1981), 75–86.

196   *Bibliography of Works Cited*

—— et al., *Aphek-Antipatris 1974–1977: The Inscriptions* (Tel Aviv, 1978).

KORNFELD, W., *Onomastica aramaica aus Ägypten* (Vienna, 1978).

KRAELING, C. H., and ADAMS, R. M. (eds.), *City Invincible* (Chicago, 1960).

KRAMER, S. N., 'Sumerian Literature: A General Survey', in G. E. Wright (ed.), *The Bible and the Ancient Near East: Essays in Honor of William Foxwell Albright* (Garden City, NY, 1961), 249–66.

KRISPENZ, J., *Spruchkompositionen im Buch Proverbia* (Europäische Hochschulschriften Ser. 23 349; Frankfurt, 1989).

LANG, B., 'Schule und Unterricht im alten Israel', in M. Gilbert (ed.), *La Sagesse de l'Ancien Testament* (BETL 51; Louvain, 1979), 186–201.

LAYTON, S. C., 'The Steward in Ancient Israel: A Study of Hebrew (*ʾăšer*) *ʿal-habbayit* in its Near Eastern Setting', *JBL* 109 (1990), 633–49.

LEMAIRE, A., 'A Schoolboy's Exercise on an Ostracon at Lachish', *TA* 3 (1976), 109 f., pl. 5. 2.

—— *Inscriptions hébraïques, i. Les Ostraca* (Paris, 1977).

—— 'Abécédaires et exercises d'écolier en épigraphie nord-ouest sémitique', *JA* 266 (1978), 221–35.

—— 'Fragment d'un alphabet ouest-sémitique du VIIIe siècle av. J.-C.', *Semitica*, 28 (1978), 7–10, pl. I.

—— 'Notes d'épigraphie nord-ouest sémitique', *Semitica*, 30 (1980), 17–32.

—— *Les Ecoles et la formation de la Bible dans l'ancien Israël* (OBO 39; Freiburg (Sw.) and Göttingen, 1981).

—— 'Sagesse et écoles', *VT* 34 (1984), 270–81.

—— and VERNUS, P., 'Les Ostraca paléo-hébreux de Qadesh-Barnéa', *Orientalia*, 49 (1980), 341–34.

—— and VERNUS, P., L'Ostracon paléo-hébreu no. 6 de Tell Qudeirat (Qadesh-Barnéa), in M. Görg (ed.), *Fontes atque Pontes: Eine Festgabe für Hellmut Brunner* (ÄAT 5; Wiesbaden, 1983), 302–26.

LENZEN, H. J. (ed.), *XVIII vorläufiger Bericht über die von dem Deutschen Archäologischen Institut und der Deutschen Orient-Gesellschaft aus Mitteln der Deutschen Forschungs-gemeinschaft unternommen Ausgrabungen in Uruk-Warka* (Berlin, 1962).

LICHTHEIM, M., *Ancient Egyptian Literature* (Berkeley, Calif., Los Angeles, and London, 1973, 1976, 1980).

—— *Late Egyptian Wisdom Literature in the International Context: A Study of Demotic Instructions* (OBO 52; Freiburg (Sw.) and Göttingen, 1983).

LIDDELL, H. G., SCOTT, R., and JONES, H. S., *A Greek–English Lexicon*[9] (Oxford, 1940), with supplement edited by E. A. Barber *et al.* (Oxford, 1968).

LIDZBARSKI, M., *Phönizische und arämaische Krugaufschriften aus Elephantine* (Berlin, 1912).

LINDBLOM, J., 'Wisdom in the Old Testament Prophets', SVT 3 (1960), 192–204.

—— *Prophecy in Ancient Israel* (Oxford, 1962).

LINDENBERGER, J. M., *The Aramaic Proverbs of Ahiqar* (Baltimore and London, 1983).

LIPIŃSKI, E., 'Scribes d'Ugarit et de Jérusalem', in H. L. J. Vanstiphout *et al.* (eds.), *Scripta Signa Vocis: Studies about Scripts, Scriptures, Scribes and Languages in the Near East, Presented to J. H. Hospers by his Pupils, Colleagues and Friends* (Groningen, 1986), 143–54.

LUSCHAN, F. VON, and ANDRAE, W., *Ausgrabungen in Sendschirli V* (Berlin, 1943).

MACALISTER, R. A. S., *The Excavation of Gezer 1902–1905 and 1907–1909* (London, 1912).

MCCARTER, P. K., *II Samuel*, (The Anchor Bible; Garden City, NY, 1984).

MCKANE, W., *Prophets and Wise Men* (London, 1965).

—— *Proverbs: A New Approach* (London, 1970).

—— Review of R. N. Whybray, *The Intellectual Tradition in the Old Testament*, JSS 20 (1975), 243–48.

MALFROY, J., 'Sagesse et loi dans le Deutéronome: Etudes', VT 15 (1965), 49–65.

MARQUART, J., *Fundamente israelitischer und jüdischer Geschichte* (Göttingen, 1896).

MAZAR (= Maisler), B., 'The Scribe of King David and the Problem of the High Officials in the Ancient Kingdom of Israel', BJPES 13 (1946/7), 105–14 (Heb. Eng. summary: iv–v).

—— 'The Excavations at Tell Qasîle', IEJ 1 (1950/1), 194–218.

—— 'King David's Scribe and the High Officialdom of the United Monarchy of Israel', in *The Early Biblical Period* (Jerusalem, 1986), 126–38.

MESHEL, Z., *Kuntillet 'Ajrud: A Religious Centre from the Time of the Judaean Monarchy on the Border of Sinai* (Jerusalem, 1978).

METTINGER, T. N. D., *Solomonic State Officials: A Study of the Civil Government Officials of the Israelite Monarchy* (CB OT Series 5; Lund, 1971).

MILLARD, A. R., 'Epigraphic Notes, Aramaic and Hebrew', PEQ 110 (1978), 23–6.

—— ''BGD . . . —Magic Spell or Educational Exercise?', *Eretz-Israel*, 18 (1985), 39*–42*.

—— 'An Assessment of the Evidence for Writing in Ancient Israel' in J. Amitai (ed.), *Biblical Archaeology Today: Proceedings of the International Congress on Biblical Archaeology, Jerusalem, April 1984* (Jerusalem, 1985), 301–12.

MILLER, J. M., and HAYES, J. H., *A History of Ancient Israel and Judah* (London, 1986).

MORAN, W. L., *Les Lettres d'El-Amarna: Correspondance diplomatique du Pharaon* (Paris, 1987). Revised English edn.: *The Amarna Letters* (Baltimore and London, 1992).

MORGAN, D. F., *Wisdom in the Old Testament Traditions* (Atlanta and Oxford, 1981).

MÜLLER, H.-P., 'Magisch-mantische Weisheit und die Gestalt Daniels', *UF* 1 (1969), 79–94.

MURPHY, R. E., *The Tree of Life: An Exploration of Biblical Wisdom Literature* (Anchor Bible Reference Library; New York, 1990).

NAVEH, J., 'A Paleographic Note on the Distribution of the Hebrew Script', *HTR* 61 (1968), 68–74.

—— 'Some Considerations on the Ostracon from 'Izbet Ṣarṭah', *IEJ* 28 (1978), 31–5.

—— *Early History of the Alphabet* (Leiden, 1982).

—— 'Writing and Scripts in Seventh-Century BCE Philistia: The New Evidence from Tell Jammeh', *IEJ* 35 (1985), 8–21.

NEL, P. J., *The Structure and Ethos of the Wisdom Admonitions in Proverbs* (BZAW 158; Berlin 1982).

NICOL, G. G., 'The Wisdom of Joab and the Wise Woman of Tekoa', *St. Th.* 36 (1982), 97–104.

NORTH, C. R., *The Second Isaiah* (Oxford, 1964).

OESTERLEY, W. O. E., *The Book of Proverbs* (London, 1929).

PARDEE, D., 'Letters from Tel Arad', *UF* 10 (1978), 289–336.

—— *Handbook of Ancient Hebrew Letters* (SBL Sources for Biblical Study 15; Chico, Calif., 1982).

PARKINSON, R. B., *Voices from Ancient Egypt: An Anthology of Middle Kingdom Writings* (London, 1991).

—— 'Tales, Teachings and Discourses from the Middle Kingdom', in S. Quirke (ed.), *Middle Kingdom Studies* (New Malden, 1991).

PECK, J., 'Note on Genesis 37: 2 and Joseph's Character', *ET* 82 (1970/71), 342 f.

PFEIFFER, R. H., *Introduction to the Old Testament* (1st British = 2nd US edn.; London, 1952).

PLÖGER, O., 'Zur Auslegung der Sentenzensammlungen des Proverbienbuches', in H. W. Wolff (ed.), *Probleme biblischer Theologie: Gerhard von Rad zum 70. Geburtstag* (Munich, 1971), 402–16.

—— *Sprüche Salomos (Proverbia)* (Neukirchen, 1981–4).

POSENER, G., *Littérature et politique dans l'Egypte de la XIIIᵉ dynastie* (Paris, 1956).

—— 'Quatre tablettes scolaires de Basse Epoque (Aménémopé et Hardjédef)', *RdE* 18 (1966), 45–65.

PREUSS, H. D., 'Das Gottesbild der älteren Weisheit Israels', SVT 23 (1972), 117–45.

PUECH, E., 'Abécédaire et liste alphabétique de noms hébreux du debut du IIe s. AD', *RB* 87 (1980), 118–26.

—— 'Response to Lemaire and Levine', in J. Amitai (ed.), *Biblical Archaeology Today: Proceedings of the International Congress on Biblical Archaeology, Jerusalem, April 1984* (Jerusalem, 1985), 354–65.

—— 'Les Ecoles dans l'Israël prèexilique: donnèes épigraphiques', SVT 40 (1988), 189–203.

RAD, G. VON, 'Der Anfang der Geschichtsschreibung im alten Israel', *AK* 32 (1944), 1–42. ET in *The Problem of the Hexateuch and other Essays* (Edinburgh and London, 1965), 166–204.

—— 'Josephsgeschichte und ältere Chokma', SVT 1 (1953), 120–7. ET in *The Problem of the Hexateuch and Other Essays* (Edinburgh and London, 1965), 292–300.

—— *Die Josephsgeschichte* (Biblische Studien, 5; Neukirchen, 1954).

—— *Das erste Buch Mose, Genesis* (Göttingen, 1956). ET: *Genesis: A Commentary* (London, 1959).

—— *Theologie des alten Testaments*, i. *Die Theologie der historischen Überlieferungen Israels* (Munich, 1957). ET *Old Testament Theology*, i (Edinburgh, 1962; London, 1975).

—— *Weisheit in Israel* (Neukirchen-Vluyn, 1970). ET *Wisdom in Israel* (London, 1972).

RANKE, H., *Die ägyptischen Personennamen* (Gluckstadt, 1935, 1952, 1977).

REDFORD, D. B., *A Study of the Biblical Story of Joseph*, SVT 20 (1970).

—— 'Studies in Relations between Palestine and Egypt during the First Millennium BC, i. The Taxation System of Solomon', in J. W. Wevers and D. B. Redford (eds.), *Studies on the Ancient Palestinian World Presented to Professor F. V. Winnett* (Toronto, 1972), 141–56.

RICHTER, W., *Recht und Ethos: Versuch einer Ortung des weisheitlichen Mahnspruches* (St. ANT 15; Munich, 1966).

RÖMHELD, D., *Wege der Weisheit: Die Lehren Amenemopes und Proverbien 22, 17–24, 22* (BZAW 184; Berlin, 1989).

RUDOLPH, W., *Jeremiah*² (HAT 12; Tübingen, 1958).

RÜTERSWORDEN, U., *Die Beamten der israelitischen Königszeit* (BWANT 117; Stuttgart, 1985).

SCHMIDT, J., *Studien zur Stilistik der alttestamentlichen Spruchliteratur* (AA 13, 1; Münster, 1936).

SCHMITT, H.-C., *Die nichtpriesterliche Josephsgeschichte* (BZAW 154; Berlin, 1980).

SCOTT, R. B. Y., 'Solomon and the Beginnings of Wisdom in Israel', SVT 3 (1955), 262–79. Reprinted in J. L. Crenshaw (ed.), *Studies in Ancient Israelite Wisdom* (New York, 1976), 84–101.

—— 'Folk Proverbs of the Ancient Near East', *TRSC* 15 (1961), 47–56.

—— *Proverbs, Ecclesiastes* (The Anchor Bible; Garden City, NY, 1965).

—— 'Wise and Foolish, Righteous and Wicked', SVT 23 (1972), 146–65.

SEIBERT, P., *Die Charakteristik*, i (Wiesbaden, 1967).

SELMS, A. VAN, 'The Origin of the Title "the King's Friend"', *JNES* 16 (1957), 118–23.

—— 'Isaiah 28: 9–13: An Attempt to Give a New Interpretation', *ZAW* 85 (1973), 332–9.

SKEHAN, P., 'A Single Editor for the Whole Book of Proverbs' (revised version), in P. Skehan (ed.), *Studies in Israelite Poetry and Wisdom* (CBQMS 1; Washington, DC, 1971), 15–26. Original version in *CBQ* 10 (1948), 115–30.

SKLADNY, U., *Die ältesten Spruchsammlungen in Israel* (Göttingen, 1962).

SOLL, W. M., 'Babylonian and Biblical Acrostics', *Biblica*, 69 (1988), 305–23.

TALEB, M. ABU, 'The Seal of plty bn m'š the Mazkir', *ZDPV* 101 (1985), 21–9.

TALMON, S., 'The "Comparative Method" in Biblical Interpretation— Principles and Problems', SVT 29 (1977), 320–56.

TEIXIDOR, J., 'Bulletin d'épigraphie sémitique 1978–1979', *Syria*, 56 (1979), 353–405.

—— 'Les Tablettes d'Arslan Tash au Musée d'Alep', *Aula Orientalis*, 1 (1983), 105–8.

THOMAS, D. WINTON, 'Textual and Philological Notes on Some Passages in the Book of Proverbs', SVT 3 (1955), 280–92.

TIGAY, J. H., *You Shall Have No Other Gods* (HSS 31; Atlanta, 1986).

TOY, C. H., *A Critical and Exegetical Commentary on the Book of Proverbs* (ICC; Edinburgh, 1899).

TUFNELL, O., *et al.*, *Lachish III* (London, 1953).

USSISHKIN, D., 'Excavations at Tel Lachish 1973–1977: Preliminary Report', *TA* 5 (1978), 1–97.

VAUX, R. DE, 'Titres et fonctionnaires égyptiens à la cour de David et de Salomon', *RB* 48 (1939), 394–405. Reprinted in *Bible et Orient* (Paris, 1967), 139–201.

—— *Histoire ancienne d'Israël*, i (Paris, 1971). ET *The Early History of Israel*, i (London, 1978).

VOLZ, P., *Hiob und Weisheit* (SAT iii/2; Göttingen, 1921).

WARNER, S., 'The Alphabet: An Innovation and its Diffusion', *VT* 30 (1980), 81–90.

WEEKS, S. D. E., 'Joseph, Dreams and Wisdom', M. Phil. thesis (Oxford, 1989).

WEINFELD, M., *Deuteronomy and the Deuteronomic School* (Oxford, 1972).

WELLHAUSEN, J., *Der Text der Bücher Samuelis* (Göttingen, 1871).

WESTERMANN, C., *Genesis*, iii. *Genesis 37–50* (Neukirchen, 1982). ET: *Genesis 37–50: A Commentary* (London, 1986).

WHYBRAY, R. N., *Wisdom in Proverbs* (SBT 45; London, 1965).

—— *The Succession Narrative: A Study of II Samuel 9–20; I Kings 1 and 2* (SBT 2nd series, 9; London, 1968).

—— *The Intellectual Tradition in the Old Testament* (BZAW 135; Berlin, 1974).

—— 'Yahweh-Sayings and their Contexts in Proverbs 10¹–22¹⁶', in M. Gilbert (ed.), *La Sagesse de l'Ancien Testament* (BETL 51; Louvain, 1979), 153–65.

—— 'Poverty, Wealth and Point of View in Proverbs', *ET* 100 (1988/89), 332–6.

—— 'The Social World of the Wisdom Writers', in R. E. Clements (ed.), *The World of Ancient Israel* (Cambridge, 1989), 227–50.

—— *Wealth and Poverty in the Book of Proverbs* (JSOTS 99; Sheffield, 1990).

WILSON, F. M., 'Sacred and Profane? The Yahwistic Redaction of Proverbs Reconsidered', in K. G. Hoglund *et al.* (eds.), *The Listening Heart: Essays in Wisdom and the Psalms in Honor of Roland E. Murphy, O. Carm.* (JSOTS 58; Sheffield, 1987), 313–34.

WIRGIN, W., 'The Calendar Tablet from Gezer', *Eretz-Israel*, 6 (1960), 9*–12*.

YADIN, Y., 'Four Epigraphical Queries', *IEJ* 24 (1974), 30–6.

—— 'The Historical Significance of Inscription 88 from Arad: A Suggestion', *IEJ* 26 (1976), 9–14.

YEE, G. A., '"I Have Perfumed my Bed with Myrrh": The Foreign Woman (*'iššâ zārâ*) in Proverbs 1–9', *JSOT* 43 (1989), 53–68.

YEIVIN, S., 'A Hieratic Ostracon from Tel Arad', *IEJ* 16 (1966), 153–9.

YOHANNAN, J. D., (ed.), *Joseph and Potiphar's Wife in World Literature: An Anthology of the Story of the Chaste Youth and the Lustful Stepmother* (New York, 1968).

ZEVIT, Z., *Matres Lectionis in Ancient Hebrew Epigraphs* (ASOR Monograph Series, 2; Cambridge, Mass., 1980).

Index of Passages Cited

FROM THE OT AND APOCRYPHA

Index of Authors

General Index

DATE DUE